Reupholstering
for the
Home Craftsman

Reupholstering
for the
Home Craftsman

Michael E. Torelli
and
Ellen K. Haggerty

Drawings by Dennis Griffin

Chilton Book Company
Radnor, Pennsylvania

Published in Radnor, Pa., by Chilton Book Company
and simultaneously in Don Mills, Ont., Canada
by Thomas Nelson & Sons, Ltd.
Designed by William E. Lickfield
Manufactured in the United States of America

Library of Congress Cataloging in Publication Data

Torelli, Michael E
    Reupholstering for the home craftsman.

    Includes index.
    1. Upholstery. I. Haggerty, Ellen K.,
joint author. II. Title.
TT198.T67   684.1′2   77-4586
ISBN 0-8019-6568-3
ISBN 0-8019-6569-1 pbk.

2 3 4 5 6 7 8 9 0   6 5 4 3 2 1 0 9 8

To
> Lucy Torelli
> Tom Haggerty
> *and*
> Lionel Kaufman

Contents

Introduction, ix
  Reupholstering Makes Sense, ix
  Finding Your Treasures, ix
  Using this Book, x
  The Slow Step-by-Step Method, x

Part One
Tools of the Trade

Chapter 1
Overview of a Chair, 3
  A Cross Section, 3
  The Outside Pieces, 4
  The Reupholstery Process, 4

Chapter 2
Tools and Equipment, 11
  Basic Reupholstery Tools, 12
  Fabric Preparation Tools, 18
  Frame and Wood Preparation Tools, 18
  Equipment, 20

Chapter 3
Supplies, 22
  Basic Reupholstery Supplies, 22
  Fabric Preparation Supplies, 33
  Frame and Wood Refinishing Supplies, 34

Chapter 4
Sources of Tools and Supplies, 39
  One-Stop Shopping, 39
  A Variety of Stores for
    a Variety of Needs, 39

Chapter 5
Selecting Reupholstery Fabrics, 41
  Durable Fabrics, 41
  Velvets, 41
  Prints, Plaids and Stripes, 42
  Vinyl Plastic and Leather, 43
  Needlepoint, 43

Chapter 6
Your Workshop, 44
  Work and Storage Space, 44
  Adequate Light and Height, 44
  Moving Furniture, 45

Part Two
Reupholstering Techniques

Chapter 7
Preparing Reupholstery Fabric, 49
  Labeling Upholstery Pieces, 49
  Measuring Fabric Pieces, 54
  Marking and Cutting Fabric, 58

Chapter 8
Taking the Chair Apart, 62
  Examining the Chair, 62
  Working Section by Section, 62

Chapter 9
Repairing the Frame, 65
  The Foundation, 65
  Attachment Rails, 65
  Disassembly, 67
  Reassembly, 68

Chapter 10
Replacing Webbing and Heavy Burlap, 72
  Jute Webbing, 72
  Heavy Burlap, 72
  Steel Webbing, 72
  Webbing, Burlap and Cardboard, 73
  Rubber Webbing, 73

Chapter 11
Light Burlap and Seat Edgings, 75
  Attaching Burlap Foundations, 75
  Seat Edgings, 75
  Stitches and Knots, 76
  Reupholstering Shaped Wooden Edges, 78

Chapter 12
Repairing Springs, 79
  Replacing Damaged Spring-Coil Twine, 79
  The Return Tie, 80
  Common Coil-Spring Repair, 81
  Coil-Spring Seats and Backs, 82
  Repairing a Marshall Unit Back, 83
  Repairing a Platform Rocker Back, 83
  Repairing No-Sag Springs, 84

Chapter 13
The Old and New Stuffing, 88
  Sterilizing Sprays, 88
  The First Layer, 88
  The Second Layer, 89

Chapter 14
Machine Sewing, 90
  Before You Begin, 90
  Curved Seams and Corners, 90
  Making and Using Welt, 91
  Pull Strips, 93

Chapter 15
Putting On Reupholstery Fabric, 95
  The Professional Look, 95
  Packing and Pintacking, 95
  Major Upholstery Cuts, 96
  Pleats, 97
  Double Welt and Gimp, 97
  Ornamental Nails, 97
  Decorative Buttons, 98
  Hand Sewing, 98
  Reupholstering Loose Wood Panels, 99
  Reupholstering Common Arms, Backs and
    Seats, 101
  Making Skirts, 103
  Tacking on Cambric, 107
  Making Arm Covers, 108

Chapter 16
Upholstered Cushions, 110
  Cushion Shapes and Parts, 110
  Making a Cushion Cover, 110
  Stuffing a Cushion, 116

Part Three
Reupholstery Projects

Chapter 17
Dining Room and Kitchen Chairs, 119
  The Parts, 119
  Recovering a Chair with Vinyl Plastic, 119

  Metal Office Chairs, 124
  Highchairs, 124

Chapter 18
Overstuffed Chairs, 125
  Introduction, 125
  Our Project and Your Overstuffed Chair, 125
  Reupholstering an Overstuffed Chair, 125

Chapter 19
Wing Chairs, 135
  Introduction, 135
  Reupholstering a Wing Chair, 135

Chapter 20
Colonial Chairs, 145
  Introduction, 145
  Reupholstering a Colonial Pillow Back, 145

Chapter 21
Channel-Back Chairs, 149
  Introduction, 149
  Reupholstering a Channeled Back, 149

Chapter 22
Tufted-Back Chairs, 155
  Introduction, 155
  Reupholstering a Tufted Back, 156
  Tufted Couches, 159

Chapter 23
Convertible Sofas and Recliners, 160
  The Convertible Sofa, 160
  Reupholstering a Convertible Couch, 161
  Recliners, 164
  Section-Assembled Chairs and Couches, 165

Chapter 24
Bottomless Rocking Chairs, 168
  Introduction, 168
  Upholstering a Rocking Chair, 168

Chapter 25
Footstools, 170
  Introduction, 170
  Reupholstering an Attached-Pillow
    Footstool, 170
  Recovering a Hard-Edge Foam Footstool, 172

Glossary, 174
Index, 176

Introduction

There are many books about upholstering; that is, building a new, stuffed chair or couch from the bare frame to the finished cover. This handbook is about *re*upholstering—rebuilding a wobbly, threadbare chair or couch into a sturdy, handsome piece of furniture that you'll be proud to own. Whether you are restoring an antique or a well-used piece of modern furniture, you'll need to take off the old fabric, repair the insides and fit the new upholstered cover just like the original one.

Anyone can learn to reupholster—a young mother, a retired person, a high school dropout, a college graduate, a weekend craftsman, a homemaker. Reupholstering courses are available in community colleges, adult education schools, high schools, technical schools and professional upholsterers' shops. It can be taught as a professional trade or as a rewarding, worthwhile home craft. The techniques of using basic upholstery tools—the tack hammer, tack lifter, scissors, curved needle and the webbing stretcher—are not difficult and the basic processes can be mastered slowly, one step at a time.

Reupholstering Makes Sense

Economics, more leisure time, enjoyment and appreciation of the old-but-still-good are the main reasons why people reupholster furniture.

Well-built new upholstered furniture is extremely expensive. Young couples often feel that they must choose between buying a home or good furniture. An older couple may believe that their budget dictates living with a worn couch; a single person often feels that the quality and comfort of upholstered furniture depends directly on the amount of money he or she can afford to spend. By reupholstering, these people can save fifty percent or more.

Most of us have more leisure time available —shorter workweeks, shorter workdays and longer vacations. Homemakers have extra time on their hands because of modern conveniences and smaller families. Many older people realize that retirement means keeping alive their interest in doing and learning new things. With the energy shortage, more and more people are staying home. When they tire of watching television, they look to their hobbies for many hours of self-fulfillment and to express their own creativity.

Reupholstering is a craft, similar to woodcraft, leathercraft, knitting. It gives an individual the opportunity to make something from start to finish. The popularity of crafts represents a backlash against the products of mass manufacturing and mechanization. When a person reupholsters a favorite easy chair, he is expressing his unique taste; there is no other chair exactly like it. He's proud to have a product of his own workmanship in his living room. He knows the joy of bringing out the potential in a worn piece of furniture with many years of use ahead.

Many discarded and worn upholstered chairs and couches have solid oak frames and handcrafted tufts that the modern upholstery manufacturer cannot afford to produce. People sometimes throw away worn but high quality upholstered furniture only to replace it with new but cheaper quality goods. But today our throwaway society is steadily becoming a recycling society. People are taking a second look at what they have. Junking is in and "one man's junk is another man's treasure."

Finding Your Treasures

The first place to look for treasures is in your own home. There may be a favorite chair in your living room, attic, basement, backroom, garage or barn that needs redoing. Are there any worn treasures tucked away in family or friends' homes? Do you have any family heirlooms that you'd be especially proud to display?

If you have to go treasure hunting outside familiar grounds, here are some ways to acquire bargains.

Garbage Day. Almost every town or city designates days during the spring and autumn when residents can discard their junk. Find out when from your town hall, sanitation department or local newspapers. Most residents won't mind if you get there before the garbage pickup. In an exclusive neighborhood, one lady did not mind when a "garbage hunter" knocked on her door and politely asked for the missing piece of a French style desk. The "garbage hunter" later found out that he had an antique worth $1500!

Dump. On the other side of the rainbow on garbage day is the community dump. Always look for a good frame, a style you like and a clean cover. If you're in doubt about the cleanliness of the insides of the chair or couch, you can buy sterilizing spray from your local professional upholsterer.

Garage Sales. Many people hold sales in their garages, barns, basements and on their lawns. They'll often be delighted to sell a comfortable easy chair—just the kind you've been looking for—at a small price.

Auctions. A bidder at an antique auction offered a dollar apiece for two beautifully crafted wing chairs. She won her treasures because nobody wanted to pay $200 each to have them professionally reupholstered. Prices at auctions vary greatly, depending on how much competing bidders are willing to spend. People are reluctant to buy upholstered furniture, particularly if they aren't aware they can reupholster it themselves. For guidance in selecting worthwhile bargains, read L. G. Hewitt's *All About Auctions.*

Secondhand Furniture Stores. The Salvation Army, Goodwill Industries, thrift shops and privately owned secondhand furniture stores can be found in most communities.

By law, any store selling upholstered furniture to the public must display a "yellow tag." This yellow tag guarantees that the furniture has been sterilized.

Using this Book

It's most important that you come away from this introduction knowing that you can do it. This book will guide you through the reupholstering process, using a slow step-by-step method.

An overview of a chair and what's inside it are discussed at the beginning of Part One. Once you're familiar with the purpose of each component, the subsequent chapters discuss in detail the tools, equipment and supplies you'll need for your project—as well as those which are optional. Detailed descriptions of fabrics, their characteristics and suitability for reupholstery projects are included in this section, which concludes with a chapter on setting up your workshop area to best advantage.

Part Two will show you how to do it. Following the many illustrations and descriptions of upholstery processes, you'll build a good knowledge base for tackling your first reupholstery project.

Part Three gives you a chance to follow actual reupholstering projects from start to finish. You can see the slow step-by-step method of reupholstering in action.

If you study this book carefully and perform each reupholstery step patiently, there is no reason why you can't reupholster your chair or couch almost as well as, or maybe even better than, some professional upholsterers.

The Slow Step-by-Step Method

Learning to master any new skill is a slow process and learning to reupholster involves mastering new skills. You probably know how to handle most of the basic upholstery tools—hammer, tack lifter, mallet, scissors, yardstick, chalk, screwdriver and sewing needles. Some tools, such as a webbing stretcher, a stuffing regulator and pipe clamps, will appear new and strange. You may need a bit of time and practice to master them.

You should thoroughly understand each reupholstery process. The flow and number of processes will vary from project to project and some are harder than others. Go through each process on your project slowly, one step at a time. Don't be afraid to learn from your mistakes. Repeat a procedure until you're satisfied with the job. Then, go on to the next step. In the end you'll be far more pleased with the results.

After carefully examining a chair and taking it apart, reupholstering involves rebuilding a foundation for the stuffing and the new upholstered cover. If the frame is weak, the finished product will be weak. If the webbing sags or the springs are loose, those faults will be apparent. If the stuffing is not carefully prepared, the chair may be lumpy in areas and uncomfortable. If the new cover is not put on with regard to "the tricks of the trade," then the reupholstered project will look amateurish.

But, if you carefully study and perform the processes detailed in this book, you will be amazed by the professional appearance of the finished article.

Part One

Tools of the Trade

Chapter 1

Overview of a Chair

Every project in this book is a chair. A couch is simply a wider or extended version. If you draw a vertical line down the center of the chair, you can see that the left and right sides are symmetrical. The same is true of the couch. The main difference between the two is that the couch will have two or more cushions, a wider inside and outside back and seat.

A Cross Section

Have you ever thought about what's inside a chair? Many first-time reupholsterers are amazed at how many layers of material make up the seat alone. Figure 1–1a is a cross section of the seven layers. In the order they're used in reassembling a chair, they are:

1. Webbing or heavy 17-oz. burlap (the weight of a medium-grade webbing), which acts as the foundation for the springs and the stuffing.
2. Springs to give buoyancy or resiliency for a comfortable, soft seat.
3. The piece of 10-oz. burlap that keeps the stuffing from falling through the springs to the webbing.
4. First insulating layer of stuffing (hair, tow, moss, foam rubber or polyurethane rubber) covers the springs.

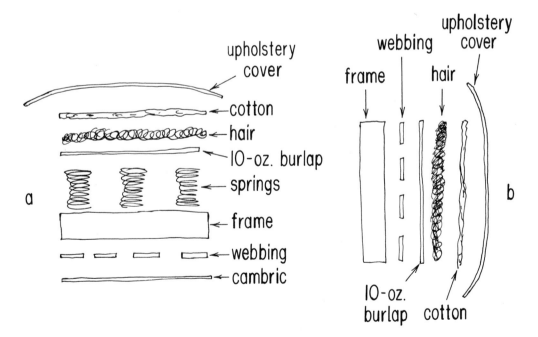

Fig. 1–1 Inside look at the many layers of material found in a chair. *a.* Seat of the chair. *b.* Back of the chair.

5. Second soft layer of stuffing (usually cotton felt) to give a soft, comfortable look and feel.
6. Reupholstered cover.
7. Cambric dust cloth to give the finishing touch on the bottom of the seat. It covers unsightly webbing and collects any dust that falls through the chair.

What's inside a chair back varies from piece to piece. Some overstuffed chairs, your favorites to relax in, have the same layers of material as the seat, except that the bottom of the back (actually the back of the back) is upholstered fabric. The back shown in Figure 1–1b has only four layers—a webbing and 10-oz. burlap combination (no springs), hair, cotton stuffing and upholstery fabric.

The Outside Pieces

Since you want to learn to reupholster like a professional, you should be familiar with the jargon used in an upholsterer's shop. Figure 1–2 shows the simplest kind of chair, with only three pieces to label. In a colonial couch, you could have as many as thirty-one pieces of upholstery fabric to cut out, sew and tack on! You'd be terribly confused if every piece did not have a name to identify it. In Chapter 7 you will learn their names and how to attach them to the more elaborate chairs.

The Reupholstery Process

Every reupholstery project, no matter how big or small, how simple or complicated, requires the same basic approach. To give you the feel of the process—what to do before getting involved in the details of how to do it—the illustrations in this chapter take you into the shop to see how the chair in Figure 1–2 is reupholstered, from start to finish.

Step 1: Examine the Chair

You'll notice in Figure 1–3 that the only upholstered portions are the seat and back. The arms and legs have exposed show wood that needs a complete refinishing job. The wood finish has deteriorated and is dull, badly marred and scratched. The frame is rigid: No pieces have to be taken apart, reglued, redoweled or reclamped.

The foundation of the seat, the webbing and the cambric have rotted with age and the springs are popping out the bottom. You'd find the chair unsafe and uncomfortable to sit on. Both the webbing and cambric must be replaced. From the holes in the fabric you can see that the stuffing is not rotten, moldy or shredded, and it shapes the seat well. The springs need to be retied.

The back of the chair is the same age as the seat. The webbing is not rotten and the burlap does not need to be replaced. The stuffing is good.

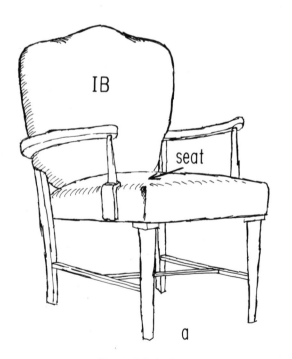
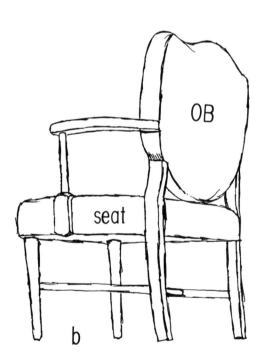

Fig. 1–2 Labeling the outside fabric pieces of the chair. *a*. Front view. *b*. Rear view.

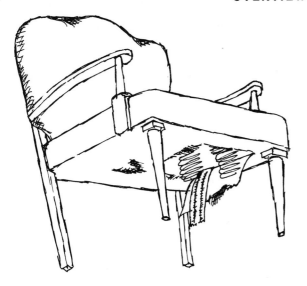

Fig. 1–3 Examine the condition of the chair.

Step 2: Make a Measurement Chart

With a tape measure, record the vertical and horizontal measurements of the inside back (IB), outside back (OB) and the seat. These measurements (Fig. 1–4) are the first step toward making an all-important cutting diagram.

Step 3: Make a Cutting Diagram

A cutting diagram is like a puzzle (Fig. 1–5). The many fabric pieces must be fit together on your small diagram and all must face in the right direction. The trick is to fit the small pieces in so you

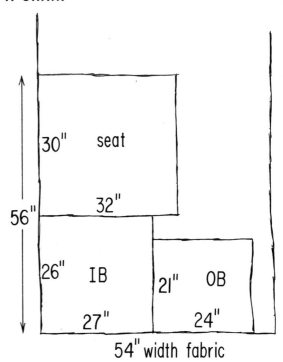

Fig. 1–5 Cutting diagram shows how the new upholstery fabric pieces will be chalked and cut. Adding the vertical measurements, 26″ and 30″, will show you need to buy 1²/₃ yards of fabric.

have the least possible waste. This step is very helpful in determining the exact amount of upholstery fabric you'll need. Some couches will use up to 14

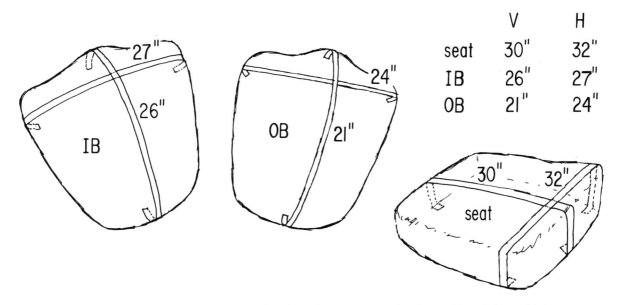

	V	H
seat	30″	32″
IB	26″	27″
OB	21″	24″

Fig. 1–4 A chart of all vertical and horizontal measurements for the outside upholstery fabric covers. Tape measures include 1″ extra on each side of the IB and seat for tacking to the frame and ¹/₂″ extra on each side of the OB to turn under before hand sewing.

yards of fabric, with the cost per yard varying from $10 to $40. If an estimate chart in the fabric store says you need 16 yards, but your exact cutting diagram calls for only 14 yards, you'll save yourself a lot of money.

Step 4: Measure and Rough-Cut Fabric

Chalk the fabric, using a yardstick as a straight-edge. Cut the fabric with a heavy pair of scissors.

Step 5: Refinish the Wood

Loosen the old upholstery fabric around each joint of exposed wood in the arms and legs. Strip the wood down with paint and varnish remover and a rough-textured cloth. Rub with denatured alcohol and another clean, rough cloth. Refinish with one to two layers of a stain and varnish combination.

Step 6: Start Taking Notes

There are two ways to reupholster, the hard way and the easy way. The hardest way is to take the chair apart completely, relying on memory or a couple of week-old notes to finish the chair. The easiest way is to completely reupholster one section at a time; i.e., remove the old seat cover, repair the webbing and burlap, retie the springs, tack on the new cover and then start the back. You have closely observed any hand sewing, cuts in the fabric, places where the pieces are tacked down. Your notes are clear and your memory is fresh. If you cannot start the back of the chair for another day or week, you need not worry about forgetting anything.

Step 7: Take the Seat Apart

Turn the chair upside-down. With a mallet and ripping chisel, tack lifter or screwdriver, remove the tacks securing the cambric and the old seat upholstery cover. Remove the torn, rotten webbing (Fig. 1–6). Remove the springs by pulling out the tacks on the frame. *Do not* cut any spring twine unless it is rotten or broken between two springs. Two sets of spring tying, old and new, are better than one.

Save the old cover as a guide to how it was pleated, cut and tacked. Take notes on any points you might want to remember when you're ready to put on the new cover. Take out the stuffing and set it aside for reuse. *Never* throw it away. It custom fits the chair and is often hard to duplicate. A fresh new layer of cotton felt can always be added.

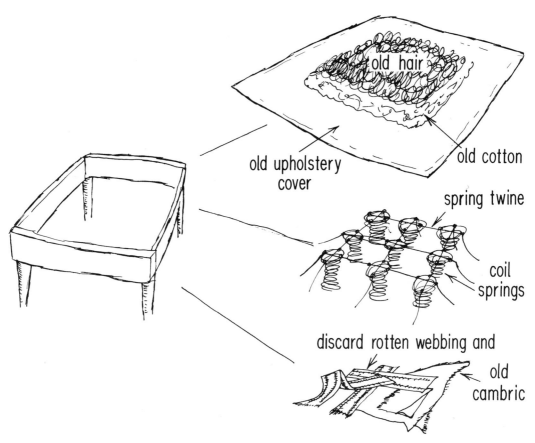

Fig. 1–6 Take the seat apart and separate the contents into three piles. Never throw away old stuffing; set the springs aside as a unit and do not cut spring twine.

steel webbing

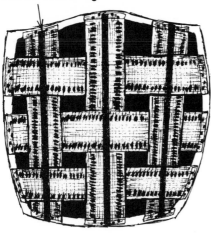

Fig. 1–7 Tack on the new webbing.

Step 8: Tack on New Webbing

This project calls for new webbing in the seat. You'll need a tack hammer, #14 tacks and a webbing stretcher to complete this step. To insure no more popped spring problems, you might want to tack on three strips of steel webbing to give added strength (Fig. 1–7). All reupholstering jobs with coil springs are given the extra strength and insurance of steel webbing.

Step 9: Sew Springs in Place and Retie

Turn the chair right-side-up. You can see that most of the spring twine has rotted and the springs need to be put in place, anchored to the webbing and completely retied (Fig. 1–8).

With a 6″ curved needle or a 10″ straight needle and stitching twine, sew the springs into place. Retie and reanchor the springs to the frame using spring twine, #14 tacks and a tack hammer.

Step 10: Cover the Springs with Burlap

Measure and cut 10-oz. burlap to the vertical and horizontal measurements of the seat-with-springs. The burlap will act as a foundation for the stuffing. Attach with #3 tacks (Fig. 1–9).

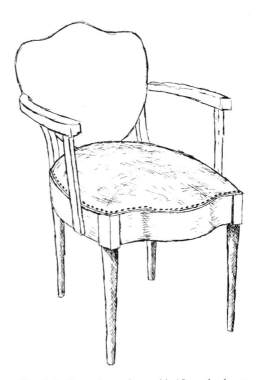

Fig. 1–9 Cover the springs with 10-oz. burlap to keep the stuffing from falling through.

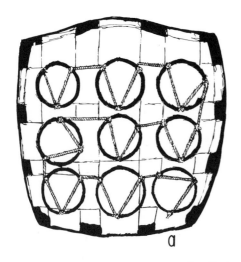
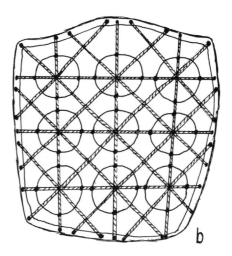

Fig. 1–8 Reinserting the springs. *a.* Sew the bottom of the springs to the new webbing. *b.* Retie and reanchor the tops of the springs to the seat frame with a four-way tie (spring twine crosses each spring four ways).

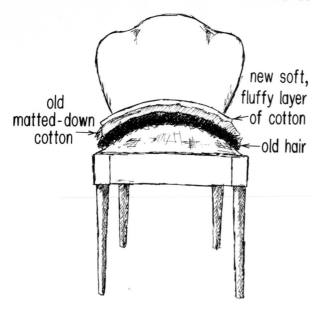

Fig. 1–10 Restuff the seat.

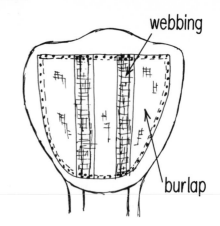

Fig. 1–12 Restretch and retack the 10-oz. burlap and webbing.

Step 11: Restuff the Seat

Put on the old seat stuffing as it was. Add new cotton felt, a half to a full layer, for a soft, new look (Fig. 1–10).

Step 12: Tack on Reupholstery Cover

Study the pleats and cuts of the old seat fabric. With #3 tacks, secure the new fabric just as the old had been (Fig. 1–13). Now, you are finished with the seat.

Step 13: Remove the Back

Cut the hand-sewn stitches on the outside back (OB). Remove the tacks anchoring the inside back (IB). Gently, take out all the stuffing and lay it aside, noting the top, bottom and sides (Fig. 1–11).

Step 14: Retack Burlap and Webbing

The old 10-oz. burlap and webbing are not rotten or torn and do not need to be replaced. Restretch the webbing first, then the burlap. Retack with #6 tacks where there are double layers of webbing and burlap; use #3 tacks where there is only burlap (Fig. 1–12).

Step 15: Restuff the Back

In a few places, tack the old stuffing, which has been properly positioned (Fig. 1–14). Lay on fresh new cotton felt, a half to full layer.

Step 16: Tack on the IB and OB

Study the pleats and cuts of the old IB cover. Using #6 tacks, pintack the new IB (driving the tacks in halfway). If you need to make any adjustments, you can easily knock a few tacks out and retack. Figure 1–15 shows the stages in fitting the fabric. When you are pleased with your finished product, drive the tacks in all the way. The OB will

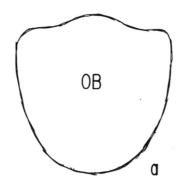
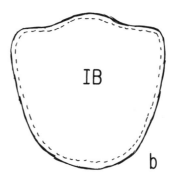

Fig. 1–11 Take off the back, separating contents into three piles: OB, IB and stuffing. *a.* Remove the hand stitches holding on the OB cover. *b.* Take off tacks holding on the IB. Remove the back stuffing and rotten burlap.

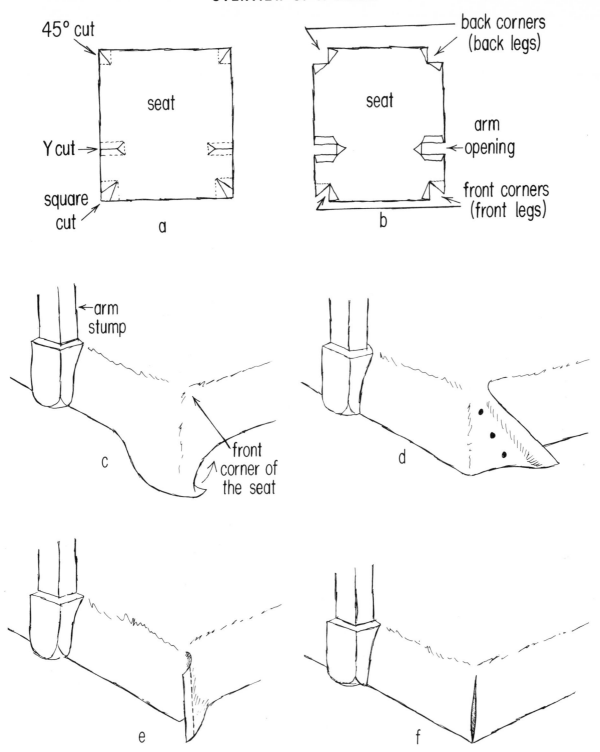

Fig. 1–13 Fitting new fabric to the seat. *a*. The solid lines of the seat fabric cover are the cutting lines. The dotted lines are the fold lines. *b*. Seat with the cuts folded back. *c*. The square cut around each front leg must be folded four ways. First, the side of each front corner is turned under and tacked on the bottom of the seat frame. *d*. Excess fabric is turned toward the middle of the seat and tacked in place. *e*. Excess fabric is folded toward the outside of the chair. Trim the fabric so that only a ¹/₂″ will be turned under in step *f*. *f*. Excess fabric is turned under to finish the corner. The corner is more than 3″ high, so it is closed with hand stitches.

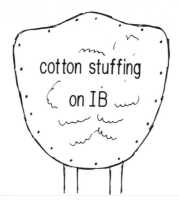

Fig. 1–14 Pintack the cotton into place.

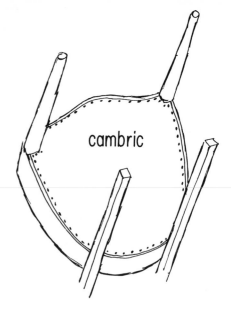

Fig. 1–16 Tack on the cambric dust cloth.

be tacked on the top and bottom, hand sewed on the sides.

Step 17: Tack on the Cambric Dust Cloth
Turn the chair upside-down. Tack on the cambric, using #3 tacks (Fig. 1–16).

Pat yourself on the back—you deserve it. The most rewarding step in the reupholstering process is when you stand back to admire the finished product.

Now, you have a feel for what to do. It is time to move on and learn exactly how to do it, and get a firm grasp of the reupholstering tools, supplies and processes.

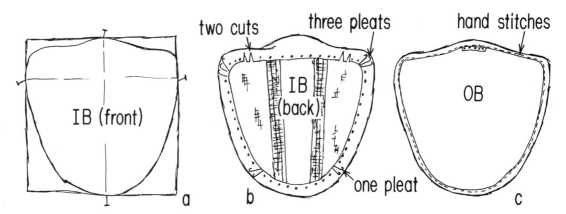

Fig. 1–15 Attaching the new back cover. *a.* Pintack the IB on each side. *b.* Back view of the IB tacked on the frame. *c.* The OB is added and stitched into place.

Chapter 2

Tools and Equipment

As a beginner or home craftsman, you must decide for yourself how many upholstery tools you need to complete your unique project: This book will guide you in that selection. If you plan to do more than one repair job or to completely reupholster more than one project, get into the spirit of the craft by buying quality tools. If you were going to take up golf or tennis as a serious sport, you would most likely invest in the proper equipment so you would thoroughly enjoy the game.

Chapter 2 introduces you to the tools, teaches you how to handle them and when to use them. Figure 2–1 shows the basic reupholstery kit.

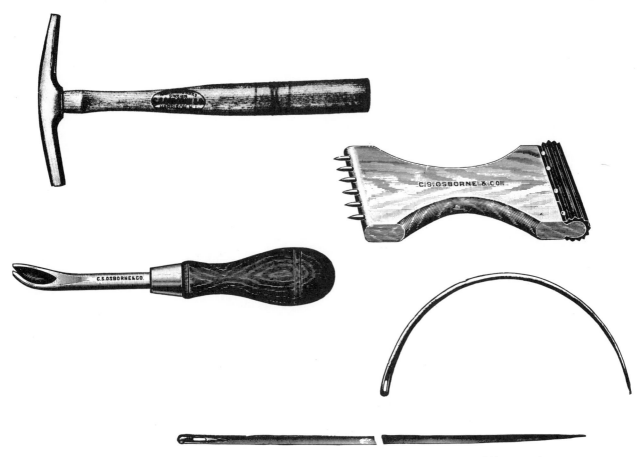

Fig. 2–1 The basic reupholstery kit contains a light upholsterer's hammer, a webbing stretcher, claw tool, and curved and straight upholstery needles. (*C.S. Osborne & Co.*)

Basic Reupholstery Tools

Upholsterer's Hammer

The upholsterer's hammer, also called a tack hammer, has one magnetic side and one hammering side. The professional upholsterer puts a small handful of tacks in the left side of his cheek and one by one, as he needs a tack, he guides it with his tongue to the front of his mouth so the head comes out first. The magnetic end of the hammer draws the tack right out. This system gives the upholsterer a third hand. The left hand is pulling the material to be tacked, while the right hand is holding the magnetic hammer and drawing the tack from his third hand—his mouth! Whatever the benefits of putting tacks in your mouth, the dangers are obvious; use utmost caution if you decide to do this.

With light pressure, the upholsterer drives the tack in so that it sticks to the fabric and wood. He never tries to drive the tack in all at once. Then, he rotates the hammer and uses the hammering end to pintack (drive the tack in lightly, not all the way) or drive it in completely.

If you do not elect to place the tacks in your mouth, you can keep them on a table very close by, reaching for them one at a time. If you never handled a hammer or feel strange holding one, it's a good idea to take a few tacks and pintack them into a piece of corrugated cardboard. You can reuse these tacks because they are easy to pull out by hand. You'll bend the tacks if you practice hitting them into hardwood, and tacks can be expensive.

The upholsterer's tack hammer is approximately 10″ long and weighs 8 oz. It is designed specifically for the upholsterer's comfort. It is light enough to be used all day without tiring you out and small enough to drive tacks in narrow, hard-to-reach corners without fear of marring any show wood.

We recommend that you use the proper tools. If you are reluctant to purchase a tack hammer for

Fig. 2–3 Small, light claw hammer sufficient for your first reupholstering project. (*C.S. Osborne & Co.*)

your first project, you could use a small, light claw hammer (Fig. 2–3) or any other small hammer. In order to put the tacks in the upholstery, pull the material with your left hand, focus your eyes on the spot you wish to tack, hold the hammer in your right hand and the tack between your thumb and index finger. Push the tack in where needed with your fingers so that the tack stands upright and, with several taps, pintack or drive the tack in. If you have to tack in narrow or unreachable locations, place a long narrow bolt on the head of the tack, using the bolt as a nail punch, and lightly tap the bolt several times. The pressure will drive in the tack.

Ripping Tools

In an upholsterer's shop, you find two kinds of ripping tools: the claw chisel or tack lifter, and the ripping chisel. Both tools are designed to remove the old tacks without ripping the fabric. You will want to use the old fabric as a pattern or guide, so it is very important to remove it carefully. You also want to make sure that you do not disturb the stuffing.

Claw Chisel or Tack Lifter

The claw chisel shown in Figure 2–4 can be used for removing large webbing nails or tacks. It is also used for removing pintacks. The claw is offset about 45 degrees from the handle so that you can keep the striking end away from the material and hold it comfortably in your hand. The claw chisel is

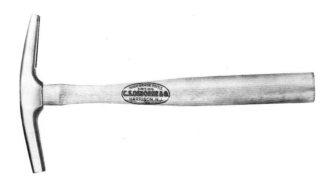

Fig. 2–2 Lightweight upholsterer's tack hammer with one magnetic end. (*C.S. Osborne & Co.*)

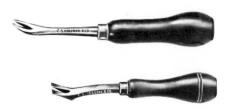

Fig. 2–4 Claw chisel for removing tacks. (*C.S. Osborne & Co.*)

almost the same as a ripping chisel except that it has a V shaped opening like a claw hammer, making it easy to get under tacks and lift them up.

Ripping Chisel

The ripping chisel (Fig. 2–5) is used primarily for prying off old tacks and material. If you feel you have to limit your purchase of tools, an 8″-long, ¼″-wide screwdriver will be sufficient.

Fig. 2–5 Ripping chisel for prying off old tacks and fabric. (*C.S. Osborne & Co.*)

Wood Mallet

The mallet is made completely of hardwood. It is approximately 11″ long, with a head 5″ wide and 2″ deep (Fig. 2–6). The wood mallet is used to hit non-metallic tools. The head of the claw or ripping chisel is made from wood or a durable type of plastic. The chisel, being hit by wood, gives the concentrated power to remove the tack. The mallet can also be used to knock apart the frame of a chair that has to be reglued or repaired (*see also* Rubber Mallet).

Fig. 2–6 The wooden mallet is used in combination with a chisel to remove tacks and fabric. (*C.S. Osborne & Co.*)

Using Wood Mallet and Chisels

If you are righthanded, the most effective way to use a mallet and chisel is to hold the mallet in your right hand and the chisel in your left. Hold each tool in a fist, not too tight but just comfortably. Always aim the ripping tool in the direction of the grain of the wood, never against it, especially when a tack is on the edge of the wood. If you strike the tack against the grain, you could split the wood.

Webbing Stretchers
Making Your Own

You can either buy a webbing stretcher or make one. Take a block of wood approximately 3½″

Fig. 2–7 Webbing stretcher tightens webbing that will be tacked to the frame. (*C.S. Osborne & Co.*)

wide, 6½″ long and 1″ to 1½″ thick. The grooves on each side of the purchased one in Figure 2–7 make it easier to grasp. Drill six ½″-deep holes, ½″ apart and ½″ from each end. You will need six 8 or 10-penny nails. Drive the nails in the holes until they are secure. Cut each nail to within ½″ of the board with a wire cutter or hacksaw. Sharpen each nail to a point with a metal file. You might want to pad the other end with rubber or cloth so it does not mar any finished woodwork. You now have a webbing stretcher as good as a professional one.

Using a Webbing Stretcher

There are several uses of a webbing stretcher: to put on new webbing; to tighten old webbing; and as a substitute to tighten heavy burlap.

1. Putting on New Webbing

Tack one end of the webbing onto one side of the chair. Let the rest of the webbing hang loosely over the other side of the chair. Hold the webbing stretcher up at about a 45-degree angle, placing the padded end of the webbing stretcher (the footing) on the opposite side of the chair (Fig. 2–8). Dig the teeth of the stretcher into the webbing. Push the stretcher down with your right hand. Hold it in place with your left hand. Then your right hand is free to use the tack hammer to tack the end down. The webbing stretcher makes the webbing taut so there is a firm foundation for the springs. Taut webbing also strengthens the frame of the chair.

2. Tightening Old Webbing

If the old webbing is not weak or rotten and looks as if it could take many more years of heavy use, it can be restretched and reused. Examine each strip of webbing separately. Leave one end of the webbing tacked down, removing the tacks from the opposite end. In order to make the webbing long enough to use a webbing stretcher, pin an extra strip of webbing or heavy material to the old webbing with upholsterer's pins or a finishing nail at least 3″ long. Now, use the webbing stretcher as if you were tacking down new webbing (Fig. 2–9).

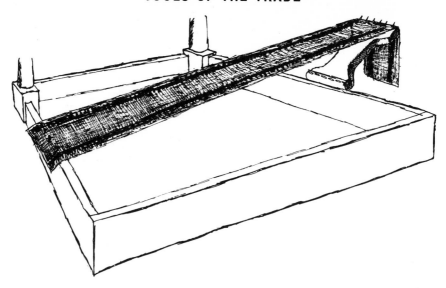

Fig. 2–8 New webbing stretched on the frame.

upholsterer's pin or 3" finishing nail

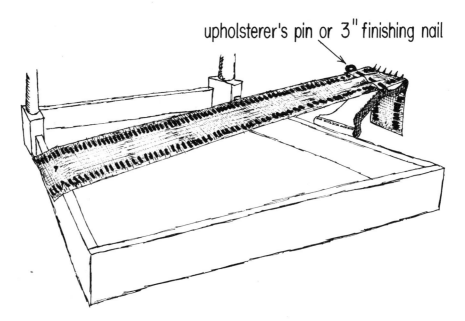

Fig. 2–9 Strong old webbing can be stretched by first attaching a short extra strip of webbing, burlap or any other heavy strong fabric. The old webbing is now long enough to use the webbing stretcher.

3. A Substitute for Tightening Burlap

The professional way to tighten heavy 17-oz. burlap when it is used instead of webbing for the foundation of a chair is to use a sagless webbing stretcher (Fig. 2–10). The foot of the teeth of the stretcher is even with the top of the chair's frame. Push the stretcher down with the teeth in the burlap, then tack the burlap.

The homemade webbing stretcher can be a good substitute for the sagless webbing stretcher. The

Fig. 2–10 Sagless webbing stretcher is a professional tool used to stretch heavy 17-oz. burlap when it is used instead of webbing as a foundation for the springs and stuffing. (*C.S. Osborne & Co.*)

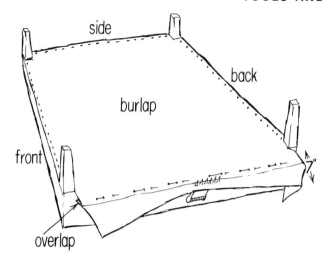

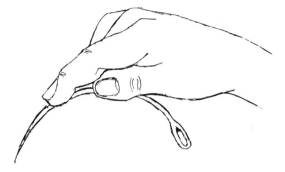

Fig. 2–13 How to hold a curved needle.

Fig. 2–11 An extra piece of burlap is pinned to the 30″-wide, 17-oz. burlap to use the standard or homemade webbing stretcher instead of the professional tool, the sagless webbing stretcher.

width of 17-oz. burlap is usually 30″. The width of most chairs is approximately 27″ or 28″. In order to stretch the burlap the width of the chair, having enough room to fold over on both sides, pin on a scrap piece of heavy burlap with upholsterer's pins or 3″ or 4″ finishing nails. Stretch and tack (Fig. 2–11). The length of the heavy burlap should be cut long enough to use a webbing stretcher. One side is tacked down and the opposite side is approximately 7″ longer than the frame of the chair.

Needles

Curved Needles

Curved needles are used for hand sewing seams that cannot be closed any other way, and anchoring springs, stuffing and edging (Fig. 2–12). There are two types of curved needles—the round-point and the three-square-point. The three-square-point needle is sharper and can rip through heavy material

easily. As a home craftsman or beginner you should have two curved needles: a number 5″ round-point for sewing seams and a number 6″ three-square-point for sewing springs into place on the burlap, sewing loose stuffing onto the light burlap to keep it from shifting around and for sewing stuffed edgings onto heavy burlap.

Hold the needle as illustrated in Figure 2–13, comfortably and loosely. The larger the needle, the easier it is to hold. Curved needles come in sizes from 3″ to 8″.

Straight Needles

The 10″ straight needle is used for tufting, attaching buttons, sewing stuffing to burlap, sewing edges and anchoring the springs in place. If you will not be attaching any buttons and you need to choose between buying a 6″ curved needle or a 10″ straight needle, purchase the 6″ curved needle.

There are four types of straight 10″ needles (Fig. 2–14): a round-point with one point; a three-square-point with one point; and a round or three-square-point with two points, one on each end. If you want to buy only one needle, buy a double-point needle. The double point is used to attach buttons or repair a chair where a button has fallen out. As mentioned

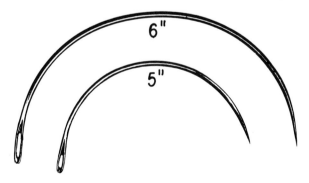

Fig. 2–12 Curved needles used for hand sewing. (C.S. Osborne & Co.)

Fig. 2–14 Straight needles used for hand sewing: (*from top*) double round-point, single three-square-point, double three-square-point. (*C.S. Osborne & Co.*)

above, the three-square point has more penetrating power than the round point.

Straight needles come in sizes from 6″ to 18″ long. A 10″ needle is sufficient in most cases. For some old furniture with thick backs, you might need a longer needle to attach buttons.

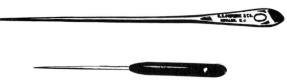

Fig. 2–15 Both the professional regulator, with one wedge end, and the regulator with a plastic handle, similar to an icepick, are used to move cotton to take out lumps or close up holes. (*C.S. Osborne & Co.*)

Stuffing Regulator or Icepick

A stuffing regulator looks like an icepick (Fig. 2–15). The name tells you that it regulates the cotton felt stuffing. After you put on the new cover, you may notice when running your fingers lightly over the surface that certain areas—sides, corners and pleats—are lumpy and other areas are shallow. Poke the stuffing regulator through the new reupholstery fabric and move the cotton from an overstuffed area to an understuffed area or take away cotton from an overstuffed area until the outside surface feels smooth to your touch. Any icepick will do. The professional regulator has a pick on one end and a small wedge, similar to a screwdriver wedge, on the other end for making corner pleats and tufting. It is not necessary to own a professional regulator.

Upholsterer's Pins and Skewers

Upholsterer's skewers are a very handy tool (Fig. 2–16). One use was already mentioned—pinning extra webbing and burlap onto the original for stretching. Another function is to shape the upholstery fabric to the exact curve of a chair. This is done by pinning the edges of the new material with skewers. If the material is not too thick, you can use regular sewing pins, but most upholstery fabrics will bend them.

Fig. 2–16 Upholsterer's pins and skewers are the heavy-duty complement of dress pins. (*C.S. Osborne & Co.*)

Another use for skewers is pinning the outside back or outside arms in place for hand sewing. The material could be pintacked with number 6 tacks, but the smooth round skewers will not rip the fabric the way sharp tacks might. Skewers also come in handy for repair work when a small area in the side of a cushion or chair needs to be held in place for hand sewing.

Trimming Knife

A trimming knife is a razor blade with a long handle on it for easy, safe handling (Fig. 2–17). You use it where it is awkward or difficult to use scissors. If your project uses either gimp or double welt, you can trim the newly stretched upholstery fabric to the desired length and width with a trimming knife.

When you are taking apart certain chairs where the shape is simple and you do not need the old pattern as a guide, you can use a trimming knife to help rip off the old fabric. An example would be kitchen chairs with plastic fabric stapled on. It would be a difficult job to take each staple out, one at a time. An easier way is to slit the plastic with the trimming knife all the way around the base of the seat or back, then grab a strip with pliers and yank it off, staples and all.

Trimming knives can also be useful in what surgeons might call "exploratory work." On certain chairs, such as overstuffed and wing chairs, there are hidden pieces of upholstery fabric in the back part of the arms and wings. To conserve expensive upholstery fabric, you will want to get accurate measurements of the arms and wings. When you slit the outside back, you can look inside and see how far back the tacking post is for the back of the arms and wings. You can also slit the cambric dust cloth on the underside of the chair to see if any

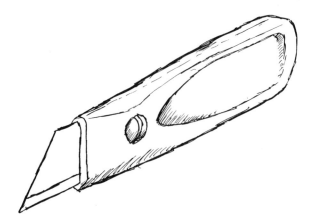

Fig. 2–17 A trimming knife is handy where scissors would be awkward to use.

spring or webbing repair work is needed. You can size up the job faster and easier before you tackle it.

Another use of the trimming knife when taking apart a chair is for cutting hand and machine-sewn stitches, especially when you want a neat cut in order to use the old upholstery fabric for a pattern.

The last important use is for trimming cardboard. Many modern furniture manufacturers use cardboard instead of webbing and burlap in certain areas, such as arms, where there is little or no weight to be supported. You may need to take the cardboard out for an easier reupholstery job. When you go to put it back into place, you may notice that it appears to be too big. Trim it with a trimming knife.

Staple Guns and Staples

A staple gun and staples can be used wherever you would use a hammer and tacks (Fig. 2–18).

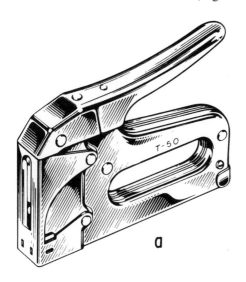

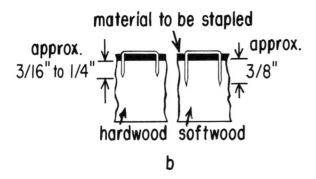

Fig. 2–18 Staple gun and staples are the alternative to hammer and tacks for fastening the fabric in place. (*Arrow Fastener Co.*) *a*. Staple gun. *b*. The size of the staple is determined by the length of the legs. Staples driven into softwood should be bigger than those driven into hardwood.

There are many advantages and disadvantages to using staples instead of tacks.

Staples are an advantage in that they penetrate the pores of the wood frame and the pores fasten the round, pointed staples in place. Tacks make wedges in the wood frame. Every reupholstery job requires finding new bare wood to drive the tacks into. After the fourth or fifth reupholstery job, the frame begins to crack. Staples are wide, cover more area than a tack and do a smoother job.

As a beginner, you may find it difficult or clumsy to use a tack hammer, constantly reaching for tacks. A staple gun is easier to operate and control. The staples and stapler are held in one hand. The staples are driven into the wood in one operation.

Modern furniture factories use staple guns extensively because it is easier to train new workers to use a staple gun than a tack hammer, and also because of speed. Staple guns do a faster job. However, factories use electric air-driven staplers. Yours will be hand powered, not as fast and easy to operate.

You might feel that certain pieces of modern furniture are not well made because staples are used to hold the fabric in place. In many cases it is not the staples or tacks that do the poor job, but the operator. Poor design will also decrease the quality of furniture: joints that are not properly glued and clamped; frames that are not fitted, doweled and glued properly; incorrect thickness of wood used; softwoods that are not properly seasoned, or have knots and aircracks, instead of solid hardwoods. When it comes to putting on burlap and upholstery fabric, staples of the proper size have more holding power.

There are two basic disadvantages to using staples. The first is that, since staples have more holding power, they are very difficult to remove. Furniture companies may have workers who are trigger happy: They have a good time shooting in an over-abundance of staples that you will have to remove. Also, some companies buy large quantities of staples of one size. They may use large $1/2''$ staples to tack down one layer of material instead of the proper size, the easier to remove $5/16''$ size. The second disadvantage is that you cannot easily readjust the new reupholstery fabric after you have stapled it on. If the pattern in the fabric is not centered properly or not tacked on tightly enough and you want to readjust it, you will have to struggle to pry out the staples and start all over again. With a hammer and tacks, you can pintack the fabric, driving the tacks in halfway so they are easy to remove.

We recommend that you use a combination of

staples and tacks to get the best of both methods. Pintack first, after centering and tightening the fabric, then staple the fabric tightly to the rest of the frame.

Staples for upholstery come in six different sizes: $3/16''$, $1/4''$, $5/16''$, $3/8''$, $1/2''$ and $9/16''$. Use $1/4''$ or $5/16''$ for stapling one thickness of material. Use $1/2''$ for stapling two or more layers, blindtacking and welting. These measurements indicate the leg length of the staples (*see* Fig. 2–18*b*). Besides keeping in mind the thickness of the materials, you must consider whether you are working with hardwood or softwood. As a general rule, the staple lengths itemized are good for tight-pored hardwoods. To get sufficient holding power in softwoods, use the next larger size staple for the job. However, if the size staple you are using stands away from the work, this means that the staple leg is too long. Use the next shorter leg length for the desired results.

If you do not own a staple gun and want to buy one, try to buy one that takes all the different staple lengths. Some guns will take only two or three sizes.

Fabric Preparation Tools

Paper Stapler or Straight Pins

Any home or office paper stapler can be a fantastic substitute or complement to straight sewing pins. Instead of pinning the old patterned upholstery fabric to the new rough-cut fabric for precise shaping, staple it! The legs of the staples are between $1/4''$ and $3/8''$, the width is between $3/8''$ and $1/2''$. Paper staples are easy to pull out of thick fabrics.

Tape Measure and Yardstick

A tape measure is used to determine the length and width of the different parts of the chair or couch—seat, cushions, arms. Since it is made of cloth, paper or a pliable metal, it can be bent to the

Fig. 2–19 Tape measure for obtaining accurate dimensions.

shape of the chair part for accurate measurements (Fig. 2–19).

Your new upholstery fabric will most likely be $54''$ wide and several yards long. The yardstick makes it easy to measure and mark the large fabric pieces—the seat, outside back, inside back and arms. Also, the long edge of the yardstick gives a perfect guide for drawing a straight line.

Chalks and Crayons

Depending on the color of the fabric, use white chalk, colored crayon or pencil as a marker—whatever shows up best. It is important to have a sharp point on your marking tool, so you know exactly where to cut after marking.

Upholsterer's Scissors of Shears

The upholsterer most frequently uses $10''$ bent shears (Fig. 2–20). The handle is bent to allow the upholsterer to cut fabric on a table without raising the cutting edge and the fabric too high off the surface. If you have a large pair of fabric-cutting scissors around the house, you can use them.

Fig. 2–20 Upholsterer's scissors are utilized for smooth, easy cutting. (*C.S. Osborne & Co.*)

No matter what kind of scissors you use, they should be *sharp*. You will be cutting heavy materials, such as burlap, webbing, twine and the upholstery fabric. The sharper the scissors, the easier and cleaner the cut. If your scissors are dull, sharpen them with an approved scissor and knife sharpener, such as a metal shop file, a Carborundum oil stone or an electric sharpener. Also, add a drop of oil to the pivot and cutting edge of the scissors. Wipe the excess oil off. Your scissors should glide across the material.

Frame and Wood Preparation Tools
Rubber Mallet

A wobbly frame, a loose joint, a broken leg, arm or wing might need repair. To reglue and repair the dowels and strenthen the joints, you may have to knock a portion or all of the frame apart. You can

Fig. 2–21 Rubber mallet used to knock apart a frame without marring the wood finish. (*C.S. Osborne & Co.*)

use a wood mallet, but if the furniture you are repairing has a wood finish you do not want to mar, a rubber mallet should be used to strike the pieces apart (Fig. 2–21). The rubber mallet can be purchased from an auto parts department or shop.

Screwdrivers

You may need a screwdriver, either a Phillips (two slots) or regular (one slot), to loosen and tighten frames and corner blocks. Some small chair legs, colonial furniture wings and upholstered furniture frames are screwed together, instead of utilizing dowels.

Clamps

Pipe Clamps

A pipe clamp is a clamp that uses a pipe for an extension, usually a ³/₄″ water pipe or black galvanized pipe. The clamp set is sold without the pipe. You may be able to get discarded pipes from your local heating and plumbing company. One end of the clamp is threaded with a crank to take up the final adjustment. The other end has a ratchet which goes back and forth and bites into the pipe to anchor

itself. If you are going to repair wobbly frames, you should have at least two sets of pipe clamps.

Pipe clamps are used to assemble two pieces of wood so they are very tight (Fig. 2–22). In furniture repair, this means putting joints together as tightly as possible. Besides tightening all parts of the frame—seat, back, arms, wings and legs—pipe clamps are used to square the frame.

Bench clamps are similar to pipe clamps. Instead of pipe, they have a long flat piece of good steel, ¹/₄″ thick by 1″ wide by 36″ long.

C Clamps

C clamps are used on smaller joints (Fig. 2–23). They perform the same job as pipe clamps, but over

Fig. 2–23 C clamps are used for a smaller area than pipe clamps. (*Adjustable Clamp Co.*)

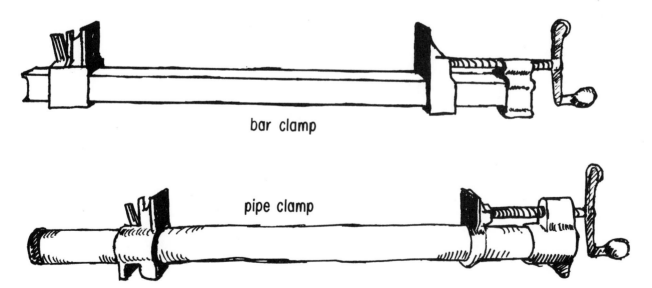

bar clamp

pipe clamp

Fig. 2–22 Pipe clamps and bar clamps utilized to retighten frame joints. (*Adjustable Clamp Co.*)

smaller areas. For major frame repair, you will most likely use a combination of pipe clamps and C clamps.

Equipment

To complete your reupholstery project, it is unnecessary to own either an industrial sewing machine or a button-making machine. Your local professional upholsterer will gladly supply these services for a minimal charge. Anything that needs to be machine sewn—cushions, backs or sides—should be precut and ready to sew. Any questions you might have about your project could also be answered by your upholsterer. It is good business sense for him to be courteous and helpful to potential customers or friends of potential customers. You might want to point this out to him, especially if he appears disagreeable. When you need custom-made buttons for your project, know how many buttons you will need and bring in scrap pieces of fabric to cover the metal molds.

Sewing Machines

Some upholstery projects can easily be completed using a home sewing machine. There are three main differences between the home machine and the industrial machine. First, the home machine has a small motor. If you are sewing several layers of heavy upholstery fabric, use the proper tension and sewing needle (probably a coarse size, 8 stitches per inch, or the coarsest size, 6 stitches per inch) as indicated in your owner's manual. Go slowly, turning the wheel by hand where necessary. Your strength in turning the wheel may supplement the power from the small motor. The home machine, though, may not be powerful enough to sew through many heavy upholstery fabrics. The industrial sewing machine has a larger, more powerful motor (Fig. 2–24). When you step on the power pedal, you have to make sure you do not sew too fast so you have control over the speed.

Second, the industrial sewing machine has a welt foot for making neat welt cording. The home sewing machine's counterpart is the zipperfoot. If you sew with care, you can also make neat welt cording with this setup.

Third, there are some fabrics that only the industrial sewing machine can sew properly and neatly. It is not necessarily the thickness of the upholstery fabric that calls for an industrial sewing machine, but the pile. Fabrics with a high woven pile are velvets, corduroys and friezes. Piles have a tightly woven base with other synthetic or natural threads woven on top. Two pieces of pile material have a tendency to creep like a caterpillar while they are being sewn together. If the proper pressure foot and feeder are not used, the top layer has a tendency to

Fig. 2–24 Upholsterer's industrial sewing machine with a powerful motor. (*Chandler Machine Sales Co., Inc.*)

stretch and the bottom layer to shirr up so that the ends of the two layers do not match. The upholsterer's industrial sewing machine has a "walking foot feeder" with one or two sets of teeth. If the machine has only one set, it is in the pressure foot section and called a walking foot. If there are two sets of teeth, one set is in the pressure foot section on top of the material and the other set of teeth is underneath the fabric in the head of the machine. These pressure "walking foot feeders" prevent the piles from stretching and shirring up. The home sewing machine has no feeder with teeth in the pressure foot section, only in the head underneath the fabric. When the pressure foot is applied, the two pieces of fabric are held together, but nothing keeps them from creeping.

Smooth fabrics such as denim, rayons, nylons, broadcloth and practically every single pile upholstery fabric—even several thicknesses—may be sewn on the home sewing machine. If you run into too much touble, it is easier to let your local upholsterer, tailor, seamstress or laundry sew your pre-cut, prepinned fabric on a heavy-duty industrial sewing machine.

Button-Making Machines

The button-making machine is a hand press which uses various sets of dies in the top and base (Fig. 2–25). There are two dies in every set and they come in different sizes. The buttons come in two pieces: the top part is like a cup; the bottom part is a cup with a loop underneath. The bottom cup fits into the top cup. These two cups, with the aid of the dies, hold the upholstery fabric so that the button matches the new upholstery cover. The operator pushes down the handle of the press and the pressure on the dies forms the two cups with upholstery fabric into a custom-made button. The cups and fabric are held together by a crimping action.

Fig. 2–25 Making covered buttons. (*Handy Button Machine Co.*) *a.* Button-making machine with the dies to cut the fabric and press the fabric into the button molds. *b.* Finished covered button.

Chapter 3

Supplies

A reupholstery project almost talks to you and tells you what components it has, what needs to be replaced and what needs to be added. Every project has special requirements. Your chair or couch is something of a teacher.

You should never throw away the old "dirty" upholstery supplies you find when you take a chair or couch apart. The *only* supplies that you should ever throw away are old bent tacks, rotten webbing, burlap and cambric and, eventually, after the project is finished, the old upholstery fabric. *Never* throw away the springs or any layer of stuffing. Always replace missing springs and add new stuffing to the old. Dirty stuffing can be sterilized with a spray purchased from your local professional upholsterer. After the stuffing is removed from the seat of the chair, you can vacuum any dust and loose fibers resting on the webbing.

This chapter describes all upholstery supplies you're likely to use in a project.

Basic Reupholstery Supplies

Upholstery Tacks

Although upholstery tacks come in fourteen different sizes, there are only three basic ones that you will need: number 3 oz., number 6 oz. and number 14 oz. (Fig. 3–1). Number 3-oz. tacks are used to tack down one or two layers of material—upholstery fabric, burlap and cotton felt stuffing. They are also used for pintacking. To tack down two or more layers of materials or for "blindtacking" outside backs and arms, use number 6 oz. Number 14-oz. tacks are used to secure webbing and heavy burlap and to anchor spring twine onto the frame.

Most tacks are sterilized by the manufacturer so that they can be placed in the side of the upholsterer's mouth, making it a third hand.

Gimp and Gimp Tacks

Gimp is a decorative trimming used to cover up the tacks where the upholstery fabric is fastened

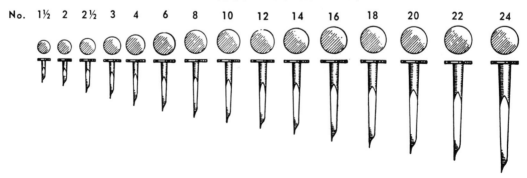

shown actual size

No.   1½   2   2½   3   4   6   8   10   12   14   16   18   20   22   24

Fig. 3–1 Upholstery tacks for tacking webbing, fabric, burlap and cambric on the frame. (*W.W. Cross*)

next to exposed show wood (Fig. 3–2). Because it is a trim, it must be put on neatly and accurately. The color of the gimp must match the new upholstery fabric or, in the case of a pattern or stripe, match one color. Most gimp comes in solid colors and is made from cotton, rayon or silk, or a combination of these.

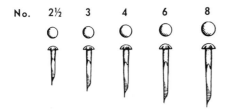

Fig. 3–2 Gimp as a decorative trimming for covering up tacks.

The most popular weave of gimp is called scroll gimp. One of its best features is that it can be glued on without glue seeping through the openings of the weave.

Gimp tacks were used by the old upholsterers to hold gimp in place (Fig. 3–3). The modern upholsterer attaches the gimp with white glue, pintacking the gimp every few inches. When the glue dries, the tacks are removed carefully.

No.   2½   3   4   6   8

Fig. 3–3 Gimp tacks used to hold gimp in place until glue dries. (*W.W. Cross*)

Other methods have been introduced that make gimp tacks obsolete. Modern design furniture is hand sewed, blindtacked, machine sewed with single welt and double welted. Insead of gimp, some designers use ornamental nails on corners of the chair or perhaps the whole outside back and arms.

Ornamental Nails

There are three types of ornamental nails: steel, brass or nickel plated; solid brass; and colored plastic nails to match plastic upholstery fabric or imitation leathers. Ornamental nails can be used on legs, outside arms, outside backs, or where the gimp goes on antiques. It is a matter of taste when and where you use ornamental nails (Fig. 3–4).

If your project already has ornamental nails in it, take them out and look closely at the frame to see if there are several nail holes in a relatively small area. New ornamental nails have to be anchored

into new holes. If the chair has been reupholstered several times, chances are the wood would split if you used new nails. Instead, try blindtacking, handsewing or gimping. You may like the "new look" even better.

Fig. 3–4 Ornamental nails for covering tacks, holding down fabric and decoration. (*W.W. Cross*)

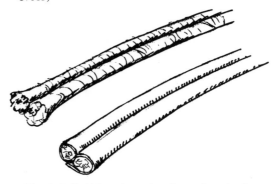

Fig. 3–5 Double welt used as decorative trim instead of gimp.

Double Welt

Double welt is used in place of gimp on modern furniture when there is exposed show wood. Do not use double welt on antiques because the style is inappropriate and detracts from the finished product.

A professional upholsterer has a special sewing machine foot for making custom-made double welt to match your upholstery material (Fig. 3–5). It is best to have him make as much as you need for a minimal charge.

Springs

The springs in a chair or couch are found in the seat and back. They give upholstered furniture resiliency and elasticity. A chair is not rigid and hard. When you sit down on it, the springs "give," producing a soft, comfortable feel—provided that the chair is properly designed and padded.

There are three kinds of springs: the double-cone coil spring, the single-cone coil spring and the No-Sag spring.

Fig. 3–6 Double-cone coil spring used for seat or back. (*Kay Manufacturing Corp.*)

Double-Cone Coil Springs

The double-cone coil spring is the best type of spring construction (Fig. 3–6). It is very rare to find a boken one. Because of its resiliency, the coil spring can absorb the shock of constant compression and expansion. However, coil springs do have a tendency to compress too much after many years of use. They can be stretched out and pulled to original height.

Coil springs come in different sizes. The size of the spring depends on the design of the chair and the location of the spring. Designers try to make the top of the seat of an overstuffed chair used for reading and relaxing 16″ to 18″ off the floor (Fig. 3–7). As a general rule, the taller the spring, the greater the elasticity and the softer the feel. Seat springs come in heights from 4″ with 5 turns (or circles) to 11″ with 10 turns. Older chairs were usually designed with short legs and 10″ or 11″ springs. The overstuffed chair was close to the floor, extremely comfortable and very hard to get out of. Some chairs, such as wing chairs, had long legs where a 7″-high spring might be needed. Many designs in modern furniture have long legs. If the modern chair has short legs, the springs may be attached to a wood board several inches up from the bottom of the chair, instead of being attached to the webbing at the base of the chair, as in older furniture. This type of construction calls for shorter springs.

Springs also vary in thickness or gauge. Seat springs are thicker than back springs because they support more weight. When describing the gauge of a spring, the smaller the number, the thicker and heavier the spring. Seat springs come in gauges from 9 to 10½. Back springs may come in 13 or 14 gauge, or heavier.

One type of double-cone coil spring you might find in an older chair is a Marshall Springs Unit. These springs are 4″ high with 4 turns and a gauge of 13 or 14. They are sewn and clipped in a muslin bag with a pocket for every individual spring.

Single-Cone Coil Springs

The single-cone coil spring is found in modern furniture (Fig. 3–8). Essentially, it is a double-cone coil spring cut in half. The cones are attached to a wood base or metal strips. They are used in upholstered furniture with high legs.

Fig. 3–8 Single-cone coil spring found in seats and backs of some modern furniture. (*Kay Manufacturing Corp.*)

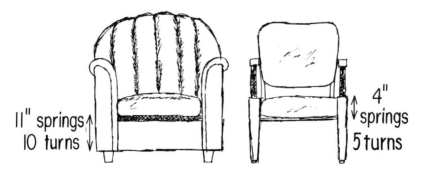

Fig. 3–7 Different style chairs have different size coil springs, resulting in varying degrees of comfort.

Spring Twine

Spring twine is used to tie down the coil springs and keep them from shifting. It is important to use top quality spring twine, since the life of the chair depends in part on the condition of the seat. Poor quality twines break and wear out sooner. The best and strongest spring twine stocked by your local upholsterer comes from a vine that grows in the swamps of Italy. It is tough and durable.

No-Sag or Zig-Zag Springs

No-Sag springs are used in most modern furniture. The steel spring has a gauge of 6 or 8. Each loop is 1″ from its neighbor (Fig. 3–9). Each length of No-Sag is 4½″ apart on center. This is a standard width between springs. No-Sag springs are used both in the seat and the back. They are attached with No-Sag clips (Fig. 3–10). The clip is a piece of steel 1″ by 1½″ bent over to form a catch. One nail and hole is mounted to the frame. Two or three other nails and holes are used to close in the No-Sag spring.

There are advantages and disadvantages to using No-Sag springs and clips. No-Sag springs are faster and simpler to install than coil springs. You do not need webbing or heavy burlap for a foundation. However, No-Sag springs do not stand up as long as coil springs. They have a tendency to snap after years of use and pressure due to inadequate resiliency. No-Sag clips also break off the frame and, after much use, you might hear a squeak in the springs. There is a layer of paper adhesive attached to the inside of the clip to keep the steel spring from rubbing against the steel clip. When this paper wears down, the friction between the spring and the clip produces a squeaky noise.

Helical Springs

Helical springs are used between the frame and rows of No-Sag springs (Fig. 3–11). There are two different sizes, one used between the frame and the spring, the other between two sets of springs. Your

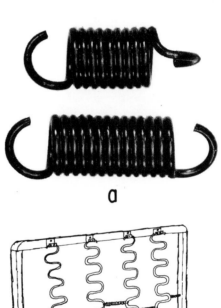

a

Fig. 3–9 No-Sag or Zig-Zag springs are found in most modern furniture. (*Kay Manufacturing Corp.*)

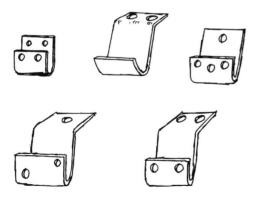

Fig. 3–10 No-Sag clips anchor the No-Sag springs to the frame. Replace clips with the same type as the original ones. (*Kay Manufacturing Corp.*)

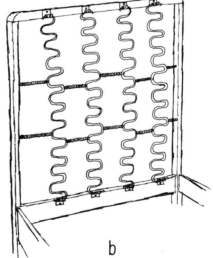

b

Fig. 3–11 Helicals are springs used between the rows and frame of No-Sag springs. (*Kay Manufacturing Corp.*) *a.* Two sizes of helicals. *b.* Helicals are placed in the middle of the back or seat, where most of the user's weight is located.

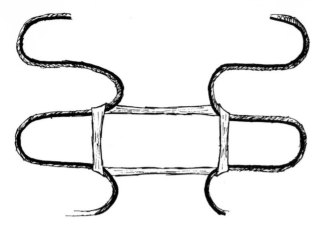

Fig. 3–12 Upholstery rubber bands can be used instead of helicals between each row of No-Sag springs.

Fig. 3–14 Jute webbing is used as a strong foundation for the seat, back and arms.

local upholsterer will be able to supply you with any replacements for broken or lost helicals.

There are many functions of helicals. The first function is to prevent the springs from tipping sidewise. Helicals also make the springs work together as one unit, distributing the weight so that two or three springs do not carry the whole burden. Helicals prevent the burlap from sagging between the rows of springs. Lastly, helicals make the No-Sag springs unit feel as close to coil springs as possible.

There are two substitutes available for helicals. There are tough, strong $2^{1}/_{2}''$ by $4^{1}/_{2}''$ rubber bands (Fig. 3–12). Another substitute is spring twine, tied at the frame and between the rows (Fig. 3–13)

Webbing
Jute Webbing

Jute webbing acts as a foundation for the springs, padding and fabric of a chair (Fig. 3–14). Your project may need one, more or all strips of webbing replaced. Jute webbing is a strong, coarse material made from the jute plant grown in India. It comes in rolls $3^{1}/_{2}''$ or $4''$ wide, and in various weights and grades. It is best to get the highest grade available, since webbing acts as a foundation for the chair.

Rubber Webbing

Rubber webbing is used on Danish modern furniture which has a lot of exposed wood. The only upholstery used is loose cushions. Rubber webbing comes in rolls $2''$ wide. It is made with two plys of cloth wrapped with a layer of rubber on each side (Fig. 3–15). A flat or V-type bite clamp is attached to the rubber webbing and the frame. Rubber webbing has a relatively short life. After four or five years it rots or stretches out too much, sagging and not acting as a good support for the cushions. How-

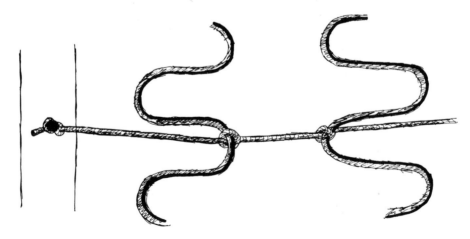

Fig. 3–13 Spring twine also keeps No-Sag springs from tilting sidewise and helps the springs work together as a unit.

Fig. 3–15 Rubber webbing is used on Danish modern furniture.

ever, both the rubber webbing and the loose cushions can be easily reupholstered.

Steel Webbing

There are two kinds of steel webbing—strap steel webbing and Neversag steel webbing.

Strap Steel Webbing. Strap steel webbing is used in a chair with coil springs (Fig. 3–16). After the webbing is tacked on and the springs are tied in place, the chair is turned upside-down. A strap of steel ¾″ wide, insulated with paper so it is not noisy, is nailed across each row of coils. It is used only in one direction. The purpose of the strap steel webbing is to give added support to the jute

Fig. 3–16 Strap steel webbing gives added support to jute webbing and heavy 17-oz. burlap.

webbing or heavy 17-oz. burlap used as a foundation for the seat. It is especially good for repair when the seat previously caved in.

Neversag Steel Webbing. Neversag steel webbing is very rarely used, but you might come across it in one of your projects. It is used in place of jute webbing for coil-spring construction. It is a strip of corrugated steel 1¼″ wide that is woven over and under each side of a coil spring. The major disadvantage to this construction is that the corrugated steel has a tendency to stretch out, weakening the foundation for the springs.

Burlap and Upholstery Cardboard
Heavy 17-oz. Burlap

Heavy 17-oz. burlap, also called Neversag burlap, is used for the same purpose as jute webbing—a foundation for the springs. Heavy burlap is like a medium-grade webbing also made from jute. It comes in rolls 30″ wide. In reupholstery work, where the old webbing is worn and must be discarded, we recommend that you use new Neversag burlap in combination with strap steel webbing for the best results. Neversag burlap is easier and faster to put on than webbing. Unlike a webbing construction, it has no airholes.

Cardboard

Some manufacturers use strong brown or grey cardboard instead of burlap and webbing. Upholstery cardboard is between $1/16''$ and $3/32''$ thick, much stronger than corrugated cardboard. It is used on the inside arms to keep the stuffing from falling through. It is also used on the outside arms and outside backs of some curved-back chairs. On top of the cardboard goes a layer of cotton stuffing, then the upholstery cover.

If you have any damaged cardboard in your project, replace it with a combination of webbing and 10-oz. burlap, or just 17-oz. burlap. Usually, over a long period of time the tacks have fallen out of the cardboard edges. In this case, replace the tacks. The cardboard sometimes stands up better than the webbing.

10-oz. Burlap

Light 10-oz. burlap is primarily placed over the seat and back springs as a foundation for the stuffing, so it has a base and does not fall through the springs. If the light burlap is not worn too badly or torn and looks as if it will give years of service, you can reuse it. Otherwise, you will need to replace it.

In curved-back furniture, 10-oz. burlap is used

along with webbing in the outside back and outside arms. It helps maintain the roundness in the chair. Light burlap is also used to make a pattern and sack for a channel-back chair that is then placed on top of the webbing.

Note where light burlap was used, for your chair will dictate when and where you will need to use light 10-oz. burlap.

Blind-Tack Tape

Blind-tack tape is a brown cardboard tape that comes in two widths, $^3/_8''$ and $^1/_2''$. Most upholsterers stock only one size, probably $^3/_8''$. The process of using blind-tack tape is called blind tacking (Fig. 3–17). The most common use of blind tacking is on the tops of outside backs and certain outside arms. Blind-tack tape is placed on the wrong side of the outside back, right up against the welt or close to the top. The tape and material are tacked, giving a neat line appearance that follows the shape of the chair. Blind-tack tape can also be tacked to the welt to keep the welt stiff and neat. It is important when blind tacking to tack or staple at the top of the tape; otherwise, when you turn the upholstery fabric over, the seam looks as if it will open up.

Another use for blind tacking is to avoid double sewing. Double sewing requires the upholsterer to hand sew through four thicknesses of fabric. For example, the outside back, the inside back and two thicknesses of welt. Single sewing involves sewing through only two layers of fabric. In the example

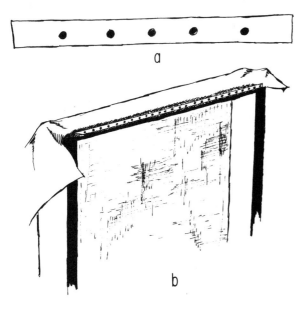

Fig. 3–17 Using blind-tack tape. *a*. Tape is brown cardboard, usually $^3/_8''$ wide. *b*. Blind tacking hides the tacks and gives straight edges or follows the curve of the chair.

given, the inside back is tacked down, then the top of the outside back is blind tacked. On the sides, the welt is tacked. The outside back is flipped over, with the face of the fabric showing, then $^1/_2''$ seams are folded and pinned on the sides. The outside back sides are hand sewn to the first layer of welt. Single sewing requires half the effort and half the time used for double sewing.

Another use of blind-tack tape is to tack on base welt, where the design of the chair calls for it. Tack the welt and tape on the edges of the chair bottom. Tack the cambric dust cloth on top.

Muslin

Muslin is an inexpensive white cotton fabric similar to a bedsheet. In the old days, muslin was used extensively. A chair or couch was completely upholstered with a muslin cover, ready for the final cover. A customer walked into a furniture store, picked the fabric and the style of chair or couch, then the upholstered furniture was custom-made. This is no longer done. Upholstering with muslin essentially meant upholstering a chair twice.

Depending on the age of your chair, you may find a layer of muslin on it. You will find that the first upholstery job on all antiques had muslin. When an antique is reupholstered for the first time, it is not necessary to recover it with the old muslin or to put new muslin on it. It is a matter of taste. If you want to the follow the old methods, you can put it on, but you will be reupholstering twice.

Between the 1940s and the 1960s, muslin was used on modern furniture instead of light burlap to pad the outside back and outside arms where there were no springs. If this muslin needs to be replaced in your project, you can replace it with light 10-oz. burlap.

The most common use of muslin today is for upholstered skirt linings. This concept is very much like drapery lining and will be discussed in the section on skirt linings.

Another use of muslin is fastening foam rubber or polyurethane foam to the frame of a chair. The width of the muslin is the width of the foam plus 1" or 2" extra, and the length is the perimeter of the rectangular or round foam. The muslin is rubber cemented to the sides of the foam. When the cement dries, the muslin is tacked down on the sides of the seat or back frame, wherever the foam is placed. The foam can be placed on top of springs or where there are no springs. This process avoids a bulky look on the sides (Figure 3–18).

There are times when you may want to make a pattern with muslin, then transfer it to the real

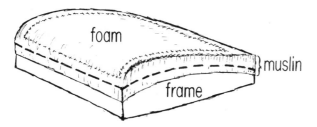

Fig. 3–18 Foam on the typical recliner seat is held down by muslin. Xs show where the muslin is attached to the foam.

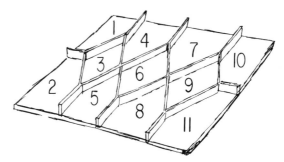

Fig. 3–19 Wood forms are the basis of modern three-dimensional fabric designs.

upholstery fabric. You do not want to learn by trial and error, and muslin is relatively inexpensive compared to upholstery fabric. If you ever want to redesign a chair, try experimenting first with muslin, pintacking it, then removing it and using it as a pattern.

Another use for muslin is in making three-dimensional designs. These designs are factory made and hard to duplicate. As an example, let us take a diamond design. This design will not be tufted. An operator at a furniture factory makes a wood form using strips of wood $1/2$ inch thick (Figure 3–19). He lays the form on top of a base, perhaps a piece of plywood. Then he cuts blocks approximately 1″ deep the shape of the diamonds and channels (Figs. 3–19, 3–20). He lays the upholstery fabric right-side-down on top of the form, then presses the blocks in their proper slots. The blocks form the three-dimensional design on the fabric. The operator removes the blocks and puts in 1″ precut polyfoam or foam rubber diamonds and channel shapes identical to the wood blocks. Now he paints the whole surface of the foam and upholstery fabric with rubber cement. Then he adds a layer of muslin on top of the wet cement. When the muslin gets wet, he brushes out the wrinkles and rolls the muslin smooth. When it dries, he has an inside back with a three-dimensional look (Fig. 3–20).

Instead of using a wood form and rubber cement, another way to make raised three-dimensional designs is by using stencils, special crayon and a special sewing machine. Let us use the same diamond example: The right side of the upholstery fabric is marked in a stencil-type manner, using a crayon made with phosphorus so that the stencil will glow under a special purple light. The fabric is turned around, right side down on the table. A precut layer of foam is centered on the fabric. Muslin, the same size as the fabric, is placed on top of the polyfoam. With a plier-type stapler, the three layers are stapled on all four sides to keep the layers from shifting. Then the fabric is turned right-side-up so that the marked design faces the operator. There is a special sewing machine made just for this purpose (Fig. 3–21). It has a three-foot neck to accommodate the whole inside back. It also has a special purple fluorescent bulb which makes the diamond markings glow. The operator of the sewing machine follows the lines of the pattern. The result is a sewn-in design of any shape desired, again giving a three-dimensional look.

A similar method is quilting. The design can be free-form, the operator creating a design while he is sewing; or he can follow a design outline that is printed in the fabric.

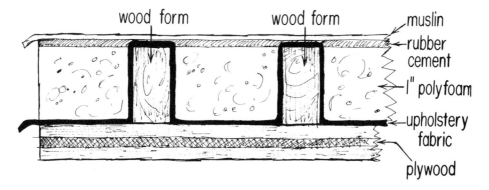

Fig. 3–20 A three-dimensional design with fabric, foam and a muslin backing.

Fig. 3–21 A special sewing machine used to make raised three-dimensional designs. (*Chandler Machine Sales, Inc.*)

Such craftsmanship is hard for an amateur or professional reupholsterer with limited machinery to duplicate. If your project has a raised three-dimensional design, you might consider consulting your local upholsterer for advice, change the inside back to a flat look or try to find prequilted upholstery fabrics on the market.

Cambric

Cambric is black cotton cloth tacked onto the bottom of the chair to catch the dust that accumulates. A chair breathes out when you sit down and in when you stand up. The air it breathes in also has dust particles. Over a period of time, an inch-thick layer of dust and stuffing particles will fall through to the webbing. Besides keeping this dust in, the cambric gives the bottom of a chair a finished look.

Stuffings

The purpose of stuffing is to make the chair comfortable. When there are springs, the stuffing eliminates the feel of sitting directly on top of them. There are many different kinds of stuffings, different combinations and different feels. Following are descriptions of stuffings you might find in, or add to, your project.

Cotton Felt

There are three grades of cotton felt padding. The best and highest grade is staple cotton. This is a pure white cotton containing no seeds. It has a soft, resilient, bouncy feel. It should be used with very fine fabrics, such as a silky rayon. If you use the second-grade cotton with seeds, you'll be able to see and feel the seeds through the rayon. It is off-white and comes in rolls 27" wide and 15" to 16" in diameter. You can regulate the thickness of the cotton by the number of layers you use. The roll itself is layered with paper every 3/4". Smaller layers can

be peeled off as desired. Cotton felt with seeds is used throughout the chair. In reupholstery work, use a new layer of this cotton so the chair has a fresh, soft feel. The third grade, reclaimed cotton, is used in cheaper furniture. It is grayish-black, very stringy and made from rags. It does not have a soft feel to it and it is easily matted down. Reclaimed cotton is used in outside backs, outside arms and on borders.

Tow and Moss

Tow and moss have very similar characteristics. Both look like very coarse steel wool. Moss is a natural fiber that grows on trees in the southern states. Tow is made from palm fibers. Both are used as first layers of stuffing, directly on top of the springs and burlap. The fibers are hand picked. They have to be laid on uniformly and stitched to the burlap so that the stuffing does not shift. Either tow or moss is used; they are not used in combination. This first layer of stuffing is covered with cotton felt. You find this combination primarily in older furniture with an overstuffed, comfortable look and feel.

Hair

Curled horse hair looks similar to moss and tow. It comes from horses' tails and manes and is sorted according to color and texture. Hair can also come from cattle and hogs. Hair is completely processed after it has been sterilized, spun, curled, dried and seasoned. Hair comes in a large bag. It must be handpicked and matted into place. Like tow and moss, hair acts as an insulator so you cannot feel the springs in the seat and inside back.

Curled hair is one of the longest-lasting stuffings available. Just about every antique has horse, cattle or hog hair for a stuffing. Besides being used on the back and seat, hair was used in some old cushions, where it is usually found in a casing of muslin. If your chair has a hair cushion that is not water damaged and there are no holes in it, you can reuse it. To give a fresh new look and feel, just wrap a layer of cotton around the muslin casing.

Rubberized Hair

Rubberized hair is a mixture of horse, hog and cattle hair, curled and rubberized with rubber cement. It comes in rolls or sheets of different thicknesses, 1" or 2", and light or medium density. It can be held in place by hand sewing, tacking, gluing or attaching muslin to the sides and frame. Rubberized hair is used as a first layer of stuffing on the inside back, seat and arms. It is easier and faster to work with than curled hair. It was used a lot about twenty-five years ago. Furniture manufacturers today do not use rubberized hair. They have replaced it with polyurethane foam and foam rubber.

Sisal

Sisal is a natural fiber grown in the Philippines. The fibers for upholstery are the same as the ones used to make sisal rope. A heavy-density pad is used on the seat with a lighter density on the inside back. Sisal can be placed on top of the burlap without being sewn. Some furniture manufacturers put the sisal right on top of the springs, with only a small strip of burlap attached to the front so the cotton cannot work its way into the springs.

Foam Rubber

Foam rubber was first introduced after World War II. The natural product, the latex or sap of the rubber tree, is the base of foam rubber. There are two types of foam rubber: solid and pincore foam (Fig. 3–22). The pincore foam rubber has holes $1/8''$ in diameter every square inch. Pincore foam rubber breathes better than solid foam rubber. During a hot, sticky day, you'd perspire if you sat on a cushion made from solid foam rubber, just as if you sat on a plastic cushion.

Foam rubber comes in seven different thicknesses: $1''$, $2''$, $3''$, $4''$, $5''$, $1/2''$ and $1/4''$. Each size has a special function.

Foam rubber in thicknesses of $1''$, $1/2''$ and $1/4''$ is used on arms and backs to increase the padding and make it easier to get out of a chair. This is especially helpful for older people. These thicknesses are also used on some seats as a second, soft layer of stuffing.

Dining room and kitchen chairs use $2''$-thick foam rubber. It is also found in combination with cotton on tufted backs on modern furniture.

Foam rubber $3''$ thick is used in Danish modern furniture and trailer furniture for loose cushions in the seat and back.

Pincore crown foam rubber, $4''$ flat and $4''$–$5''$, is used to make loose cushions. They are both better than $3''$ foam rubber because of their greater depth and body. The $4''$–$5''$ pincore crown foam rubber is $4''$ thick on the sides and $5''$ thick in the middle. When you sit on a cushion, most of the compression occurs in the middle. A thicker middle gives a more comfortable, fuller feel and a longer buoyant life. To make a better cushion with the $4''$ flat foam, some companies cement a $1''$-thick foam strip all around the sides of the cushion to give it a full look. Pincore crown, however, is recommended as best for cushions. It comes in sheets $109''$ long and $23''$ to $25''$ wide. You can purchase medium density for the seat and soft density for the back.

Foam rubber produced in previous years used a different formula with more rubber latex than that produced today. The new foam rubber has a tendency to disintegrate more readily. The new synthetic polyurethane foam, also called polyfoam, has been replacing foam rubber in quantity. The new high-density polyfoam has replaced it in quality.

Polyurethane Foam or Polyfoam

Polyurethane foam is the synthetic equivalent of foam rubber. There are three densities: soft, medium and the new high density.

The soft-density polyfoam, the least expensive, is used for loose back cushions. It has a soft, mushy feeling like feathers. It is nice when you first get it, but it does not have a long life. Sometimes it is wrapped with Dacron to give it an even softer feel.

The medium-density polyfoam is slightly more durable. It is used for seat cushions, alone or wrapped with Dacron. Medium-density polyfoam does not equal the high-density polyfoam in comfort or quality.

The new high-density polyurethane foam is as

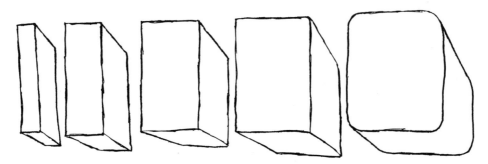

Fig. 3–22 Both polyurethane foam and foam rubber come in five common thicknesses: $1''$, $2''$, $3''$, $4''$ and $4''$–$5''$ pincore crown.

good as the best foam rubber. When you go shopping, try your local professional upholsterer for this high-quality, long-lasting product.

Polyurethane foam comes in the same thicknesses as foam rubber (*see* Fig. 3–22): 1″, 2″, 3″, 4″ and 4″–5″ crown, and ¹/₂″ and ¹/₄″ on special order. (*See* the preceding section on foam rubber for descriptions of the uses of each size.)

The manufacturer, the small professional upholsterer, the home craftsman and the beginner can use any leftover pieces of new and old foam rubber and polyfoam. Foams are expensive and need not be wasted. Leftovers should be shredded—picked by hand or cut with a serrated bread knife—into small square-inch pieces, and put aside in a cardboard box or plastic bag for future use.

One of the most common uses of leftover foam is for stuffing loose throw pillows, and pillows attached to the arms in some upholstered furniture designs. Sometimes upholsterers and manufacturers pack the shredded foam in preshaped muslin bags and use them for stuffing the inside backs and inside arms, or they might use the shredded stuffing without the muslin bag. Channels in a channel-back chair are often stuffed with a mixture of shredded foam and picked leftover Dacron, eased into place by a metal form.

Dacron

Another stuffing used for the second soft layer in a chair seat or inside back is Dacron. A soft, puffy stuffing, it is sold in two forms: wrapped with muslin or without muslin (Fig. 3–23). The Dacron wrapped with muslin comes in a roll 27″ wide with layers ¹/₂″ to ³/₄″ thick. Muslin is stitched to the Dacron every 4″ along its length. This Dacron is mostly used to revitalize old foam rubber or polyurethane cushions. The Dacron is wrapped around the old foam and hand stitched closed. The other form of Dacron is not wrapped with muslin and comes in a roll. It is uniform in thickness and more puffy than Dacron wrapped with muslin. It is rubber cemented onto the foam rubber on seats and inside backs.

Kapok

Kapok, also called "silk floss," is a natural, soft, silky fiber. It is mostly found in channel-back chairs and cushions. It is still sold today and you might find it in your chair, but very few upholsterers use it. If it is loose, it is so light and silky that it will get all over you. You can easily breathe it in. It is similar to feathers, but has less body and does not pack down as much. If the kapok comes in a casing and appears to be in good shape, it can be reused and covered with a layer of Dacron wrapped with muslin, to give it a new, fuller feel. Kapok does not absorb moisture. For this reason, it is extensively used in boat cushions and life preservers.

Feathers and Down

Down is the feathers of young birds, primarily the young goose, and the undercoating of the adult goose and duck. Down has practically no quill, because the fibers radiate from a center quill point. Feathers have soft, silky fibers growing from a tough, stemlike quill (Fig. 3–24). Down is much softer and lighter than feathers. Both are found only in antiques or very expensive custom-made furniture. Neither is recommended for use around people with allergies.

In the old days, goose, duck, chicken and turkey feathers were used as cushion and furniture

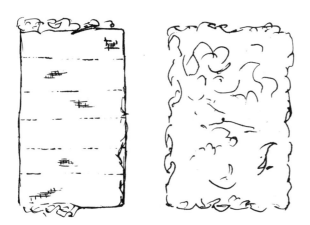

Fig. 3–23 Dacron comes wrapped in muslin (*at left*) or without muslin.

Fig. 3–24 Feathers (*at right*) have quills and are not as soft and light as down.

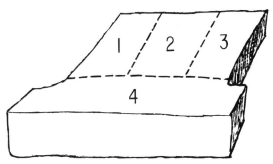

Fig. 3–25 Four-chambered casings stuffed with feathers and sewn together made up the old cushions.

stuffings. There were special vacuum cleaners that would suck the feathers into the many-chambered casings that made up a cushion (Fig. 3–25). The casings were made from ticking material, a very tightly woven muslin. Perhaps you had a very soft feather pillow when you were a child. You may remember how, even with the tightly woven casing, a few of the quills managed to stick out.

The nicest thing about a feather cushion is that, when it is placed on a chair with the proper-sized seat springs, it can be the most comfortable chair there is. When you sit on it, the cushion shapes to your body. A new cushion has a soft, mushy, heavenly feel. However, over the years, moisture gets into the feathers. Imagine a wet feather! It loses all its softness. Many layers of moist feathers pack down and the cushion becomes very hard. It is too difficult and time consuming to rejuvenate a hard feather cushion. But a feather cushion in pretty good shape, packed down but not hard, can be put into better shape. In the old days, women used to hang the cushions out on a sunny, dry day and beat them with a wire paddle (Fig. 3–26). You can try this method, with or without the wire paddle. The drier the feathers, the fluffier the cushion. If you are

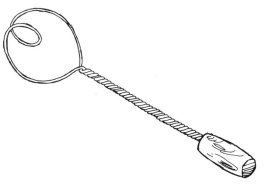

Fig. 3–26 Wire paddle used to beat feather cushions.

satisfied with the results, reuse the feather cushion. If you are not satisfied, it will be very costly and difficult to find an upholsterer willing to tackle the job. So, your best alternative is to replace the feather cushion with a foam rubber or polyurethane foam cushion.

Fabric Preparation Supplies

Threads

Hand Sewing

Hand sewing involves sewing seams on the outside back, the outside arms and on pleats. Upholsterers use either cotton or nylon carpet thread, number 18 gauge. Carpet threads are waxed to prevent knotting, twisting and shriveling. If you have a problem with your carpet thread, you can wax it yourself by rubbing the thread with soap or beeswax. Carpet threads also come in assorted colors. In the old days, an upholsterer used only two colors: tan for light-colored fabrics; black for dark-colored fabrics. If you sew ''the'' upholsterer's hand stitch—the blind stitch—carefully, you could use any color. The beginner may want to purchase carpet thread to match one of the dominant colors in his fabric.

Machine Sewing

As with hand-sewing threads, there are both cotton and nylon threads. The strongest and best cotton thread for sewing heavy upholstery fabrics is 16–4—16 gauge diameter and 4 ply. The medium strength is 20–4; the least expensive and least durable strength is 24–4. The nylon machine thread for upholstery is number 69. It is very fine and very strong, stronger than the 16–4 cotton machine thread. When it comes to threads, nylon is definitely stronger than cotton in a given gauge-strength group.

Never use machine threads intended to sew clothing on upholstery or even slipcover work. The threads break too easily and the seams rip apart under pressure. Upholstery and slipcovering also involves sewing through may layers of fabric, which are often quite bulky.

Flax Stitching Twine

Flax stitching twine, also called mattress twine, is used to stitch burlapped edges and the first layer of stuffing into place. This flax twine has a thicker gauge and is stronger than nylon and cotton threads used to hand sew fabric. You can also purchase nylon stitching twine for sewing burlapped edges and for tufting.

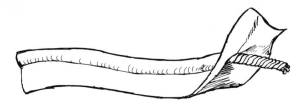

Fig. 3–27 White cotton or paper welting cord covered with fabric is tacked or sewed onto the edges of the cushions, back, arms or seat to give the chair a finished, tailored look.

Welting
Welting Cord

Welting cord is a cotton or paper cording covered by a 1½-inch-wide strip of upholstery fabric and sewed on the inside edge of the cording (Fig. 3–27). Its main function is to give the upholstered chair or couch a finished, tailored look. Throughout this book, when we mention *welt* we are referring to fabric-covered welting cord.

There are two kinds of welt cord: cotton slip-cover welt cord and paper upholstery "fiber welt cord." Cotton slipcover welt cord looks exactly like the four-ply twisted cotton yarn used to make old-fashioned mops. It is soft, pliable and, above all, washable. It can also be used for upholstery. The fiber welt cord is stiffer and is made by companies that manufacture toilet paper. The paper is twisted tightly and meshed with the thread cover to hold it together. It should *not* be used for slipcovers that will be machine washed, because the paper fiber cord will disintegrate.

Cotton slipcover and upholstery welt comes in one size. The standard upholstery fiber welt cord is ¼″ or ⁸/₃₂″. It also comes in widths of ⁶/₃₂″, ⁵/₃₂″ and ⁴/₃₂″.

At one time, thick ½ inch—as opposed to ¼ inch—fiber welt cord was used extensively in modern furniture to give it a different look in design. You may have thick welt cord on your project and wish to replace it again.

Ready-Made Welt Cord

Ready-made welt cord is already covered with a decorative fabric. It comes in a few solid colors and is usually used for slipcovers. When you are doing a custom reupholstery job, one of the easiest and most satisfying parts of your project can be making your own matching welt. Nothing equals a perfect match for the tailored look.

Double Welt

In place of gimp on modern furniture where there is exposed show wood, designers use double welt.

A professional upholsterer has a special sewing machine foot for making double welt. It is best to bring a scrap of your reupholstery fabric and have an upholsterer make custom matching double welt. Double welt can be glued on and set the same way as gimp.

Do not use double welt instead of gimp on antiques. It would be out of style and detract from the finished product.

Zippers

Zippers are used in upholstery to give loose seat and back cushions a fitted look. They are also used in some ottomans where the top has a cushion effect. Zippers are used in slipcover cushions and on one side of the outside back seam to facilitate removing the slipcover for cleaning.

Fig. 3–28 Upholstery zippers come on a long roll. They are cut to order.

The size of the teeth in upholstery zippers is number 5. Upholstery zippers are usually tan. The professional upholsterer buys zippers in a roll, cutting each zipper the length needed and adding an end and pull (Fig. 3–28). You can buy any length and type zipper you need—18″, 20″, 24″, 27″, 30″, 36″, 45″, 54″ and 72″ long—at your local fabric shop or intermediate sizes in an upholsterer's shop.

Frame and Wood Refinishing Supplies

There are three basic conditions of exposed show wood in a chair or couch.
1. The show wood is in *good* shape. It does not have a lot of scratches and dents. It may look dull, but otherwise is practically brand new. The show wood just needs a good cleaning and shining.
2. The show wood is in *fair* shape. The surface is scratched, but not extensively. The wood needs touching up, as well as cleaning and shining.

3. The show wood is in *poor* shape. The surface is badly marred, dented, scratched and dull. It needs a complete refinishing job. This might include stripping, cleaning, wood filling, rebuilding, regluing, restaining, varnishing and repolishing.

There are three basic conditions of the frame in a chair or couch.

1. The wood frame is sturdy with no loose joints. The frame needs no attention.
2. The wood frame is sturdy in most areas with the exception of a loose wing, arm or leg. The frame needs minor repair.
3. The wood frame wobbles. It needs extensive repair work, regluing and reclamping most or all the joints.

This section will list all the supplies you need to prepare the show wood and the frame for the next reupholstery step. Before you do any "refinishing," you should be familiar with what goes into the "finish" of a chair's exposed show wood. There are seven basic steps in the creation of a satin-stained chair leg.

1. A block of wood—usually oak, maple, cherry, mahogany or pine—is cut to the design desired for the chair leg. A curved leg is cut with a bandsaw. A straight leg is cut by a table saw. A round leg is cut on a wood lathe.
2. The shaped leg is sanded by an electric sander. Sanding takes the marks of the saw off the wood, shapes the leg to exact dimensions (if the leg is $2^{1}/_{16}''$ wide and it should be exactly $2''$ wide to fit in the leg joints, it can be sanded) and it gives a smooth appearance.
3. Holes are drilled for doweled joints.
4. The leg is fastened, glued and clamped in the correct position in the frame.
5. The leg is stained, usually a darker color than the natural color of the wood.
6. The pores of the wood leg are sealed with the first coat of varnish, lacquer, shellac or polyurethane. The sealer acts as a barrier to prevent future applications from soaking into the wood like a sponge, disappearing from the surface.
7. Second and third layers of varnish, shellac, lacquer or polyurethane act as a protective coating to keep the wood from drying out, cracking and showing minor bumps. Sanding between applications gives a smooth, satin finish.

Supplies for Frame Repair
Flathead Screws

Flathead screws are used instead of clamps to tightly hold in place two pieces of wood until the

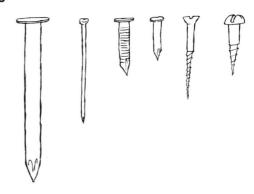

Fig. 3–29 Nails and screws used in reupholstering include, *from left,* the rozen nail, finishing nail, stronghold screw nail, No-Sag nail, flathead wood screw and roundhead wood screw.

glue at the joints dries. They can be used alone at a joint or in combination with dowels. The screw in the middle of two dowels acts as a clamp.

Flathead screws are unfinished, sharp-edged screws that are used where they will not show when the chair or couch is reupholstered (Fig. 3–29).

There are two types of heads on flathead screws: the Phillips, which is like a cross, and the slot. They come in different thicknesses and lengths. If you are missing a few screws and have an original available, take a sample to your hardware store and order the exact size, unless the person who previously repaired the chair used the wrong size screw.

Flathead screws are also used to brace corner blocks and screw in short legs.

Roundhead Screws

Roundhead screws have curved, smooth, finished heads and can be used on the outside where they may show (Fig. 3–29). One use is for attaching metal plates that the legs of modern furniture will be screwed to.

Rozen Boxed Nails

All upholstered furniture, if it has nails, has rozen boxed nails (Fig. 3–29). They are lighter and thinner than common nails and lightly coated with rozen. Rozen is a chemical that serves two functions: first, it acts as a lubricant, allowing the nail to glide into the hole; second, it acts as a glue once in the wood.

Nails are used just like screws when it comes to assembling the frame. A small hole is drilled in the frame between two dowels, and the nail is hammered into place. If you are taking apart a frame and need to replace rozen nails, you can purchase these at your local upholsterer's shop, hardware

Fig. 3–30 Dowels used in reupholstery are *(from left)* the screw-type grooved dowel, plain dowel and wood dowel plug.

store or lumberyard, or replace them with flathead screws.

Wood Dowels

Wood dowels are used to join two separate pieces of wood on a furniture frame. They are especially useful where the joint is exposed and not upholstered. Dowels are usually made from hard birch wood. There are two types: the screw-type grooved dowel and the plain dowel (Fig. 3-30). The grooves in a screw-type dowel serve two functions. First, as the dowel is driven into the wood, the grooves allow trapped air to escape. Second, the glue used to secure the dowel in the hole bites into the grooves, making the dowel even stronger. The standard furniture screw-type dowel is $7/16''$ in diameter and $1\,3/4''$ long. Antiques with thinner wood use dowels $3/8''$ in diameter and $1\,3/4''$ long. There is also a $7/16''$ by $3''$, used when three pieces of wood are glued together.

Plain dowels are the ones you usually see in hardware stores. They come in assorted diameters, from $1/8''$ to $1''$, and up to $3'$ long. They can be purchased the length and diameter desired. The standard diameter for furniture is $7/16''$; however, the hole where the old dowel set may have worn larger than $7/16''$ and a new larger dowel is needed. It is necessary to make a V groove in the dowel in order to allow trapped air to escape when the dowel is driven into the hole. Otherwise, the dowel acts like a piston, the trapped compressed air acts as a spring, the glue acts as an air sealer and lubricant, and the dowel shoots out of the hole or may crack the hole side of the wood.

Wood Dowel Plugs

Wood dowel plugs are used to seal holes at the head of screws in the exposed wood of maple and Danish furniture. They are usually made from birch or maple. In the old days, regular dowels or wood

filler were used to cover up a screw in the exposed show wood. Wood dowel plugs are easier and faster to use.

There are two different types of wood plugs (Fig. 3-30). One looks like a short cork on a wine bottle: It sinks into the wood tightly and completely. The other kind looks like a mushroom: The base of the mushroom sinks into the hole while the top sticks out. Both serve the same function and come in different diameters—$7/16''$, $1/2''$ and $5/8''$, with $7/16''$ being the standard. A little drop of glue is placed on a plug to hold it in place.

Wood dowel plugs are practically impossible to remove without damage. The only way to remove them is by driving a screwdriver or chisel into the center with a mallet. When the center comes out, the sides will fall out. The wood plugs can also be drilled out.

Glues

Glue is set between the joints of a frame to give extra strength. The joints are always clamped, screwed or nailed until the glue dries. The two types of glues used in furniture repairs are hide glue and white glue. Hide glue is the "old timer." It is made from the hides of horses. In the old days, hide glue came only in a dry sawdust-like powder that you had to mix with water in an electrically heated glue pot. Today it is an amber-colored, premixed liquid ready to use. You may have seen it also in small tubes of household cement at checkout counters in hardware stores. A thin coat is brushed on both sides of the joint, leaving a tough, shock-absorbent coat. It is water resistant and only very, very dry heat and age will weaken its holding power. An antique chair was found floating in the ocean three days after a hurricane. The joints glued with hide glue were still solid as a rock, because they were properly glued and the frame was very thick.

White glue is the more modern affixative. It is used in every wood project requiring glue. It is not waterproof and the wood projects must be kept indoors. It is strong and quick setting. It is easy to wipe off any excess with a wet cloth. White glue is white when wet and dries to a clear finish.

Corner Blocks

Corner blocks are used in the corners to keep the frame square. They are glued and screwed or nailed in place. Corner blocks give the frame a stronger, triple joint. You may need to replace or repair a corner block.

Supplies for Wood Refinishing

The following supplies should be used outdoors in the shade on a calm day or in a well-ventilated room, because their fumes are toxic. These supplies are flammable, so care should be taken never to smoke while refinishing. Throw all used rags away or place them in a fireproof metal can, never in a plastic or styrofoam container, which might melt or decompose.

Paint and Varnish Removers

Paint, varnish, lacquer, polyurethane and shellac have one thing in common—they all lie on top of the wood. Stain, when applied by itself, soaks into the wood. Paint and varnish removers strip off anything that lies on top of the wood—dirt, grease, wax, and varnish, lacquer, polyurethane or shellac. If stain was premixed with varnish or wax, the paint and varnish remover will take it off. If stain alone was applied directly to the wood, then paint and varnish removers will not remove it.

Paint and varnish removers are used when the exposed show wood is in poor shape, badly scratched and marred, and needs a complete refinishing job. Apply the remover with an inexpensive paintbrush. It evaporates very fast and should be kept out of the sun or breeze. Let the paint and varnish remover soak in for 15 to 20 minutes. Then wipe off with a coarse cloth, an old towel, scraps of burlap or coarse steel wool. You may need two applications of paint and varnish remover to get the wood clean.

Lacquer Thinner

Lacquer thinner is similar to paint and varnish remover, in that it is another cleaning agent. It cleans off oils from the sweat of your hand, dirt, wax, and old coats of varnish, shellac, lacquer or polyurethane. It opens up the pores of the wood so that new stain can soak in and a new sealer and protective coating can be applied.

Lacquer thinner is also excellent for cleaning stain and other gunk from your hands.

Denatured Alcohol

Cleaning the exposed show wood surface is the first step in refinishing. Neutralizing the wood is the second step. Denatured alcohol neutralizes the wood so that the new finish, the stain and varnish or any other sealer and protective coating, stays on the wood. Denatured alcohol alone will not remove the old finish. Apply with a cloth and 15 or 20 minutes later, wipe off.

Wood Bleach Kits

If you'd like to lighten the color of the stain, use a wood bleach kit. There are two solutions in this kit. The first solution, the bleach, makes the wood white. The second solution, the neutralizer, neutralizes the wood so that the new stain will be absorbed. The next step is to restain the wood the desired color.

Wood bleach is only needed where the old stain has penetrated into the wood. If the stain was applied as a mixture with varnish or similar products, then the paint and varnish remover will remove it.

If you do not have a wood bleaching kit, ordinary household bleach could be used for bleaching and denatured alcohol for neutralizing.

Stains

There are five combinations of stains available: penetrating oil stain, varnish with stain, wax with stain, shellac with stain and lacquer with stain. The main difference is that penetrating oil stain penetrates into the wood and the other mixtures sit on top of the wood.

Penetrating Oil Stains. Penetrating oil stain can be applied with a brush, lint-free rag, old nylon stocking or cheesecloth. Stains come in various colors, from the darkest mahogany and walnut to the lightest oak and blond maple. Every company has its own color chart, so start and finish a project with the same brand. You can also mix a lighter stain with a darker stain, experimenting until you get the exact color you need. This technique is especially helpful when you just have to touch up a few scratches and nicks.

Varnish with Stain. Varnish with stain is an oil-based varnish mixed with an oil-based stain. The first coat seals, protects and stains the wood. The second and additional coats darken the finish and give it more body. It is easier than staining first and then varnishing, because the two steps are combined. The biggest disadvantage is that it is slow drying. You can also mix different colors to get the exact color of stain with varnish desired.

Wax with Stain. Wax with stain looks exactly like a shoepolish. You rub it into the wood, just like you would a paste shoepolish. If you prefer a satin, waxed look—as opposed to a shiny lacquer, shellac or varnish look—use wax with stain.

Shellac with Stain. Shellac with stain should be avoided when possible because it has a short life. It usually loses its ability to dry properly after six months of storage in the can on the shelf.

Lacquer with Stain. Lacquer with stain comes in a fast-drying spray, making it quick and easy to apply.

Finish Coats: Sealers and Protectors

The finish coats to use when the stain is applied separately are varnish, lacquer, shellac, polyurethane and wax. The first application seals the pores of the wood so that future layers will adhere to the surface of the wood. The second and third coatings protect the wood and finish from being damaged by minor bumps and, when sanded lightly with thin sandpaper or fine steel wool, give the finish a smooth look with more body.

Varnish. Clear varnish is brushed onto dry, stained show wood. It comes in either satin or high gloss. Even when you want a satin finish, the high gloss should always be used as a first coat or sealer. The second and third layers can be the satin. Clear varnish comes in spray or cans.

Lacquer. One of the biggest advantages of lacquer is that it is fast drying. It is usually sprayed on because it dries so fast. You could put several coats on the wood in one day. Lacquer dries to a hard finish. Lacquer can be brushed on, but because it dries so fast it is necessary to add a "lacquer retardant."

Shellac. Shellac also dries very fast, but not as fast as lacquer. Several coats can be brushed on and sanded the same day. Shellac has a short shelf life. After the can is six months old, it has to be thrown out. The shellac will never dry, but will always stay sticky. It comes in two forms: white and orange shellac.

Polyurethane. Polyurethane is one of the newer finishes on the market. It is similar to varnish, and comes in a satin or gloss finish. Like varnish, polyurethane is resistant to both hot and cold water.

Wax. Wax is usually used on old furniture. If the wood is in good shape, rub the wood with denatured alcohol and fine steel wool, cleaning and neutralizing it. Before you rewax the show wood, dust it thoroughly. You do not want to wax in the dust.

Scratch Remover

Scratch remover oil and polish are used for minor retouching jobs. There are two colors, light and dark. They are oil-based stains. You should use these only if your chair has minor scratches and does not need a complete refinishing job. There are also touchup kits with several colors. Never wipe the scratch remover all over the arm or leg of a chair—it will streak. Just wipe it on the bare spots.

Wood Filler

Wood filler is a plastic synthetic wood. The best way to apply it is to mix the required amount with stain in a little cup, glass or wood. With a putty knife, apply a small amount to the opening or crack, making it a little bit higher to allow for shrinkage. When it dries, sand it or file it down. Deeper holes should be filled two or three times so it can dry hard.

Sandpaper

Sandpaper is used in upholstery work for two main purposes: to level and smooth wood filler; to smooth the finish between layers of varnish or any other protective coating. For smoothing wood filler, you can use either a medium-coarse sandpaper or aluminum oxide paper with granules that are cleaner, faster cutting and heavier duty. Fine sanding between varnish layers should be done with fine 000, 00 or 0 sandpaper. Always sand *with* the grain or you will leave scratch lines.

Fine steel wool also does the job of fine sandpaper. The rough wood grain that wants to stand up is smoothed down. Steel wooling the wood between applications of finish coat gives a glassy-smooth surface.

Chapter 4

Sources of Tools and Supplies

Reupholstering tools, supplies and small services are not hard to find if you know where to look. The quality and variety available depend on the type of store you go to, not on your proximity to a large city. Mail order firms for the shopkeeper and homemaker distribute goods and services to the suburban, small town and city dweller.

One-Stop Shopping

Local Professional Upholsterer

Throughout the book, we mention that you can purchase tools, supplies and services from your local professional upholsterer. Only the upholsterer is likely to have *all* the supplies of the craft, or access to them. Although they are in the business of reupholstering chairs and couches, most will be glad to sell supplies and order specialized tools. They feel that by offering friendly service they may win you over as a future customer or, perhaps, that you may recommend them to friends.

Your local upholsterer can be especially helpful when it comes to buying small amounts of specialized upholstery supplies like cardboard blind-tack tape, cotton felt, webbing, quality foam, welt cording, No-Sag springs and clips. The tools you can buy through the upholsterer will be the same quality tools he uses on the job.

You can also purchase services from a local upholsterer. In a small town in Vermont, a home craftsman was reupholstering a tufted recliner. For a minimal charge, the local upholsterer gladly sold him twenty fabric-covered buttons, using the new upholstery fabric and his professional button-making machine. The local upholsterer's sewing machine was too temperamental for a customer to use, so the home craftsman called a professional upholsterer in the next largest town. For a couple of

dollars, he allowed the home craftsman to use the machine for an hour while the upholsterer went about his work.

If you do not have much experience with sewing machines or your upholsterer is reluctant to let you use it, then you can have him sew it for you. Come prepared, with all the pieces cut and pinned (or stapled) and ready to sew. If one upholsterer is not interested in helping you, try another. A tailor or laundry will also have a heavy-duty sewing machine for heavy fabrics.

Your upholsterer can also be a good source of advice. Think out your project ahead of time. If you have any questions, ask him while you buy your supplies.

You can buy fabric from an upholsterer, as well. Most use the higher-priced, quality-crafted fabrics found in interior decorating shops, not cheap factory fabric that will wear out easily (as used on less expensive new furniture). The biggest disadvantage is that you choose your fabric from sample catalogues. It may take a couple of weeks or more for the fabric to come into the shop.

Whatever you need to buy, your local upholsterer offers one-stop shopping.

Upholstery Supply Houses

In many cities, there are upholstery supply houses set up to retail supplies and tools. They may be a part of the upholsterer's shop. They stock everything you will need to complete your project.

A Variety of Stores for a Variety of Needs

Mail-Order Catalogues

The large department store mail-order sections have upholstery kits (tack hammer, tack lifter, curved needle, straight needle and webbing stretcher). They also carry webbing, burlap, stuffing and a limited variety of other supplies.

Woodcraft mail-order catalogues also sell upholstery tools and supplies. They have a larger variety than the general mail-order houses. Mail order is convenient for at-home shopping. You may prefer the extra help and advice from a professional upholstery shop.

Factory Outlets

When there are flaws in the weave, these upholstery fabrics are sent directly to seconds shops. You have to carefully examine any fabric you buy to check that the flaws are few and far between—far enough apart to allow you to cut around them or place them in the least conspicuous spots on the chair. When you shop for fabric, do not go by the posted estimate charts stating how much fabric you will need. Make your own accurate measurement chart and cutting diagram by studying Chapter 7.

The factory outlet or seconds shop may also carry other upholstery tools and supplies, but it is first and foremost a fabric shop for upholstery, slipcover and drapery needs.

Fabric Shops and Departments

Local fabric shops or fabric departments in large department stores usually carry a limited variety of upholstery material. The fabrics on display are usually the less expensive materials that will not wear as well as quality fabrics ordered by the professional upholsterer. For your first project, you might feel more comfortable working with a pleasing, decorative, less expensive fabric, especially if the chair or couch does not get much use or abuse.

Some fabric shops or departments also carry sample catalogues of varying qualities for special order: usually the higher the price, the higher the quality. They may also stock webbing, burlap and perhaps cotton felt or batting. Do not buy your sewing machine thread here, because the threads are not strong enough for upholstery (unless the thread is nylon, very difficult to break and designated for heavy upholstery fabrics).

Interior Decorating Shops

Many interior decorating shops and furniture stores house a professional upholsterer. They also have numerous books of fabric samples that may keep you daydreaming about which beautiful one to use. They may also sell other upholstery supplies and be available for questions you might have about a fabric's durability and suitability for your decor.

Hardware Stores

Most hardware stores stock several sizes of upholstery tacks, decorative nails, staples, staple guns and the less expensive and lower grade tack hammer. They will also carry all the frame and wood preparation supplies you need: varnish removers, lacquer thinner, stains, wood filler, flathead screws, wood dowels and glues. Other tools they are likely to have are the claw chisel or tack lifter, wood mallet, rubber mallet, trimming knife, icepick (stuffing regulator), tape measure, yardstick, pipe clamps, C clamps and screwdrivers.

Furniture Factories

Some furniture factories, especially the smaller ones, will be willing to sell the upholstery supplies that go into making their furniture. So do not hesitate to ask if you have one nearby.

Secondhand Furniture Stores

The cheapest and maybe the easiest way to replace a broken seat rail, back post or leg is to find another old upholstered chair in need of repair or beyond repair that you can strip. Try the dump, as well as secondhand furniture stores. You can salvage coil and No-Sag springs, too. Make sure that the height and gauge of the springs are the same as those in your project.

Chapter 5

Selecting Reupholstery Fabrics

The choice of reupholstery fabric is a personal one. Your selection will depend upon whether you want your furniture to have a formal, semiformal or informal look. Different styles of furniture also tend to look better with certain fabrics.

We are not experts on fabric. We recommend that you talk to your local interior decorator, fabric shop or department store sales person about the different fabrics available, their advantages and disadvantages.

Durable Fabrics

The most common question concerning fabrics is, "Which will best survive wear and tear in a house full of active children?" Our answer is 100 percent nylon. Nylon is tough to cut with scissors for reupholstering, and just as tough on furniture used and abused by children. Either the burlap-type weave or nylon frieze—raised nylon loops with a nylon or cotton backing—is the best. These come in solid colors or in designs. Any fabric that has nylon along with other natural or synthetic fibers (Dacron, cotton, rayon, etc.) should outlast a fabric without nylon.

Another factor in fabrics with good durability is the weight. A heavy, thick fabric will most likely wear much better than a thin, light fabric. Stay away from thin, dress-weight fabrics, no matter what the composition.

Velvets

Rich, deep-colored and luxurious-feeling velvets are one of the most popular upholstery fabrics. They come crushed, cut or plain. Velvets come in 100 percent nylon and a rayon-cotton combination, with nylon the tougher of the two.

Some velvets can be railroaded, i.e., if the width of a fabric piece is more than 54″ (the standard width), as in the case of the inside back, outside back or seat of a couch, then the fabric piece can be laid sidewise. A velvet can be railroaded if the nap runs up and down the width of the fabric (Fig. 5-2).

What is the *nap* of the velvet? Remember, velvet is made of raised fibers on a backing. The nap is these raised fibers. When you rub your hand across the fibers, vertically or horizontally, there is one direction that will feel stiffer. If you run your hand from the bottom to the top of the nap, the fibers will stand on end. If you rub downward, from top to bottom, the fibers will lie flat (Fig. 5–1). When

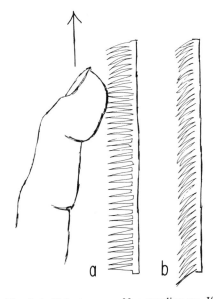

Fig. 5–1 Velvet nap. *a*. Nap standing up. If you move your finger from the bottom to the top of the nap, the fibers will stand on end. *b*. Nap lying down. If you rub downward, from top to bottom, the fibers will lie flat. A nap that lies flat points to the bottom of the goods.

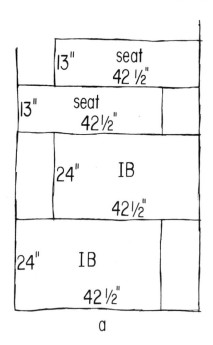 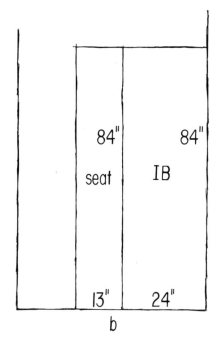

a   b

Fig. 5–2 Railroading velvets. *a*. Cutting the width of an 84″ seat and 84″ back the width of the fabric means that you must cut two fabric pieces for the seat, each 42¹/₂″ wide, joining them in the center. Do the same for the back. *b*. When you railroad velvet for a couch, you only need one piece of goods for the IB and one piece of goods for the seat, instead of two pieces each as in *a*. *Railroading* means that the width of the IB and seat is cut on the length of the fabric.

working with velvet, the nap or raised fibers should always be pointing down, i.e., lying flat. A nap that lies flat points to the bottom of the goods.

Figure 5–3 shows which way the nap should run on individual fabric pieces when working with velvet. The nap should always point down because, if the nap is brushed up, the color will look like another shade.

Prints, Plaids and Stripes

The directional arrows in Figure 5–3 also apply to the top and bottom of each fabric piece with prints, plaids or stripes. When you unroll the fabric you bought, the cut ends are the top or bottom and the selvage ends are the sides (unless the fabric is woven for railroading). An upside-down pattern is usually easy to spot. If there is a flower, the stem should always go to the bottom. Upside-down plaids or stripes usually will look a different shade or do not match at all. Remember, when you label and cut your individual fabric pieces, to mark them immediately with OB, OA, etc., and follow Figure 5–3.

For your first reupholstering project, we recommend that you stay with a solid-colored fabric. If you have experience in working with fabric, you may like the extra challenge of working with prints, plaids or stripes. These tips on matching should help make the job easier.

The dimensions of the fabric pieces for prints,

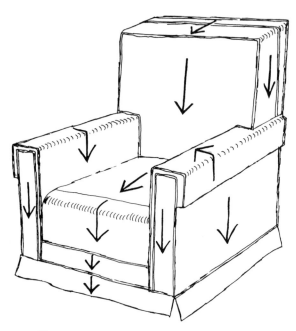

Fig. 5–3 The nap should always point down as you move your hand in the direction of the arrow for each fabric piece.

stripes and plaids will be exactly the same as solid colors. The only difference is that the pattern has to fall in a specific spot so that the stripes and plaids line up with what is above and what is below. For this reason, you cannot use the standard fabric measurement chart and cutting diagram described in Chapter 7. For every 5 yards of solid fabric measured, add 1 yard extra when you are working with prints, plaids or stripes. For example, a couch requiring 10 yards of solid fabric will need 12 yards of fabric if there are any prints, stripes or plaids to be matched.

Other tips on working with prints, plaids and stripes will be discussed in Chapter 7.

Vinyl Plastic and Leather

We recommend that you stay away from plastic for your first project, unless you are working on a relatively simple chair, such as a kitchen chair. If you reupholster a recliner, do not use plastic.

Vinyl plastic has a tendency to stretch when sewing—it almost acts like a rubber band. You want as much control over your fabric as you can have. Vinyl plastic is hard to control.

If you use vinyl plastic on kitchen chairs, remember never to railroad it (cut the length sidewise), unless it is absolutely necessary. You can railroad, or cut crosswise, your strips of vinyl for welt, because plastic stretches a little vertically, but mostly horizontally. Never cut welt strips on the bias with plastic, since it stretches so nicely on the simple vertical or horizontal cut.

You cannot hand sew vinyl plastic as easily as cloth. It is difficult to stitch and has a tendency to rip easily. If the outside back or outside arms need repair, use ornamental nails instead. If torn cushion seams need repair, always machine sew the rip.

The most important rule to remember when you work with vinyl plastic is that any holes made will remain and not close up as they do in a tweed or nap fabric. So never poke a stuffing regulator in vinyl plastic. Also, never pin or staple above the $1/2''$ seam line; always pin or staple within the line. You do not want pin or staple holes to show or to rip the finished cover.

When it is time to slide the vinyl cover over the top back of the kitchen chair or to stuff foam into a vinyl cushion cover, spray the stuffing with silicone. A silicone spray makes the vinyl glide over the foam or other stuffing. Look for a small can in your hardware store.

All the considerations that apply to vinyl plastic also apply to imitation or real leather. Leather also stretches when sewn; leaves permanent holes when pinned, stapled or sewn (so you cannot afford to make a mistake and rip out a seam); and is helped onto the stuffing by the use of a silicone spray. There is very little leather used in upholstery today. leather is very expensive and it takes a good craftsman to know how to work with it. Vinyl imitation leather is more prevalent and less costly.

Needlepoint

Every needlepoint needs to be squared. You can square it with a damp cloth and iron, or steam iron. Take a scrap of plywood or Masonite and pintack one side and the bottom first so they are square. Then stretch the top and other side into a square. You can use a carpenter's square, the corner of a square table, or you can square it by eye. In knitting and crocheting this method is called *blocking*.

When you are reupholstering a seat where all four sides will be tacked under, make sure that you center the pattern on the seat and allow $1/2''$ to $1''$ of needlepoint in place. You do not want any bare spots to show.

On the bottom of the seat (most likely the removable seat of a rocking chair or dining room chair), trim the sides of the needlepoint by cutting the backing fabric close to the woven fibers.

Any piece of needlepoint that must be sewed, as for a throw pillow, cushion or inside back, where the threads of the weave have to be cut into, is treated differently. First, mark the woven needlepoint the size you want it, allowing for the usual $1/2''$ seams on each side. Rubber cement the ends under $1/2''$. Then, when the rubber cement is dry, cut the remainder of the woven needlepoint and/or backing off. This process will keep the needlepoint from unraveling.

Chapter 6

Your Workshop

Your workshop can be in the family workshop, a spare room, the garage, the corner of a family room, the basement—any place where you have adequate work space, storage, light and height.

Work and Storage Space

You will need enough room so that you can walk around your chair or couch, working from all four sides. If you are a weekend or evening craftsman or beginner, your projects will take several sessions that may span several weeks. if you select a corner of a room, and want your project to be out of sight after each session, you can throw a big sheet on top of it and pin an intriguing "do not disturb" sign on it. If you do not mind the untidy look of an unfinished project and if no one will touch your tools and accomplishments, you might want to leave your project uncovered. (Of course, keep dangerous tools and supplies out of the reach of small children and animals.) A reupholstering project can be an interesting conversation piece. Probably the best solution is to find a workshop or spare room that you can close the door to after every session. You will just want to sweep up any loose tacks or scraps of fabric that are of no use.

Speaking of tacks, we recommend that you never work with a rug underneath your project. It is too difficult to pick up all the tacks off a woven rug, and too risky not to pick them all up. So, select a room with a bare floor.

You will also need a fabric-cutting table. A large dining room table is the best arrangement. You want to be able to open your fabric up at least the 54″ width and the length of one large fabric piece. You can unroll and mark the fabric a little at a time. Then, cut when you finish marking all the pieces, again unrolling the fabric a little at a time. If your dining room table is not big enough, a well-swept floor could serve as a cutting table. Avoid cutting fabric on thick pile carpets.

Adequate Light and Height

You will want to work under the most comfortable conditions possible. The best lighting for workshops is two 4′-long fluorescent lights directly over a couch or chair. You have a good view of all four sides of your project. You may be tying knots, tacking and hand sewing, and you do not want to strain your eyes more than is necessary. However, any room well lighted—either by artificial lights or natural sunlight—will be adequate.

One of the most important rules of your reupholstering work area is to have adequate height. You need a comfortable working position. You do not want to strain your back by constantly bending over to complete every reupholstering step. The ideal way of bringing your chair or couch up to a comfortable working height is to make upholstery horses. Figure 6–1 shows the specifications for making your own. Borders around the tops of the horses keep the chair legs from slipping off.

If you have regular carpenter's sawhorses, with no boards on top to hold the legs of a chair or couch, you can adjust them for upholstery use. On the top of each sawhorse, screw in a $3/4$″ board. You can remove the board when you finish the project.

Upholstery or adjusted sawhorses also allow you to reach and work underneath a chair if you need to. For example, to remove bolts of a convertible hide-a-bed. They are also versatile: horses can be placed as close or as far apart as the legs of the chair or couch are.

If you do not have or wish to make horses, a low table big enough for your project might also be

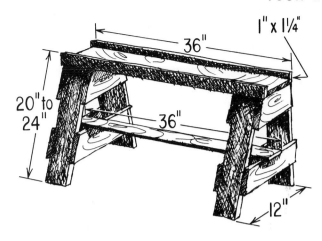

Fig. 6–1 Upholstery horses give you adequate working height. This one is made entirely from 1 x 4.

helpful in raising the chair to an adequate height. If you have carpenter's horses, you can also place a sheet of plywood on top of the horses. You can use the raised plywood as a fabric-cutting table, as well as a lift for the chair.

Moving Furniture

Carrying a 350-pound convertible couch or a 200-pound colonial sofa can be easier if you know ahead of time what you are doing, a stuggle if you do not. We are listing a few pointers that might be helpful.

1. The best arrangement for carrying furniture is two people holding a well-balanced couch or chair. Discourage the third party helper who runs in the middle of the couch to assist you. He is only rocking the boat, throwing you off balance.

2. For endurance and balance, spread your arms so that you are carrying the couch in the front and back corners at the bottom of the frame. If you are going through a doorway, place both hands just to the inside of both legs at the bottom of the frame, to save your fingers from getting squashed.

3. Another way to balance furniture is to put one hand up on the front of the arm and the other in front of the back leg.

4. The person who is walking forward should always guide the person who is walking backward.

5. Hold the weight of the couch with your legs, *not* your back. Bend at the knees with your back straight. Never bend over from your back.

6. When you go through a doorway, the angle of the back of the chair should be vertical.

7. When going around corners, either turn the back straight up and then give it a half turn, or vise-versa.

8. Sometimes a couch just won't make it through a doorway or around a corner. We have seen owners of a large colonial sofa lower it from a second story window with ropes, but these were big, husky fellows. We do not recommend this method. If a couch must be removed to a new work area, try taking off any removable legs. An extra 2″ could make a world of difference.

9. For the 350-pound convertible couch, see if the back lifts out—the modern convertibles do. Check to see if there is a wing nut under the arm or at the bottom of the back, or screws on the outside back near the back of the arm. Remove the mattress, carrying it separately. Tie a rope around the unit so that it does not open up, jamming in the doorway or throwing you off balance.

Part Two

Reupholstering Techniques

Chapter 7

Preparing Reupholstery Fabric

The first thing to do, before you can even think about how much new reupholstery fabric you will want to buy, is to study, name and label all the fabric pieces that make up your individual chair. In this section, we will look at an overstuffed chair that is labeled appropriately. There are seventeen different fabric pieces that could be found on your chair. As you study the overstuffed chair, label the fabric pieces of your chair while they are still attached to the frame. Study how each piece is shaped and attached. It is important for you to become familiar with the vocabulary in this section. We will be using it throughout the book in the instructions, especially the abbreviations (Figure 7–1). As a general rule, all boxings are sewed, borders are tacked and panels are nailed.

Labeling Upholstery Pieces

Seat

The seat is the front part of the chair, underneath the cushion. When there is a cushion, it runs from

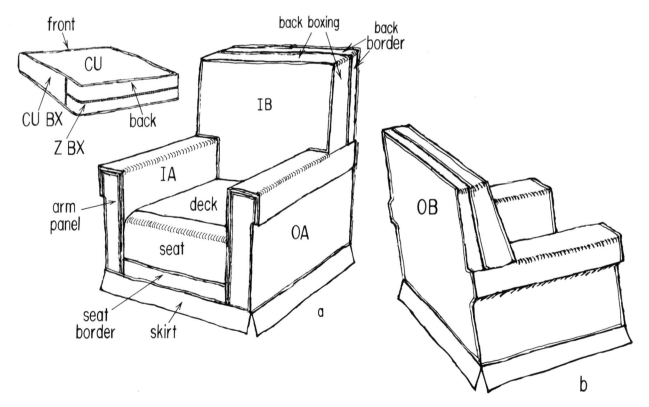

Fig. 7–1 Label all the fabric pieces. The double lines indicate welt. *a*. Front view. *b*. Back view.

49

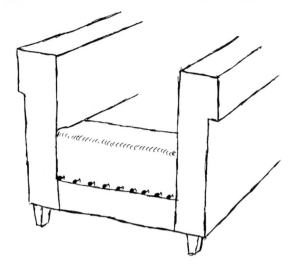

Fig. 7–2 Seat in a chair that has a cushion.

the front of the chair to 3″ or 4″ on top. In chairs without a cushion, the seat covers from front to back and side to side, overlapping on the bottom edges of the chair. The seat is tacked on the bottom or the front of some antiques (Fig. 7–2).

Seat Border

The seat border is found in the front of some chairs with a cushion. It is strictly for decoration; it serves no functional purpose. In the front of the chair, the seat is tacked on a few inches before the bottom of the frame. The seat border, usually a few inches wide, is blind tacked on the top and tacked on the bottom of the chair. It usually runs around the arms. There is a welt between the seat and the seat border. The welt is usually sewn to the border, but it could be tacked separately to the frame. The

border is tacked; then, the blind-tack strip is tacked (Figure 7–3).

Deck

The deck is machine sewed to the top of the seat and tacked out of sight onto the back and two sides of the frame (Fig. 7–4). The deck is directly underneath the cushion, and only exists when there is a cushion. The deck can be covered with special decking material, an inexpensive cotton "duck" or flannel. Decking comes in six different colors. You should choose the color closest to the dominant color in your fabric, or use a tan or gray decking material.

The other way is to make "self-decking"—using the same upholstery fabric as the rest of the chair.

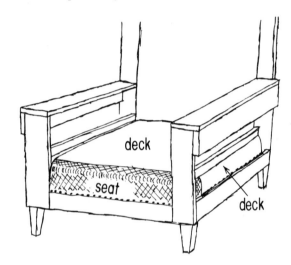

Fig. 7–4 The deck is machine sewed to the seat and tacked out of sight onto the back and two sides of the frame.

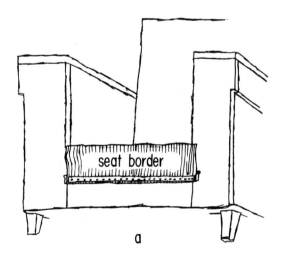

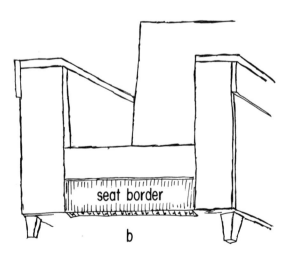

Fig. 7–3 Seat border. *a*. Border is blind tacked on top. *b*. The seat border is tacked underneath the chair.

Use your own judgment: Decking material is less expensive than upholstery fabric.

Inside Back (IB)

The inside back is the part of the chair that your back touches when you sit in it (Fig. 7–5). The IB could be plain, tufted or channeled. If it is a boxed inside back, it is machine sewed to the back boxing and tacked to the top back rail. A border will be tacked on later. On the bottom, it is pushed through the back of the seat and tacked on top of the back seat fabric.

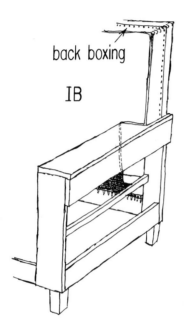

Fig. 7–5 Inside back is machine sewed to the back boxing. On the bottom, it is pushed through the back of the seat and tacked on top of the back seat fabric.

Back Panel

The back panel is made from plywood or hardwood (Fig. 7–6). It measures about 12″ high and 2″ wide. It could be shaped. It is nailed with finishing nails on the top side of the back where the inside and outside backs come together.

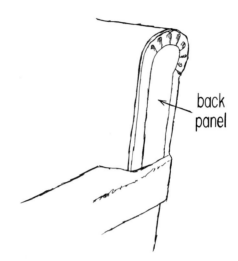

Fig. 7–6 Back panel is a fabric-covered piece of plywood or hardwood, shaped and nailed on each side of the back.

Back Boxing

The back boxing is always sewn to the IB, with a welt between (Fig. 7–7). It gives the top of the back a box-style structure. It can be tacked to the top of the outside back frame; or it can be tacked to within a couple inches of the top of the outside back so that a back border can be affixed.

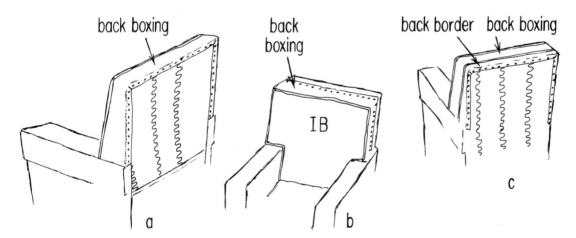

Fig. 7–7 Back boxing. *a.* Back boxing is tacked onto the outside back frame and machine sewed to the IB. *b.* Or, when there is a back border, the boxing is tacked on the top back rail. *c.* The border covers the rest of the top back rail.

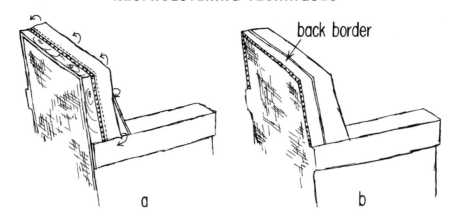

Fig. 7–8 Back border. *a.* The border is first blind tacked on the end of the back boxing. *b.* The border is then tacked onto the outside back frame.

Back Border

The back border is usually between 1″ and 3″ wide. A back border is usually found in good furniture. It adds to the tailored look of a chair. The back border runs on the sides up to the top of both arms (Fig. 7–8). It is blind tacked to the frame at the back part of the back boxing. A welt is tacked on first, next to the back boxing or sewed to the back boxing. The back border is tacked on the top. The back border is then pulled over and tacked on the top of the outside back frame and sides.

Outside Back (OB)

The OB is located behind the chair on the back. It is usually blind tacked on the top, pulled over, stretched out and tacked on the bottom (Fig. 7–9).

The sides are turned under at least ½″, and hand sewed to the welt, if any, and the border. If welt is used, it usually runs on top of the back and down the two sides.

Inside Arms (IAs)

As the name implies, the IAs are located on the inside of the arms. There are several types of IAs. Some are cut and sewed to shape the frame. Some are square or rectangular and tacked on at four places—top, bottom, front and back (Fig. 7–10). Some are pullover, i.e., pulled over the arm frame and pleated in the front. A few IAs are tufted. Some arms are made with a cap on top and the IA and OA can be in two pieces or one piece. More detailed descriptions will be given in Chapter 15.

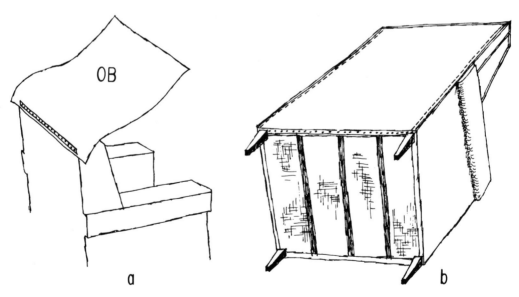

Fig. 7–9 Outside back. *a.* Fabric is first blind tacked on top. *b.* OB is then pulled over, stretched out, tacked on the bottom. The sides are turned under at least ½″ and hand sewed.

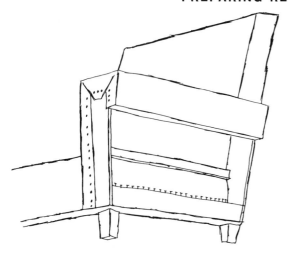

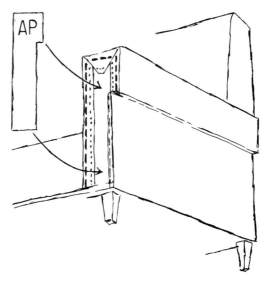

Fig. 7–10 Inside arm in this chair is tacked as shown.

Fig. 7–12 Arm panel is an upholstered, shaped piece of plywood or hardwood nailed to the front of the arm.

Outside Arms (OAs)

The OAs are located on the outside of the arms. They can be machine sewed and shaped, shaped by hand and sewed by hand, or tacked on all four sides—top, bottom, front and back (Fig. 7–11).

Arm Panels (APs)

Arm panels are located on the front of the arms (Fig. 7–12). They can be between $1^1/_2''$ and 3″ wide and the height of the front of the arm. They are upholstered with a half or full layer of cotton felt underneath the fabric. They are nailed with finishing nails. The arm panels cover the tacks from the IA and OA.

Cushion (CU)

The top and bottom parts of the cushion are cut in reverse, but identically shaped (Fig. 7–13). They are held together by cushion boxings with welt between. Along the back of the cushion and extending approximately 4″ on each side is the zipper, which is attached to the zipper boxing.

Cushion Boxing (CU BX)

The cushion boxing is usually $4^1/_2''$ high. It runs along the front and the sides, minus approximately

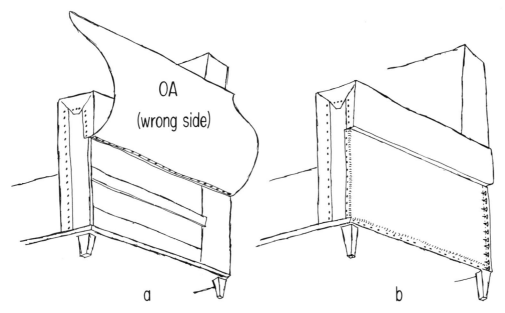

Fig. 7–11 Outside arms. *a.* OA is first blind tacked on top. *b.* OA is then tacked on the bottom, front and back.

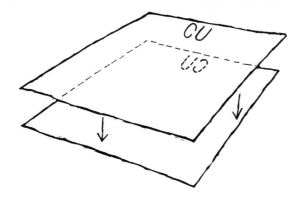

Fig. 7–13 Cushion fabric pieces are the top and bottom of the cushion.

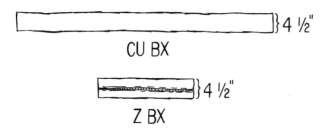

Fig. 7–14 Cushion boxing and zipper boxing are sewn together to give the cushion its height.

4″ from the back on each side. The cushion boxing is sewed to the zipper boxing (Fig. 7–14), then to the top and bottom of the cushion.

Zipper Boxing (Z BX)

The zipper boxing is always cut into two pieces, usually 3″ high and the distance of the back plus 4″ on each side (8″), plus two ½″ seams (1″). In some cases, the zipper boxing is along the back only, especially when there is an open arm and the cushions are visible on the sides. The zipper is sewed between the two 3″ zipper boxing pieces (Fig. 7–14), giving you a finished zipper boxing 4½″ high—the same height as the cushion boxing.

Skirt

The skirt dresses up the bottom of the chair and covers the legs. Sometimes the legs of the chair look very ordinary and detract from its appearance. The skirt serves a cosmetic, as well as a decorative, purpose. There are two types of skirts: the inverted V or kick pleat; and the boxed pleat. At this point, the important information about the two pleats is figuring out how much upholstery material is needed.

The inverted V or kick pleat is used on most standard chairs. The box-pleated skirt is used mainly on colonial furniture and attached pillow footstools. The inverted V skirt is usually cut $8\frac{1}{4}″$ high so that it finishes off, after sewing, at 7″. The inverted V skirt always has a lining. Under each pleat on each corner of the chair, there is usually 12″ of fabric (Fig. 7–15). As an example, a 30″-square chair would require approximately 172″ of joined fabric in the width: $30″ \times 4 = 120″ + (12″ \times 4) + (1″ \times 4)$ for seams $= 120″ + 48″ + 4″ = 172″$.

The box-pleated skirt needs fabric approximately double the perimeter of the chair (Fig. 7–16). For the example of the 30″-square chair, you will be needing double $(30″ \times 4 = 120″)$ or 240″.

For both types, a welt goes around the top of the skirt. It is usually tacked, stapled or sewed by hand. The skirt is blind tacked onto the bottom of the chair so that it hangs close to the floor.

Inside Wings (IWs)

Wings are found on wing-back chairs and colonial furniture (see Fig. 19–7). As you sit in the chair, the IWs are located on each side of your head. The IW is tacked on the top and front. The back part of the wing is pulled through a slat or opening made on the frame. The bottom is hand sewed.

Outside Wings (OWs)

The OWs are located on the outside section of the wing frame (see Fig. 19–11). The welt runs on the edge of the frame. The OW is shaped and hand sewed in the welt. The back part is tacked to the outside back.

Measuring Fabric Pieces

Correct measurements for each upholstery piece not only help you when it comes to chalking and cutting your fabric, but also when you go to the fabric shop to buy your sometimes expensive reupholstery fabric. If your fabric costs $15 a yard and you could efficiently use 5 instead of the estimated 6 yards, then you can save $15. So, before you go shopping, you should learn how to measure all the upholstery pieces, then make a measurement chart and a cutting diagram.

Measure the pieces in the order of the list just reviewed, so as to record every piece. Make a measurement chart like the ones at the beginning of each project chapter (Part Three). In the chart, all the fabric pieces are listed vertically. First record the vertical measurement of the fabric piece, then the horizontal measurement, then any welt measurement for that section of the chair.

Fig. 7–15 Inverted V or kick-pleated skirt. *a*. Determining width of fabric needed to make kick-pleated skirt for 30″-square chair. *b*. Inverted V or kick-pleated skirt is blind tacked on the bottom edge of the chair. *c*. Completed inverted V skirt has a pleat at every corner.

Fig. 7–16 Box-pleated skirt. *a*. How to determine the amount of fabric needed for a box-pleated skirt: $30'' \times 4 = 120'' \times 2 = 240''$. *b*. Box-pleated skirt is blind tacked on the bottom edge of the chair. *c*. Several pleats are on each side of the chair, as well as at the corners.

All measurements should be done *before* the chair is taken apart. If a chair should have a hole in the seat with most of the stuffing missing, then you can estimate how the shape of the stuffing will be when finished. Or, you could wait until the new stuffing is in place and measure then. Another thing to remember is that every piece that is measured is going to be rough cut. All rectangular pieces, to be tacked to the chair on all four sides, are rough cut and fitted on the chair by the pulling and pintacking process. The only pieces that are rough cut using the measurements in your chart, then true cut using the old fabric pieces as a pattern, are *shaped* pieces like some IBs, IWs, IAs and cushions.

We do not recommend that you use every old upholstery fabric piece as a pattern for the new. First, it is time consuming and not necessary. Second, the old fabric may be stretched out of shape after years of use and may be too big. Also, the old fabric must be resquared so that the vertical and horizontal threads of the fabric are not slanted. Use the old fabric pieces only where necessary to get a distinctly shaped piece.

Tips on How To Measure

When measuring a fabric piece that has machine sewed seams on all four sides, add $1/2''$ on each end to the measurements. Example: To get the measurements for the top of a cushion that is 22″ by 24″, add $1/2'' + 22'' + 1/2'' = 23''$ for the vertical measurement; $1/2'' + 24'' + 1/2'' = 25''$ for the horizontal measurement. For any tacked-on side of a fabric piece, allow 1″ extra. Example: The OA of the overstuffed chair is tacked on all four sides. If the OA measures 27″ by 32″, then add $1'' + 27'' + 1'' = 29''$ for the vertical measurement; $1'' + 32'' + 1'' = 34''$ for the horizontal side.

If you have a fabric piece that is both machine sewed and tacked on different ends, then combine the $1/2''$ and 1″ rules. Example: The back boxing of the overstuffed chair is machine sewed to the IB on the top and tacked down on the sides and bottom (*see* Fig. 7–7). If the rectangular strip for the back boxing measures 8″ by 36″, then add $1/2'' + 8'' + 1'' = 91/2''$ for the vertical measurement and $1'' + 36'' + 1'' = 38''$ for the horizontal measurement.

Always use a cloth or flexible metal tape measure. Do not use a yardstick. You want to be able to follow the distinct curve of the chair to get an accurate measurement. When measuring sewed edges, measure from seam line to seam line, allowing extra for the seams. When measuring tacked-on

edges, measure from exposed edge to exposed edge, adding extra for pulling and pintacking.

Another important tip to remember is to measure deep enough on certain hidden fabric pieces. A few good examples would be determining the horizontal measurements of the back boxing in the overstuffed chair, the inside wing of the wing chair or the vertical measurement of the IB in the overstuffed chair. In the overstuffed chair, the side ends of the back boxing are hidden below the inside arms. They are pulled down and tacked onto the seat rail. The bottom of the IB is pulled under the seat and tacked on the seat rail. The inside wing of the wing chair is hidden under the IB and tacked on the frame on the outside of the wing.

There are two ways to get measurements of hidden sections. One way is to stick your hand and tape measure deeply enough into the hidden fabric piece to determine where the fabric end is tacked and where the seam is located. In cases where the fabric is hidden deep in the chair before it reaches a rail to be tacked onto, a "pull strip" of inexpensive burlap or other strong scrap upholstery fabric is often attached to the end of the fabric piece. In this case, determine how deep into the chair the seam is that joins the fabric piece to the pull strip. If you do not feel that you can get an accurate measurement by sticking your hand and tape measure in hidden places, then loosen the tacks on the hidden end and then take your measurements. Take as many measurements as you can first, because you will have to take the outside pieces off (OAs, OB) to get to the hidden inside ends.

All the fabric pieces should be measured into inches. It is less confusing when you measure everything in one unit, linear inches. Another reason is to enable you to use the Welt Chart.

Determining Welt Quantity

There are two ways to cut your fabric for welt. One way is to make $11/2''$ strips running either the width or length of the fabric. The best way is to make $11/2''$ strips running along the bias or diagonal of the fabric. Fabric stretches easily along the bias. When you cover the welt cording with fabric that stretches, it will take curves and corners easily, with a minimum of snipping. Also, fabric cut on the bias will last longer, not wearing out as fast.

After you measure the linear inches of all the welt that you will need in each section of your project and mark down in the third vertical column on your Measurement Chart, then add up the third column. You will have the total number of linear inches of welt needed to complete the whole project

WELT CHART

Square Piece of Fabric (inches)	Inches of Welt Needed (Approximate)
15 by 15	150
18 by 18	216
21 by 21	294
24 by 24	384
30 by 30	450
32 by 32	512
34 by 34	578
36 by 36	756
39 by 39	1092
45 by 45	1350
48 by 48	1536
54 by 54	1944

(see the Measurement Charts for each project, Part Three).

The Welt Chart tells you how large a square of fabric to cut in order to give you "so many" inches of welt cover. If the total length of welt needed is 512", cut a square piece of fabric 32" by 32". The welt will be 1¹/₂" strips cut on the bias. Chapter 14 will go into detail on how to make welt. If you cut narrower than 1¹/₂" strips, you will have a skimpy cover for the welt cording. If you cut your strips a little wider than 1¹/₂", then you will not have a long enough piece of welt cover when the individual strips are sewed together. The Welt Chart takes into account the extra needed for the ¹/₂" seams that join the welt pieces.

After you cut all the fabric pieces, you may discover that you do not have a 32" by 32"-square piece of fabric to make the 512" welt cover mentioned in our example. In this case, try to join two leftover fabric scraps in order to have a 32" by 32"-square piece. Cutting on the bias is preferable whenever possible.

Making a Cutting Diagram

You should now have all your measurements written down on your Measurement Chart. You figured out how much welt you will need and how much fabric is required for it. Now it is time to fit all the pieces together on your 54"-wide fabric (or whatever width) like a puzzle. The object of the game is to fit the pieces together with the least amount of waste.

On the same piece of paper as your Measurement Chart, shape out a rectangle, leaving one side open. Take all the fabric pieces with widths 27" (half of 54") or less, and try to fit two or three pieces across so that the combined widths come as closely to 54"

as possible. Example: In an overstuffed chair, the OA is 24" vertically and 27" horizontally and the cushion top is 23" vertically by 23" horizontally. If we put the cushion top next to the OA on the same horizontal section, then they will cover 50" across, leaving only 4" of waste. Study Figure 18-2 to get a better indication of how to fit your puzzle together.

Several fabric pieces should be fit in first on your cutting diagram. They are the skirt, cushion boxing, back border and seat border. These are usually made with several strips 54" wide and, when lined up one against another, there is no waste.

Your cutting diagram is an approximate scale drawing of how the fabric will look when it is marked and ready to cut. By adding up the vertical length, in inches, of the longest side of the cutting diagram, then converting the total inches to yards, you know exactly how much fabric you need to purchase. After you buy the fabric you will have all the information marked out for marking and cutting.

Figure 7-18, the sample yardage estimates, will give you an idea how much fabric is needed for similar projects. Check your measurements against those of the estimates to see that you are within a yard or two of the estimate.

Diagraming Stripes, Plaids and Patterns

You cannot make a cutting diagram for stripes, plaids and patterns. It is almost impossible to tell

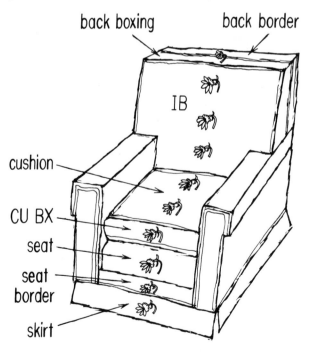

Fig. 7-17 Pattern, stripe or plaid should be repeated in a straight line.

3 yards   4 ½ yards   6 yards   5 yards

8 yards   12 yards

Fig. 7–18 Examples of the approximate fabric yardage needed for several basic furniture styles.

exactly how much fabric you will need. The pattern or stripe should be repeated down the IB, back border, back boxing, seat, cushion, cushion boxing and skirt, as shown in Figure 7–17.

For a rough estimate of the yardage needed, figure out how much fabric you would need if your material were a solid color, with no design. For every 5 yards of fabric needed, add 1 extra yard for matching and aligning the pattern, stripe or plaid. Example: If you need 10 yards of solid-colored fabric for a couch, you will need 12 yards if your fabric has a pattern, stripe or plaid. You can also get a rough estimate from the yardage estimate examples in Figure 7–18, using the same formula as above for matching.

Remember that your cutting diagram was figured using 54″-wide fabric. Most upholstery fabric is 54″ wide. If the fabric is 48″, 52″ or any other variation, then take this into account when you make up your diagram.

Marking and Cutting Fabric

The ideal situation is to have a table long enough and wide enough to spread the whole piece of fabric out at once. Maybe you are one of the lucky ones with a dining room table that opens up to seat fifteen—most likely not. If you have a clean hardwood or tile floor, you can use that instead. We do not recommend that you use a soft surface like carpeting. It is very hard to mark accurately with chalk on this surface. Cutting can be hazardous to a carpet, as well as to the fabric.

Otherwise, roll the fabric out a yard at a time—or the amount of fabric needed to mark one piece at a time. Smooth it out in all directions so there are no creases. If it's creased from being folded in half or quarters, press it out the best you can with your flattened hands, or with a steam iron.

Squaring the Bottom of the Fabric
Solids and Stripes Only

The best way to square the bottom of the fabric is to use a carpenter's square. Align the long end of the square against the long end of the fabric. Place a yardstick next to the top edge of the square. Draw a 36″ line. Slide the yardstick down to the other end of the fabric and draw the remaining part of the line (Figure 7–19). Trim the fabric. Your first fabric piece will be square—so will every succeeding piece. If you do not have a carpenter's square, you can use the edge of a square table or a piece of plywood.

It is important to square the fabric because the chair is square, not slanting to one side. You want to make sure the threads of the fabric run exactly

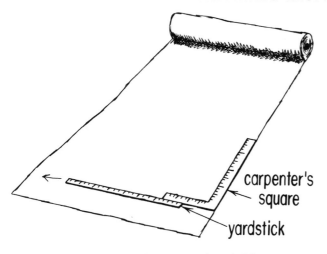

Fig. 7–19 Carpenter's square and yardstick are the best tools for squaring the bottom of the fabric.

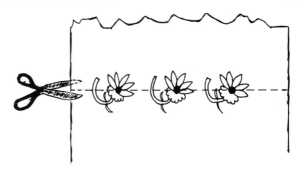

Fig. 7–21 Cut straight across, through the same spot in the pattern.

vertical and horizontal, not on a slight diagonal. Also, if you cut a rectangular cushion top and bottom $1/2''$ off, you will have a wedgelike shape.

Patterns or Plaids

It is not recommended or necessary to use a carpenter's square to square the bottom of the fabric with a pattern or plaid. Plaids are cut on the first horizontal stripe line. The horizontal line will be square to the side edge of the fabric (Fig. 7–20). However, some fabrics are woven crooked. If this is your case, then measure to the woven lines and cut on the woven line.

Patterns are cut in a similar manner. Find a pattern, a leaf, flower, etc., that runs across the full width of the fabric. Cut straight across the same part of the pattern (Fig. 7–21). Example: Cut from center to center of one particular flower pattern.

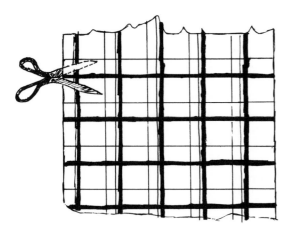

Fig. 7–20 Plaids are cut on the first horizontal line to get the first "square" line.

Checking for Flaws

Many fabric houses have sales on fabrics with flaws. Some seconds shops carry only flawed fabrics. These are factory outlet shops. They price fabric close to half price in some cases. It is very important that the inexperienced fabric buyer check carefully for flaws—imperfections in the weave of a fabric. Threads may be bunched up. A row or rows of threads may be missing. Slugs, bumps or foreign fibers or colors may have been woven into the fabric, leaving a lump. If you examine your fabric very carefully, such flaws are obvious. They may not be so apparent on the finished product (the upholstered chair) to the uneducated eye. When you do not have too many flaws, you can mark your fabric pieces around them. If there are too many to eliminate them completely, try to place your fabric pieces so that the flaws will be situated in the least noticeable spots on the chair. If the fabric is marked 50 percent off, it would be wise to buy an extra half or full yard, depending on the total amount of fabric you need.

Matching and Marking the Fabric Pieces

Always use a wedge-shaped chalk or crayon to make the thinnest line possible. A thick chalk line could be cut on the left, center or right, making the fabric piece three different possible dimensions. You will also use a yardstick to make a straight line. Make sure the yardstick is straight. If there are no flaws on a solid-colored fabric, mark on the wrong side. If there are flaws, or if the fabric has stripes, plaids or patterns, mark on the right side.

One example of finding the points and making the connecting lines to form a fabric piece is shown in Figure 7–22. To make a fabric piece 24″ by 27″, start at the base of the fabric. Measure from left to right 27″. Go up less than 24″ on the same side, making another mark. Take a yardstick. Place it even with the bottom of the fabric and next to the

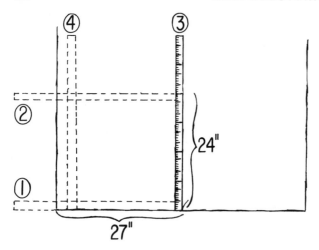

Fig. 7–22 How to measure and mark each fabric piece.

two chalked points. Join these two points and stop at 24″, then make a 1″ line at a right angle to the line you just made. Put your yardstick on the outside edge of the fabric and measure and mark 27″ out. Now you should have two lines, 24″ vertical and 27″ horizontal. You have marked a rectangular piece, 24″ by 27″.

Other pieces will require four lines. Mark all the fabric pieces in this way, according to your cutting diagram.

Caution: We cannot overemphasize how important it is to label every piece after it is marked and cut. This way you will always know which end is the top of the fabric piece, as well as which fabric piece is which. On velvets and other napped fabrics, a piece will look a different shade upside-down. All patterns should be right-side-up, as most have a top and a bottom. A few patterns may have no distinct top, bottom or sides; for example, a perfectly round flower with no stems or leaves. With plaids, if you turn one upside down, the two pieces will not match and may look very different. Labeling also prevents you from putting the fabric piece on sideways.

After all your fabric pieces are marked, from the first to the last on your cutting diagram, then you are ready to cut them. Always use a sharp pair of heavy fabric scissors.

Patterns and Plaids

You should mark and cut each fabric piece one at a time when you work with plaids and patterns. This is in direct contrast to doing all your marking first, then all your cutting, when working on solid-colored fabrics. All the marking for patterns and plaids is done on the face of the fabric. The main pieces—the larger ones—should be marked and cut first. The seat, cushion, cushion boxing, IB, back boxing, back border, seat boxing and OB have to line up in the center of the chair. Whatever you decide will be center, follow through all the pieces. Wherever there are two of each kind of fabric piece—two IAs, two OAs, cushion top and bottom—they should be identical to each other.

When chalking and cutting, do so at a particular spot in the pattern, all the way across, as mentioned above, vertically and horizontally. After you cut a pattern or plaid, chalking the face of the fabric, immediately turn each piece over and label it.

Matching Pieces Horizontally

Sometimes, plaids, stripes and patterns have to be matched horizontally. This is true where there are two or three fabric pieces sewn together to form one continuous width of goods, e.g., the IB, OB, seat or skirt of a couch.

We have found an easy way to make a perfect match. When cutting your fabric, find the center. Mark with chalk on the fabric face up, 27″ from each end of the width of the fabric (half of 54″). If you matched the left selvage with the right selvage, it would be the same as the center. Usually there is another pattern between the center and each end. Estimate what you want to use as the center. Study the fabric and the width of the fabric piece you need. Example: If the fabric piece is 48″ wide, then the center of the piece will be the center of the fabric. If the fabric piece is 24″, the center could be between the center of the fabric and the end of the fabric (Fig. 7–23). Now, you have a rough estimate of where the fabric piece will be cut.

To get the exact line for cutting, here is what you do. Your center line is established. Add ¹/₂″ seam allowances as shown in Fig. 7–24. If this is cut correctly, then if you sew a ¹/₂″ seam, the design should be perfectly matched.

Matching Top and Bottom Seams

Once the fabric pieces are cut so that the pattern is going vertically, with any one pattern repeating from the top of the chair to the bottom of the chair, as in Figure 7–18, you have finished matching from top to bottom. The top and bottom seams will not match identically. Patterns, in most cases, repeat anywhere from 8″ to 27″. You would waste too much expensive upholstery fabric matching top and bottom seams. Example: It is often difficult to match the pattern of the top of the IB and the bottom of the IB boxing. Of course, vertical lines on stripes and plaids always match, while horizontal lines may not.

Another tip concerns welt: If there is welt between two fabric pieces (as in the IB of a couch), use the vertical ends of the fabric for the center welt.

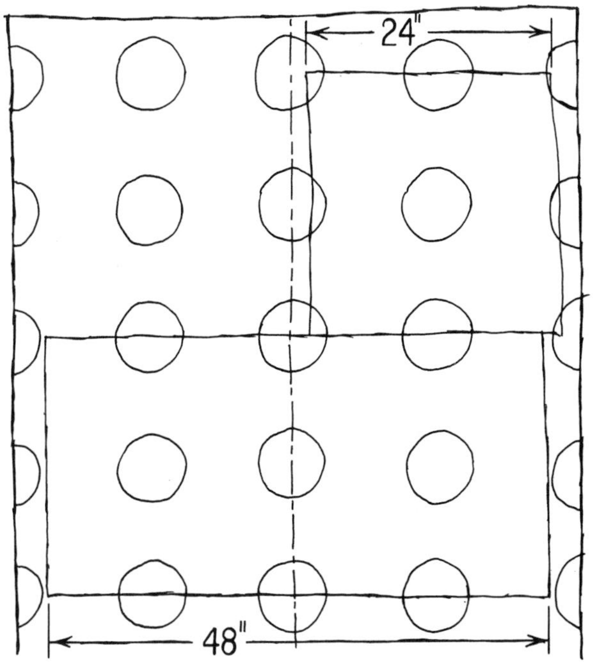

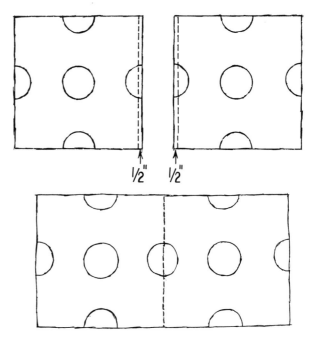

Fig. 7–23 Cutting and matching patterned fabric pieces (each circle represents a pattern).

Fig. 7–24 Matching two fabric pieces horizontally. The two $1/2''$ allowances are taken up by the seam.

Chapter 8

Taking the Chair Apart

Examining the Chair

Before you take the chair apart, you will want to size up the amount of work you will have to do. You will most likely be replacing the old upholstery cover with a new one. The previous chapter showed you how to measure, chalk and cut your new fabric cover. Now you can get an idea of how much work has to be done on the frame, webbing, burlap and stuffing. One of the first steps in every project is examining the chair.

It is important to determine whether a frame is loose or rigid. If the frame is loose or shaky, the glue in the joints may have dried. In this case, the chair has to come apart completely in one operation, as in the project chapter on the wing chair. If the frame is rigid, then you will want to take the chair apart the easy way, section by section.

Working Section by Section

Never strip the whole chair apart in one operation unless you have to do extensive frame repair. Your impulse when you tackle your first project will probably be to confidently take your mallet and tack lifter or ripping chisel and start stripping the chair from top to bottom. *Do not do this*. This is the hardest way for the beginner—or experienced professional—to tackle a project. The joy of carefree removal of the dirty old upholstery fabric will quickly flee when you realize several days or weeks later that you cannot remember how to put it back together. It is much easier to work on one section of a chair from start to finish. Your memory is fresh and your notes are clear on how the section was put together. When reupholstering arms, you can leave one arm intact to study while you reupholster the other. The old arm is an excellent teacher. The new reupholstered arm then becomes a guide for redoing the old one. The only time you will want to strip the chair completely is when you have to do any frame repair: Chapter 19 gives some tips on making the job easier when you have to strip the chair.

Whenever you feel the need, take notes, especially when you plan to stretch your project out over several weekends. Make a sketch of your chair (at least try to). Label the outside pieces. Make your measurement chart nearby, along with your cutting diagram. Note where your chair has welt. As you take each section of the chair apart, note where a fabric piece was blind tacked, hand sewed, tacked under, had gimp or double welt, or where cuts were made for perfect corner fits or two pieces were machine sewed. Ask yourself, ''What kind of skirt is on the chair? Do I need to use the old, shaped upholstery cover as a pattern? Are most of my fabric pieces going to be rectangular in shape?'' The more you study your chair and the more data you write down before you pick up your mallet and tack lifter, the easier your project will be and the more professional the result.

Removing the Old Upholstery Cover

When you take a chair apart, the first thing you do is turn it upside-down, resting it on sawhorses or a low table. After you remove the cambric, loosen the bottom of the OAs and OB, and all four sides of the seat. Then turn the chair right-side-up. Take off the rest of the OB by cutting any side stitches and removing the blind-tack strip from the top. Also, remove the stitches and blind tacking holding on the OAs. Now all the outside pieces are off. You have opened up your chair.

If the chair needs extensive frame repair, take off

the IB, IAs, seat border, then the seat, in that order. The chair will be reupholstered in the reverse order. Carefully take the stuffing and old upholstery cover off as one piece, placing it on the floor so that you remember which is the top of the seat and can tell right from left arms. It might be helpful to label each piece on the outside with a chalk or crayon.

If the chair does not require any frame work, and you can reupholster it section by section, then you can take off and reupholster in the following order. First, all the outside pieces are removed—OAs, OB, perhaps the OWs. Now you can get to the inside pieces, reupholstering one section at a time: first, the seat; second, the arm; third, the other arm; fourth, any IWs; fifth, the IB.

A more detailed description of removing the old upholstery cover might be helpful. After all the outside pieces are off, loosen the bottoms of the IB and IAs. They are tacked on top of the seat cover. Pin-tack the bottoms of the IB and IAs on the back and arm rails, so they are out of your way when working on the seat. Now you can loosen all four sides of the seat, take out and save the old stuffing, retie the springs, repair any webbing and burlap, and tack on the new seat cover. After you reupholster the seat, then reupholster one arm completely, from start to finish, using the other arm as a guide. Then reupholster the second arm from start to finish. Next the IB, then any cushion. Any borders or boxings are done when that particular section is done. Example: Do the seat border after tacking on the seat.

Reaching the Original Layer

Some upholsterers, especially during the Second World War when labor was scarce, reupholstered directly over the old layer of fabric. In some cases, a chair has four or five layers of upholstery covers, sometimes with extra padding to level out bumpy spots. The chair loses it original shape. It looks like a model that has put on too much weight.

It is important to get down to the original fabric, so that these pieces can be a guide and pattern. Throw the other layers of old reupholstery fabric away.

White and Yellow Tags

For health and sanitary reasons, your state department of health requires that any piece of upholstered furniture must display a yellow or white tag if it is sold to the public (Fig. 8–1).

The white tag is used only on *new* furniture. It lists all new clean stuffings that are found in the

Fig. 8–1 (*Left*) White tag is used on sterilized new furniture; (*right*) yellow tag is affixed to sterilized old furniture.

chair, such as sisal and cotton felt. The white tag means that the chair has never been reupholstered before. You are very fortunate if your chair has a white tag. That means that everything original is still in the chair. This rule applies especially to antique chairs with expensive original stuffing like down, feathers and curled horse hair. The white tag will also mention the manufacturer's name.

A yellow tag means that the furniture was reupholstered at least once. It states that "This article contains the same material received from the owner, to which has been added _____." Whatever has been added, such as a layer of cotton felt or a polyurethane foam cushion, will be filled in on the tag by the reupholsterer. The bottom of the tag states the "date sterilized," to kill bacteria which otherwise may smell or become a health hazard. There are several kinds of disinfectants on the market. These are stocked by your local professional upholsterer.

Since you will be doing your first pieces of reupholstering for yourself or close friends and relatives, you do not have to worry about obtaining yellow tags. We do recommend the sterilizing step mentioned in the beginning of every project chapter, for your own health. If you know your piece of furniture and feel that it is clean, then you can safely skip this step.

Be very careful if you consider doing reupholstering for other people. There is a stiff fine for violators who get caught selling reupholstered furniture without the yellow tags.

Removing Old Tacks, Cover, Stuffing and Springs

As you reupholster each section of a chair, you will want to carefully remove each layer of fabric and other materials. Use either a ripping chisel, tack lifter or screwdriver with a mallet. Try to knock the tacks out from above the fabric, so that the fabric is clear of old tacks and does not get ripped in the process. You may want to study an old fabric piece or use it as a pattern. Each section of the frame should be clear of all tacks before any reupholstering is done. You want to avoid a lumpy base, as well as the frustration of hitting the old tacks with new tacks or staples.

The stuffing should be removed with extreme care, so that you know which end is the top and which section of the chair it belongs on. Contrary to popular opinion, *never* throw away old stuffing. The stuffing is professionally shaped to the chair, so you do not want to disturb it. You will only add to existing stuffing, never take away from it.

Remember that every chair or couch is an individual. Your chair will "talk" to you, telling you how it was put together, where there was welt, where the arm piece was tacked out of sight, what new supplies are needed, where it is in need of repair. So, listen!

Chapter 9

Repairing the Frame

The Foundation

The chair frame is something akin to the skeleton or bones of man. Every board and slat has a unique function. Some boards are used as tacking strips for the upholstery fabric. Others are used exclusively to hold the webbing and burlap. Some slats are made so that fabric can be pulled through and anchored. The main function of some boards is to give the chair its unique shape. When you take apart your chair, note where fabric pieces and other materials are tacked.

Figure 9–1 will give you an inside look at a frame. We will describe where each upholstery piece is attached, on which board and through which slat, so you will have a better knowledge base before you tackle your first reupholstering project. Also, follow the illustrations carefully.

Your chair starts out with four seat rails. The seat is actually a rectangular box held together by dowels which are glued solidly into their respective holes. On the inside corners of the seat are corner blocks. Corner blocks are fastened with screws or nailed, then glued into place. The screws or nails act as clamps to hold the corner blocks in place while the white or hide glue is drying. The corner blocks help keep the seat of the chair square.

The back also starts out as a rectangular box, doweled and glued at every corner. There are vertical back slats mounted in the back frame to allow the IB fabric to be pulled through and tacked on. They give added strength to the back.

To keep the back from falling backward under pressure, the arms bridge the back and seat together to form a solid construction. The arm stump is shaped according to the design desired—round, square or any other shape. The whole arm can be even with the front rail; recessed only on top, where

you have a square cushion; or recessed completely, where you have a T cushion.

On the top outside arm of the frame, between the arm stump and the back post, is the "top arm tack board." It is mounted to the chair in order to tack the top of the IA and OA fabric pieces. It is usually a $7/8''$-square piece of wood.

The wing is a distinctive, shaped piece usually made from two pieces of wood, doweled together and fastened in two places—on the front back post on top and on the top of the arm board on the bottom. The wing is only there for appearance—it serves no functional purpose, other than giving the owner a built-in pillow on which to lay his head.

The legs in front are attached separately to the frame. The rear legs are usually an extension on the back posts.

Attachment Rails

Fastening Webbing and Burlap

Figure 9–2 indicates attachment points for webbing and burlap. For the IB, the webbing and burlap are fastened from the top back rail to the bottom back rail, and on the sides to the back slats.

For the IAs, the webbing and burlap are nailed on top to the arm board, on the bottom to the lower arm board, in the front to the arm stump and in the back to the back post.

For the seat, the webbing and burlap are nailed to the top of the four seat rails.

For the wings, the webbing and burlap are tacked on the inside wing top rail and the wing post, and back to the back post.

Attaching Fabric Pieces

This section can be helpful as a reference to use when you do not know where to tack on a certain

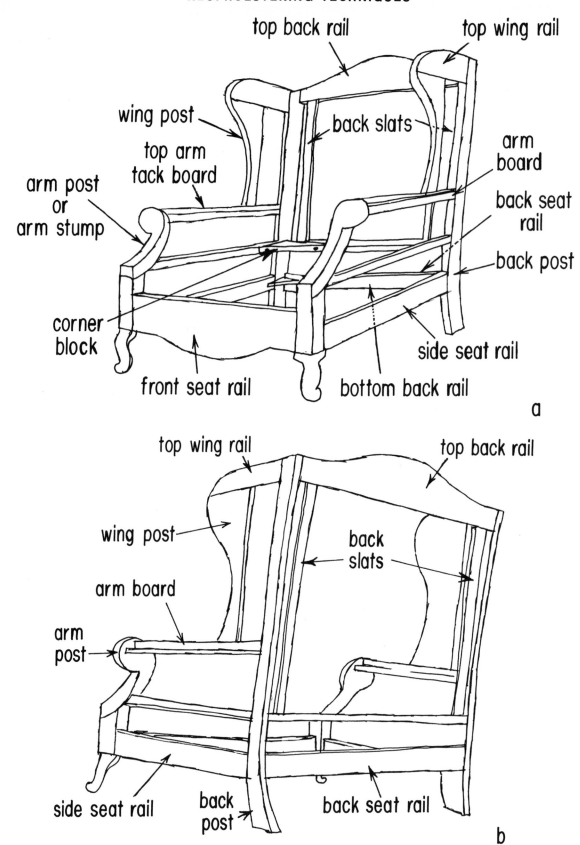

Fig. 9–1 Wing chair frame. *a*. Front view. *b*. Rear view of the frame.

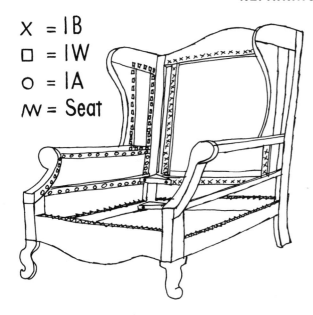

X = IB
□ = IW
o = IA
ⅿ = Seat

Fig. 9–2 Webbing and burlap are used for the foundation of each part of the chair. IB, IW, IA and seat are tacked according to this diagram.

fabric piece. Remember, every chair is an individual. In this particular recessed-arm wing chair (Fig. 9–1), the fabric pieces are attached as detailed below.

Seat and Deck

In the front, the seat is tacked underneath the front seat rail and side rails up to the arms (*see* Fig. 19–4). From the arm, the decking is tacked on top of the side seat rail. The back of the decking is tacked on the top of the back seat rail.

Inside Arms

The IAs are tacked on top to the top arm tack board (*see* Fig. 19–5). On the bottom, they are attached to the top of the side seat rail. The front is pulled around the arm stump and tacked on the outside of the stump; the back is pulled and tacked to the back post.

Inside Wings

The IWs are tacked on top of the outside top wing rail (*see* Fig. 19–7). The bottom is fastened by pulling it hard from the front and back of the welt. There is no tacking on the bottom. The IW on the bottom is hand sewed down to the IA. The front of the IW is tacked to the outside of the wing post. The back part is pulled through the slats and tacked to the back posts.

Inside Back

The top of the IB is tacked on the outside top of the back rail. The bottom part is tacked on the top of the back seat rail. The sides are pulled through the space on the inside of the back slat and tacked to the back post.

Welt

The welt is tacked from the arm tack board, up around the wing post, to the top wing rail; also, on top of the back rail, down the opposite wing post to the opposite top arm tack board (*see* Fig. 19–10).

Outside Wings

The OWs are tacked on the back of the back post. In the front, around the welt, they are hand sewed (*see* Fig. 19–11). The bottom of the OW is tacked to the top arm tack board.

Outside Arms

The OAs are blind tacked on the top arm tack board (*see* Fig. 19–12). The bottom is tacked under the side seat rail. The front part is sewed on the edge of the arm posts. The back is tacked to the back posts.

Outside Back

The OB is similar to the OAs. The OB is blind tacked to the top of the top back rail (*see* Figs. 19–14 and 19–15). The bottom is tacked on the bottom of the back seat rail. The sides are sewed to the OW and OA, where they meet on the corner.

All chairs are similar in one respect: All fabric pieces are tacked on the above-mentioned boards. If you forget where a particular piece was tacked, study this section.

Disassembly

Chairs are made with left and right sides exactly the same, only reversed. They are held together by cross pieces between the left and the right sides. With this in mind, the first logical step in knocking the chair apart is to separate left from right.

To make it easy to reassemble, we recommend that you mark the joints before knocking apart the chair. For the first joint to be disassembled, mark a "1" on each side of the joint (Fig. 9–3). When you go to put the joint back together, you have the "1" next to the "1." All other joints are labeled the same way. This tip will save you uncertainty, and is especially important if you are going to take the chair apart one day and glue it back together another day.

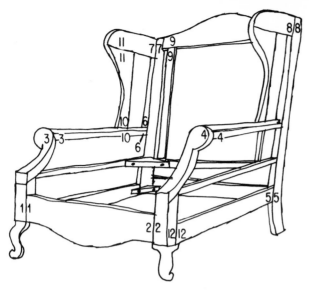

Fig. 9–3 Number each side of a joint before you knock it apart to avoid confusion.

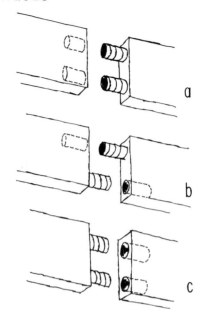

Fig. 9–4 Each joint breaks up differently. *a.* Both dowels stayed on the right board. *b.* Each dowel stayed on a different board. *c.* Both dowels stayed on the left board.

Knocking a Chair Apart

The best tool to use when you knock the frame of a chair apart is a wood mallet. A rubber mallet is especially good for exposed show wood, because it will not mar the wood. If you have no show wood, you can use a regular wood mallet.

Start at the first joint. Knock the two sides of the joint apart, making sure that you give several light blows instead of one heavy blow. Strike the mallet as close to the joint as possible to get the maximum amount of work from each stroke. After you divide the left and right sides of the chair, then knock apart one side at a time, making sure that all the joints are numbered.

When you separate a joint, you will notice that both dowels are on one side, or else there is a hole and a dowel on both sides of the joint. All joints break up differently (Fig. 9–4).

Cleaning and Checking Dowels

After the whole frame is disassembled, take a pair of pliers and one joint of the frame. Gently grip the dowel and try to rotate it to see if it is loose. If it is tight, leave it alone; if it is loose, pull the old dowel out. Try this process on all dowels, pulling out any loose ones. Throw away any dowel that is cracked or broken. They cost only a couple of pennies apiece, so replace when in doubt.

Old dowels should be scraped clean of dried glue. Take a knife or other scraping tool to remove the old glue from the hole side and the dowel side of each joint. The easiest way to scrape the hole is

with a $7/16''$ bit, making sure that you do not drive the drill bit all the way through the hole.

Reassembly

Gluing and Clamping

Before you do any gluing, make sure that you have all the new dowels needed to complete your frame repair. Whether you are working with new or old dowels, the process is exactly the same. The only difference is that you will have two ends to glue for a new dowel and usually only one end for an old dowel.

You will be gluing one section at a time—only as much as you can clamp. Put a layer of white glue, as thin as possible, in the dowel hole and on the dowel. You can use a pencil, small brush or nail to spread the glue evenly. You do not have to rush when you are working with white glue. Work at a normal pace. It takes at least a half hour to set up.

Now you are going to assemble the dowels in the joints on each side of the chair, then you will attach the two sides with cross boards. We recommend that you buy pipe or bar clamps that extend to any length desired. If you are going to take apart a chair, you could purchase two 4′ clamps. If you are going to take apart the frame of a couch, you could use either two 8′ clamps or four 4′ clamps, two joined together with a coupling (Fig. 9–5). Do not

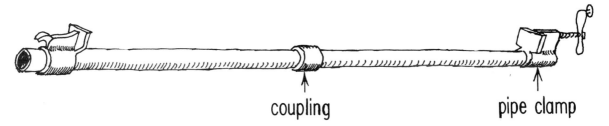

coupling   pipe clamp

Fig. 9–5 If you need an 8' clamp to hold the joints of a couch and you only have 4' clamps, you can connect two 4' lengths with a coupling.

forget that some bar clamps are sold with only the two pivot and clamping devices. Purchase as long a pipe as you need to do the job (or any other future jobs you have in mind). You should allow an hour for the glue to set up in every gluing and clamping session, more for hide glue—overnight, if possible.

The professional upholsterer who does quality work will repair a shaky frame. He may own a dozen or more different sized bar, pipe and C clamps to clamp together every size joint. The small C clamps are good for small joints. By owning so many clamps, the professional can reglue and reclamp the chair in one operation. The beginner or home craftsman only needs two C clamps and two bar or pipe clamps. Gluing and clamping the frame back together may take several one-hour sessions, making it more time consuming, but as a beginner or home craftsman you can do a good job.

When you clamp a joint, make sure the clamp is on tight. You want the dowels to set as far in the holes as possible. A loose clamping job will mean a weak joint, easily broken.

Also, after the joint is clamped tightly, wipe off all excess glue with a damp rag. You will want to make sure that the frame is clean of any excess glue.

Fixing Enlarged Holes

You may come across a chair, perhaps a rocking chair, where no amount of gluing or clamping will hold the joint or joints together. If you examine the joints carefully, then you will see that the hole into which the dowel fits is too large for the dowel. The hole is enlarged from being loose for a long time and constantly rubbing against the wood. How do you remedy this problem?

The first point to remember is to stay away from glues that claim to swell up the wooden dowel so that it will fit snugly in the hole. Any hole that is enlarged 1/16" or more must be corrected in this manner: First, redrill the hole the next size larger than the dowel, i.e., 1/8" bigger. Check to see if the

wood permits using a larger hole: 1/8" extra may run off the edges of the wood. Then cut a piece of muslin or a similar thin fabric the size of a half-dollar coin. Glue the half of the dowel that will fit in the enlarged hole and place the center of the muslin on the tip of the dowel. Smooth the sides of the muslin down. Put glue on the outside of the muslin and in the hole. Now the dowel will be large enough to fit snugly in the hole. If the muslin-wrapped dowel is not large enough, then add another layer of muslin until it fits snugly. Glue the other side of the dowel and hole. Clamp the joint together. Your repair job will make the chair as sturdy as possible.

Repairing Broken Legs

Occasionally you may find yourself with a project that has a broken leg or other frame part. In order to have a sturdy, comfortable chair, you will want to make any necessary repairs.

There is one very important tip to remember when you are working with hardwood frames—oak, maple, poplar, mahogany. Most frames are made out of hardwood; it is even good to follow this rule with softwood frames. Never put a nail or screw directly into bare wood. Always drill a pilot hole slightly smaller than the nail or screw. The drilled pilot hole will prevent the wood from splitting.

There are several things that could happen to a leg of a chair or couch. The modern round leg has a lag that goes inside the leg (Fig. 9–6). A lag is a metal rod 3/4" long, with one end forming a metal thread and the other end forming a wood thread. Sometimes the lag is too short on the leg, and the leg cracks (Fig. 9–6a). The best way to repair the broken "lagged leg" is as follows: Split the cracked leg with a chisel or screwdriver so you can spread a thin layer of glue on both sides of the crack (Fig. 9–7). You do not need to split the leg apart completely. Take a piece of cardboard or heavy paper and use it to work the glue into the crack.

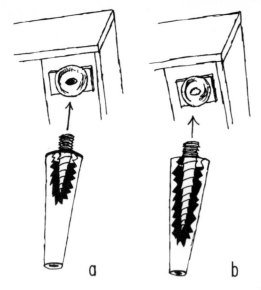

Fig. 9–6 Lags in a modern round leg. *a*. Inside look at a short lag that sometimes splits the wood. *b*. Inside look at a lag long enough to carry the extra weight of the user.

Then clamp the leg tightly with C clamps and wedge blocks (Fig. 9–8).

The hole which accepts the lag also wears. Take a ¹/₂″ drill and drill the hole deeper, about ¹/₂″ deeper than it was. Make a V glue groove on a ¹/₂″ dowel. Put the glue on the dowel and in the hole. Drive the dowel into the leg (Fig. 9–9). Wipe off the excess glue and cut off the excess dowel. You have just plugged up the hole. Now you want to make a new, proper-sized hole. Redrill the leg at the center of the dowel. The diameter and depth of the drill bit will depend on the width and depth of the lag. A typical example might be to use a ¹/₄″ bit

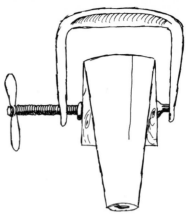

Fig. 9–8 Clamp the crack shut.

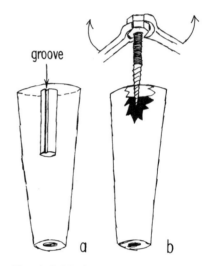

Fig. 9–9 Making a new lag hole. *a*. Plug up the old hole with a ¹/₂″ dowel. *b*. Screw the lag into the leg, using two wrenches.

Fig. 9–7 Glue the broken leg.

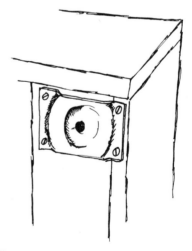

Fig. 9–10 The round leg and lag are then screwed into a metal plate mounted on the base of the chair.

for a $5/16''$ lag (the hole is $1/16''$ smaller than the lag, allowing for the lag to screw in tight), and to drill down $2''$ if the lag is $2''$ deep.

It is a little tricky to put the lag into the leg (Fig. 9–9b). Make a temporary head for the lag, using two nuts. Screw both on until they are even with the top of the lag. Using two wrenches, tighten the nuts against each other. With one wrench, screw the lag into the leg. Now the leg is ready for reuse. This type of leg is screwed into a metal plate that is mounted on the base of the chair with screws (Fig. 9–10).

Repairing Broken Frame Boards

If you have a puppy who loves to chew the wood frame or leg of your chair, a missing chunk can be refilled with plastic wood filler. Build up the leg or board a little higher than necessary, then sand it into shape. Restain and refinish the wood.

Chapter 10

Replacing Webbing and Heavy Burlap

Webbing and heavy burlap act as a foundation for the seat, back or arms. The springs, stuffing and fabric rest on this foundation. Both webbing and 17-oz. burlap are made from jute; the main difference is that the woven webbing has air holes and also takes a little longer to put on than the heavy burlap.

When do you replace the old webbing strips with new strips or the old burlap with new? When the webbing and burlap rips very easily and the fibers are rotten, it will no longer serve as a firm foundation. As a rule, if you are going to replace one or two webbing strips, it is best to replace them all.

If the webbing or burlap is sturdy and reusable, then both can be restretched and retacked on one end to eliminate sagging.

Jute Webbing

You will need number 14 tacks, a webbing stretcher and your webbing. If you are using new webbing, you will start by turning the webbing over an inch. Stagger five tacks evenly across the width of the webbing. Staggering tacks prevents the wood from splitting. On the other end, you will be using the webbing stretcher. Hold the webbing stretcher at a 45° angle to the edge of the frame. Dig the teeth into the webbing. Push down on the webbing stretcher so it is a little below the edge of the frame. Put three tacks evenly across the webbing. Cut off the remaining webbing, leaving about a 1″ overhang; fold it over. Apply four tacks, staggering them to prevent the wood from splitting.

Heavy Burlap

Tacking on 17-oz. burlap is similar to tacking on webbing. Start in the front of the chair. Turn over

1″ and drive in number 14 tacks across the front. With a sagless webbing stretcher or a regular webbing stretcher (*see* Ch. 3), follow the same technique used to stretch webbing. Tack the whole back side. Cut the excess burlap, leaving 1″ or 2″ extra. Fold and tack again, staggering the tacks. Then repeat the process on the sides.

Steel Webbing

Steel webbing is only used when there are coil springs. It gives added strength at the base of the springs. Strips of steel webbing are tacked onto the bottom of the seat frame from front to back, directly in the center of the coils. For example, the seat of an average chair has nine coils and needs three strips of steel webbing. The average couch seat has twenty-seven coils and would need nine strips of steel webbing.

When you tack on steel webbing, you always work from the roll. Steel webbing is tacked very differently to modern furniture without show wood and antique furniture with exposed show wood (Fig. 10–1). For the upholstered chair or couch with no show wood, start with steel webbing 1″ longer than necessary over the first edge. Nail in a stronghold screw nail on one side. Stretch the webbing with a steel webbing stretcher that you may be able to borrow or rent from your local upholsterer. Or buy one, if you plan to do several projects. It is very important to get a tool that will stretch the steel webbing tautly. Sagging steel webbing contributes nothing to a stronger foundation. You can also use a pair of pliers to grip the end of the webbing. You might want to have one person pull the steel webbing taut, while another person drives in the number 14 tacks.

Place the steel webbing stretcher up against the

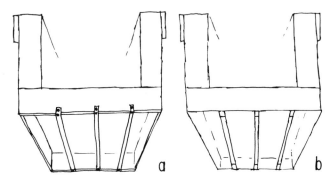

Fig. 10–1 Attaching steel webbing. *a.* For modern furniture without show wood, tack the steel webbing to the front and back boards. *b.* For antique show wood chairs, the steel webbing stays out of sight. It is tacked on the bottom of the chair. No tacks are seen because the steel webbing is turned over at the end for a smooth edge and conceals the tacks.

frame of the chair, pulling down hard on the handle until the webbing is level. Drive the nail in on the bottom edge of the frame. Then go back and nail in number 3 and 4 tacks, as shown in Figure 10–1.

For antiques with exposed show wood, start with 1″ of steel webbing hanging over the edge of the frame. The first nail is driven into one side of the steel webbing. With the stretcher, stretch the steel webbing until it is level. Drive in a nail to one side of the steel webbing. Take off the webbing stretcher. Stagger the third and fourth nails on the opposite sides of the steel webbing. Cut 1″ over the frame edge. Turn the excess over to cover the nails, hitting it with a hammer so that it lies down flat.

Webbing, Burlap and Cardboard

Any chair or couch that is fully upholstered in the arms and back needs a foundation to hold the stuffing and upholstery cover. Whatever you already had on your chair, you will put on again. If the webbing and/or burlap is rotten, replace it. If it is sturdy and can be used for another 10 or 20 years, then restretch it.

Arms and backs have three possible foundations. The first possible foundation is a webbing and light 10-oz. burlap combination. You may find one or two strips of webbing in each direction in the arm and as many in the back as in the seat. The light 10-oz. burlap is stretched on top of the webbing. Another foundation is the stretched 17-oz. burlap. This method is desirable, especially in an arm and/or back with light stuffing where you can feel the double layers of tacking, webbing first and then 10-oz. burlap. Both foundations are tacked on the inside

arm frame and either the inside or outside back frame. The third possible foundation is cardboard (*see* Ch. 3). The cardboard is tacked on the inside arm frame, forming a firm foundation. Usually, if you have a chair or couch with a loose pillow back, you will find a carboard foundation.

When reupholstering, study the webbing, burlap or cardboard carefully. Replace or stretch the foundation of the arms and back exactly the way it was.

Rubber Webbing

Rubber webbing is used only on Danish furniture. The chair or couch has an all-exposed-wood frame. Rubber webbing strips are stretched from front to back on the seat (*see* Fig. 10–2). Upholstered cushions of foam rubber or polyurethane are set directly on top of the rubber webbing. There are cushions in the seat and back. There are no springs. There is no stuffing. The only reupholstering work involved is installing new rubber webbing—which stretches easily after several years of steady use—and measuring, cutting and sewing new upholstery cushion covers. Rubber webbing foundations in Danish furniture are not constructed to last a long time. However, they are easy to reupholster, making it easy for you to redecorate your room.

Rubber webbing always runs from front to back only. There are no side-to-side strips woven be-

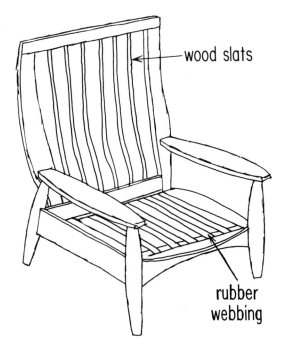

Fig. 10–2 Danish modern furniture has round wood slats on the back and rubber webbing on the seat. Back and seat cushions are placed on top.

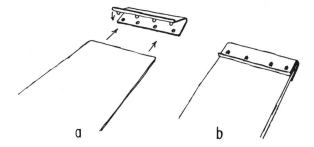

Fig. 10–3 Clamping rubber webbing. *a.* Open V clamp slides onto each end of the rubber webbing strip. *b.* The V clamp is squeezed closed with a vise or hammer.

tween. If you are doing a repair job on the rubber webbing, we recommend that you weave and tack on the side strips. First, you remove the old, over-stretched rubber webbing. On each edge of the webbing is on V clamp. Pull the old V clamps out with pliers. If you have vulcanized rubber webbing, the clamp is permanently attached to the webbing; then you have to purchase new clamps.

The frame of the Danish chair or couch has a saw cut, about 1/8″ wide, the whole length of the back seat board and the front seat board. Squeeze the V clamp closed with a vise or hammer (Fig. 10–3). Place the closed clamp in the rear frame saw cut. Pull the rubber webbing across to the front saw cut, chalking at this line, then cut. Pull the closed clamp

out of the rear saw cut. Measure the length of the rubber webbing. This is the length required for the remaining strips. At the end of the first strip, squeeze on another V clamp. Insert the new rubber webbing where the old was. If the first strip fits tautly, then cut the remaining strips the same size. If it does not, make the necessary adjustments. Now you are ready to weave the cross strips and staple or tack them to the side of the frame (Fig. 10–4).

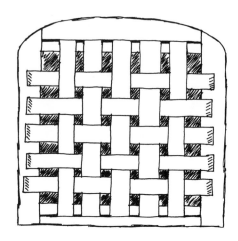

Fig. 10–4 Repaired Danish seat has rubber webbing woven in and out, similar to a jute webbing foundation.

Chapter 11

Light Burlap and Seat Edgings

Light burlap is put directly on top of the seat or back springs as a foundation for the stuffing. The upholstery cover holds the stuffing down and the burlap holds the stuffing up.

Attaching Burlap Foundations

Measuring and Cutting

The 10-oz. burlap is measured similarly to the upholstery fabric. Measure the vertical and horizontal distances needed, adding an inch extra on each side. For example, if the length is 30″ and the width is 36″, then the burlap will be 32″ by 38″.

Tacking on 10-Oz. Burlap

You will be using the cross system to tack on 10-oz. burlap. Mark the center top of the front seat rail and the back seat rail. Fold the burlap in half, notching front and back. Start in the front and turn the burlap under 1″. Place the notch on the center of the frame and drive in your first tack. Grab the notch in the back. Fold it over 1″, pull the burlap tight and drive in the second tack.

Go to the center of the right side and follow the same procedures. Then go to the center of the left side and repeat. Using this method, the burlap will be perfectly centered.

Go back to the front. Turn the burlap over 1″. Tack to the left and right of the center tack. Do the same on the back and sides, folding the two front corners square and neatly, tacking the two back corners right up against the legs. There should be no big holes for the stuffing to fall through.

Attaching Burlap to Arms and Back

The 10-oz. burlap on the arms and back serves the same foundation function for the stuffing. The burlap is measured, cut and tacked on in the same manner.

Seat Edgings

A seat edging is either cylinder-shaped burlap stuffed with rolled paper, 1″ to 1¼″ in diameter, or a roll of paper of the same dimensions without the burlap, or a shaped wooden edge (Fig. 11–1). In a chair with no seat cushion, the edging is put on the front of the chair frame so that the front has a round edge instead of a sharp edge. Edgings also help hold the stuffing in place, especially the older stuffings of hair and sisal (Fig. 11–1*b*). Many older books on upholstering recommend that you tack burlap edging on all four sides of the seat, back and inside arms. When reupholstering, we recommend that you only repair or replace edgings that were in the *original* upholstery job. Most chairs you will find have edgings only on the front of the seat frame. The stuffings are held in place by the upholstery cover. Also, you do not have the problem of falling stuffing with the modern stuffings—foam, cotton felt and rubberized hair—as you do with sisal and hair.

Edgings are used in the front of a chair with a seat cushion for two reasons. The first reason is to create a round edge. The second reason is to prevent a hole in the front of the seat (Fig. 11–2). Years ago, coil springs were used in cushions. Coil spring cushions have a high crown, about 5″ in the center and 4″ on the sides. If there were no fox edging to make up the 1″ difference, you'd have a hole in the front of the seat. Also, the edging keeps the cushion from rolling back and forth. Today, you still have crown cushions but they are made out of foam rubber or polyurethane foam.

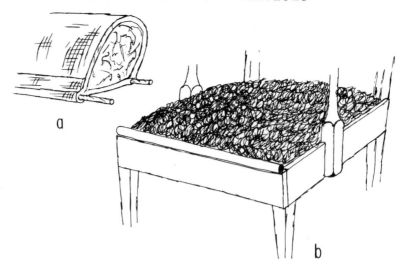

Fig. 11–1 Seat edgings. *a.* Seat edging is cylindrical burlap, stuffed with rolled paper. *b.* Front seat edgings hold hair or sisal in place.

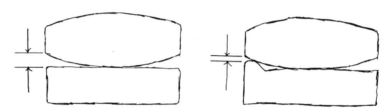

Fig. 11–2 Edging in a seat with a cushion prevents a hole in the front of the seat.

Ready-Made Fox Edgings

Many older upholstery books will explain how to make your own burlap-covered stuffed edgings from scratch. Today, this time-consuming hand-crafted edging is not necessary. You can purchase ready-made edgings called fox edgings from your local professional upholsterer.

Fox edging is about 1″ to 1¼″ in diameter. You can purchase the length you need for the chair, usually about 22″. There are two kinds of fox edging. The best is the burlap stuffed with paper. Second best is the all-paper edging with brown paper on the outside.

If the old fox edging is torn and needs to be replaced, measure and cut the new edging the length of the old. We no not recommend using the paper edging unless you have hog rings to clip the paper edging to the edge wire of an overstuffed chair. If you have paper edging on an overstuffed chair, replace it with burlap fox edging that can be hand sewn or tacked in place.

Two Ways to Attach Fox Edging
Nailed-on Edging

On the hard edge where there are no-sag springs or no springs, the fox edging is nailed down, using number 14 tacks (Fig. 11–3*a*). Nails are 1″ apart, just as they were originally on the chair. The edging should stick out over the frame about ¼″.

Sewn-on Edging

On a soft or spring edge, the fox edging is sewed on, using an overthrow or hem stitch. It is sewn in two places (Fig. 11–3*b* and *c*). It is stitched where it is sewed by machine, catching the coil springs as you hand sew across and along the front of the edge wire. The fox edging and edge wire are sewn together with an overthrow stitch.

Stitches and Knots
Overthrow Stitch

The overthrow stitch is a continuing spiral stitch, repeating every inch (*see* Fig. 11–3*c*). For sewing

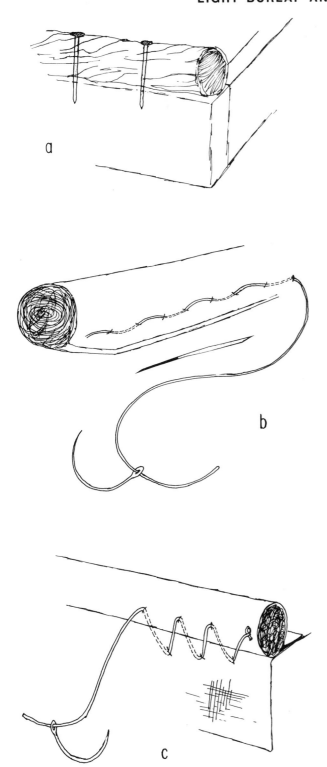

Fig. 11–3 Fox edgings. *a.* Burlapped edging can be nailed into a hard-edge seat where there are No-Sag springs or no springs. *b.* Burlapped fox edging is sewn at the machine seam, catching the coil springs. *c.* Edging is also sewn along the front of the edge wire.

on fox edging, use a curved 6″ needle and nylon or flax stitching twine. The overthrow stitch is also used where the seat and the deck joining seam is sewn to the burlap and springs.

Hem Stitch

The hem stitch is a straight in-and-out stitch with the stitches being 1″ apart (they can be closer together, but no more than 1″ apart). The hem stitch is most frequently used for hand sewing on top of the machine-sewn part of the fox edging to anchor the edging to the burlap and springs (*see* Fig. 11–3*b*) when the seat and deck seam is sewn to the burlap and springs.

Starting Knot

The starting knot for sewing the fox edging to the burlap and springs is the upholsterer's slip knot. Figure 11–4 shows the four sequential steps for making this commonly used knot.

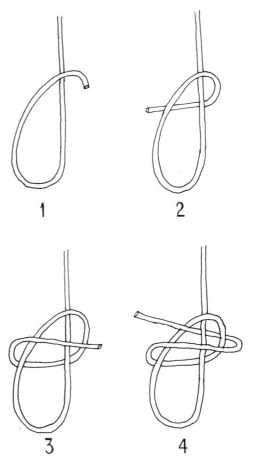

Fig. 11–4 Four steps in making an upholsterer's slip knot.

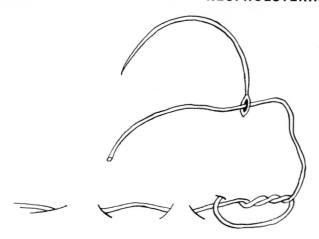

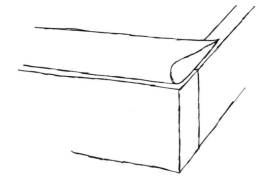

Fig. 11–6 Shaped wooden edge is used instead of burlapped fox edging.

Fig. 11–5 A three-turn slip knot is used to finish off a hem stitch.

Finishing Knot

To finish off, you will use the three-turn slip knot (Fig. 11–5). Stick the needle halfway into the fabric. On the point side, wrap the twine around the needle three times. Pull the needle through. This slip knot is in the same family as the "hangman's knot." It is used for finishing off the top and bottom ends of the fox edging; seat and deck sewn to the burlap and springs of an overstuffed chair; and sewing springs to the webbing or 17-oz. burlap.

Reupholstering Shaped Wooden Edges

What is a shaped wooden edge? A shaped wooden edge is used in place of fox edging on any chair that has a hard edge, i.e., *not* a spring edge. It is not very common. It is wedge shaped, with the round, thick side in the front. The thick front is usually from $3/4''$ to $7/8''$ wide (Fig. 11–6). It is held in place by common nails, with the holes predrilled so as not to split the wood.

The only time you'll use a shaped wooden edge is when your chair was originally upholstered with one. When you take off the old fabric, gently pry up the old common nails that hold the shaped edge in place. You do not want to split this wood.

A chair with a shaped wooden edge has a completely different type of seat construction. It is cut and sewed differently from the standard seat. You will be using the old cover as a pattern. As you remove the wooden edge and fabric, carefully study how it was put together. Cut the stitches out of the old fabric. Press each piece flat so that it can be accurately used as a pattern. Sew the new cover just like the old one. The chances of your having a shaped wooden edge on your chair are slim, but they do exist. Restuff the wooden edge with the old cotton stuffing, just the way it was when it was first upholstered.

Chapter 12

Repairing Springs

The comfort and resiliency of the seat and back of a chair or couch depend on firmly anchored springs. If the chair is older than 10 years and has not been reupholstered, you should retie the springs in the seat. Even if the springs are not popping out, do not take any chances. The seat of a chair gets the worst beating, especially if the user has a habit of collapsing into it. You don't want to retie a popped spring only a few years after your reupholstery job.

To make the job easier and longer lasting, never cut the old spring twine unless it has rotted away in some rows and is snapped, frayed and useless. New twine should be tied and nailed next to the old twine. The old twine left intact gives your spring-tying job double strength. If the frame is solid and there is no need for any frame repair, then you should not take the spring coil unit off. However, if the frame of your chair is wobbly and needs to be reglued and reclamped, then the unit must be taken out. We call the springs a unit because all the coils are tied together to work as a unit.

If the seat or back spring ties are in such bad shape that they are popping all over the place, then you will have to start from scratch. You will have to figure out where to place the springs, how to attach them to the webbing and 17-oz. burlap and how to retie the springs on the top.

To introduce you to spring placement and tying on a hard-edge chair (usually a seat with no cushion) and a soft-edge chair (a seat with an edge wire and cushion), we will first talk about the hardest, and least common, spring repair job.

Replacing Damaged Spring-Coil Twine

Step 1: Spring Removal
Chalk the locations where the number 14 tacks that hold the spring twine down are located on the edges of the frame. Make a diagram that shows how the springs were placed on the seat or back. Remove the number 14 tacks, springs and frayed spring twine. Since the springs are no longer tied together as a unit, cut off the old, frayed spring twine.

Step 2: Spring Placement
You will always place your springs the way they were originally. Be sure to take notes and make a sketch. In a small antique chair seat, you may have only five coils. There is no special distance from one spring to another. Usually the center coil is dead center. In the large overstuffed chair seat, you may have nine coils. The front, side and back coils are placed right up against the edge wire, with the

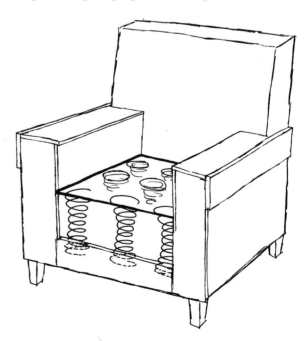

Fig. 12–1 In a spring-edge seat, the front, back and side coils are placed right up against the edge wire.

79

edge wire horizontal to the frame (Fig. 12–1). The corner springs are up against two sides. The center coil is dead center.

After the webbing or 17-oz. burlap has been repaired or replaced, chalk an X where the center of each coil will be placed. You can do this by eye or by crossing two strings vertically and horizontally where the old number 14 tacks held the old spring twine down. The twine always goes through the center of the coil.

Step 3: Stitch the Springs to Webbing or Burlap

The springs should be anchored on the bottom and on the top. By stitching the bottom of the springs to the webbing or burlap, and crosstying the top of the springs with spring twine, you will keep them from shifting in any direction.

Start out by making an upholsterer's slip knot, catching one spot on the coil at one corner of the frame. You will need flax or nylon stitching twine, and a straight 10″ or curved 6″ needle. You will probably have to string up at least two lengths of stitching twine, so cut a comfortably long piece. You will not want to make the piece of twine so long that it becomes hard to handle or so short that you have to constantly string up another.

The twine is knotted in three places on the coil. Each knot is a loop stitch that anchors the coil to the burlap. Finish stitching each coil so that you are as close as possible to the next coil to be stitched. For extra anchorage, each stitch can be knotted by wrapping the twine around the point of the needle once or twice when the needle is halfway in the burlap. This is a one or two-turn slip knot. Finish off with the three-turn slip knot at the last stitch.

Instead of hand stitching the coils to the burlap, the furniture manufacturer or professional reupholsterer will use a special tool that anchors steel clips into the springs and burlap. If the 17-oz. burlap is good, restretch it, leaving the clips in the springs. They will not need additional help from stitching twine. If the burlap must be replaced, the clips can be removed with pliers and thrown away. The coils will then be hand stitched to the 17-oz. burlap.

Step 4: Retie the Springs

You will be using two basic knots in spring tying. The starting knot, used to tie the spring twine at every point on the frame, is the figure-eight knot (Fig. 12–2). Tacks are like wedges. They have a tendency to loosen up. An ordinary knot, once loosened between the frame and the head of the tack, will slip out. A figure eight knot cannot slip, thereby giving it longer life. The second knot used in spring tying is a square knot (Fig. 12–3). Square

Fig. 12–2 Figure-eight knot, a starting knot which cannot slip.

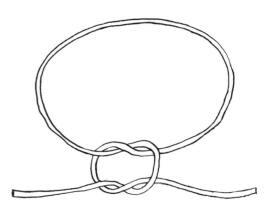

Fig. 12–3 A square knot is used every time the spring twine crosses a coil.

knots are used every time the spring twine crosses a coil.

There are two basic ties: the two-way or four-knot tie, and the four-way or eight-knot tie (Fig. 12–4). We recommend that a complete four-way tie, which includes all diagonal, vertical and horizontal ties, be done on all tied jobs, even if the original job was a two-way tie. The four-way tie does a better job of keeping the springs from shifting in any direction.

You will tie one length of spring twine at a time, from start to finish. Tie a figure-eight knot around a number 14 tack. Drive it into the frame. Tie each side of every coil so that the coil stands up straight when anchored to the opposite side of the frame. You will have to experiment a few times in order to tie the knot in the right place on the twine. On the opposite side of the frame, again tie a figure-eight knot around a number 14 tack and drive it in the frame.

The Return Tie

The return tie is used on soft spring edges (Fig. 12–5). It is used to reinforce the edge of the fox edging, i.e., to keep the edge wire even with the front of the frame. The coils will be standing up straight, not tilted down in any direction.

Start in the back of the frame with a figure-eight

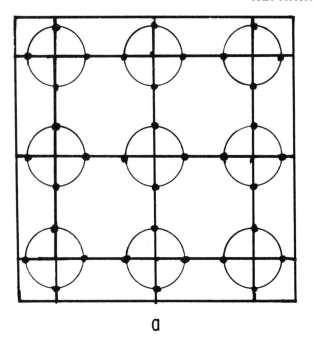

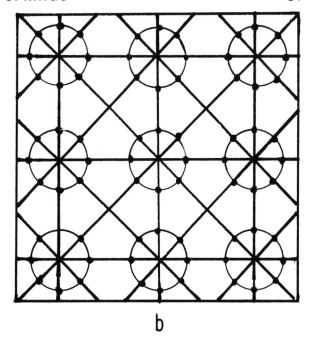

a   b

Fig. 12–4 Two ways to tie down coil springs. *a*. Two-way or four-knot tie. *b*. Four-way or eight-knot tie.

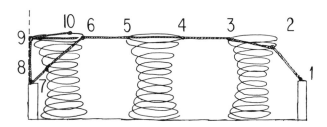

Fig. 12–5 Return tie in a spring-edge seat keeps the front coil from tilting forward. Knot #7 on the return tie is always five turns down from the top.

knot. Bring the rope up to the first coil, making sure the coil is standing up straight. Knot it. Continue knotting it until you get to the back of the front coil. Count five turns on the coil. At the fifth turn, grab the coil. Knot here. Put two nails in the frame at this point. Wrap the rope around the first nail, pulling hard until the front edge of the coil is parallel with the front of the seat rail. Then wrap the twine around the second nail. Drive the second nail in. From the second nail, grab the edge wire, starting a knot. Compress the spring until it is about 8″ from the bottom, pulling the knot tight and driving in the tack so that the height remains. Finish the knot by going from the front to the back of the coil.

Common Coil-Spring Repair

In most projects, you will not have to take out the whole coil unit in order to retie the springs. Only a

few lengths of spring twine are frayed and broken. The frame is solid, so it is not necessary to take the springs out. There are two aspects of spring repair. The idea is to anchor both the bottom of the springs and the top of the springs, so they will not shift or fall over.

The bottom of the springs may be sewn, or fastened securely with metal clips, to the bottom of the 17-oz. burlap or webbing that has *not* rotted or begun to sag. In this case, the bottom of the springs needs no attention. However, if the 17-oz. burlap or webbing is rotten, you will have to remove it. Leave the top of the springs intact. Turn the chair upside-down. Remove the tacks holding the heavy burlap or webbing. Clip the stitching twine holding the bottom of the coils to the burlap or webbing. Now your springs are dangling in place, the bot-

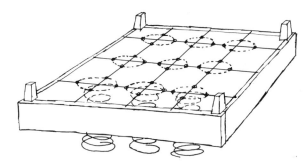

Fig. 12–6 Springs are tied in two directions on the bottom so they do not shift.

toms ready to be reanchored. Tie the bottom of the springs in two directions so they do not shift (Fig. 12–6). The goal is to keep the bottom of the springs as level as possible with the bottom of the frame. Use the same knots as you would to tie the top of the coils, i.e., figure-eight knot for starting and finishing at the frame, a regular square knot between at the coils.

The spring twine on the top of the coils may be in excellent shape, so you can leave the top alone. If several twines are snapped or frayed, retie completely on top, leaving the old twine in place for double strength.

Coil-Spring Seats and Backs

Crown Seat

A crown seat is tied as shown in Figure 12–7. The middle spring stands up straight and the two side springs are slanted toward the edge of the frame. A crown seat has no cushion. The middle of the chair receives the most weight. When you sit on the crown, it compresses the springs, giving you a soft, bouncy feel.

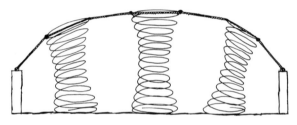

Fig. 12–7 A crown seat is tied with side springs slanted toward the frame.

To make a guide to tell you the position of the springs in a crown seat, nail a string to the frame and pull it over the springs. You will automatically get the shape of the seat. The springs only need to be compressed $1/4''$. You want only to anchor them in place, not to suppress them, taking out all the bounce and softness.

Spring-Edge Seat

Every time you have a spring-edge construction as shown in Fig. 12–8, you have a cushion on top. On a spring edge, the springs go right up to the edge wire on all four sides of the frame. The edge wire is parallel to the edge of the frame. This construction is made to give the seat a square shape. Fox edging is always sewn to the front edge wire, springs and burlap, to give a curved front edge.

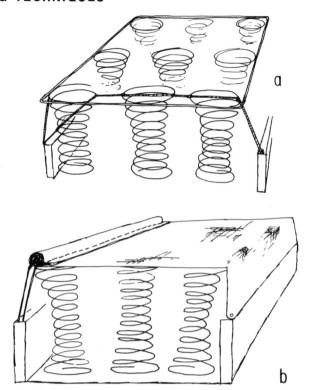

Fig. 12–8 Spring-edge seat. *a*. Seat has a return tie and edge wire. *b*. In a spring-edge seat, fox edging is always sewed to the front edge wire.

Crown or Pullover Back

The coil springs in the pullover back are tied exactly the same as the crown seat.

Spring-Edge Back

The spring-edge back is tied exactly the same way as the spring-edge seat. The top of the back, with return ties, is tied exactly like the front of the seat. The spring-edge back is used for a boxed back, where there is an upholstery cover boxing alone or a boxing and a border.

Marshall Unit Back

Marshall unit backs are not used today in new furniture. They require too much labor. They make a very comfortable chair. Several soft, small coils are used close together instead of a harder, larger coil. The Marshall unit back gives a more uniform, more comfortable feel than the regular spring-edge back.

Each small spring is made in bags $16''$ in circumference, sewn as long as needed, depending on the height of the back (Fig. 12–9). The shape of the back also depends on how the pockets are sewn

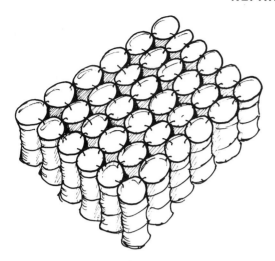

Fig. 12–9 Marshall springs unit found in some older chair backs.

together. The back or cushion could be either square or T shaped.

Repairing a Marshall Unit Back

The Marshall unit back needs repair if the muslin has torn or rotted from age. The best repair job is rebuilding the whole casing. If the bottom is rotten, the top will soon be rotten.

Step 1

Take the measurements of the old Marshall unit back to use as a guide. Note how many pockets are in each tier. Make a diagram. As when reupholstering any other casing in a chair, take apart the old muslin cover. Study it to see how it is made. You will notice that every tier has several—6 or more—pockets, $3^1/_2''$ wide.

Step 2

Start out with a strip of fabric 16" wide and the length of the back of the chair. Fold the two sides together and sew a $^1/_2''$ seam on the machine. Also, sew one end closed.

Step 3

Bring all the loose Marshall springs with you to the machine. Insert one spring next to the closed end of the muslin strip. On the machine, sew closed the other end of the spring. Now you have one pocket. Make all the other pockets in the tier in a similar fashion, until you get the length of the old Marshall unit.

Step 4

Tiers are hand sewed together, using a three-turn slip knot between every pocket. After all the tiers are sewn together, and the new repaired Marshall

spring back resembles the old one, then you are ready to stuff it in the IB cover.

Step 5

The IB cover is constructed like an attached cushion. You will have already cut out and laid aside the IB cover, the top and side IB boxings, and welt. The backing for the attached cushion can be made out of burlap or muslin. It is the same size and shape as the IB cover, except that a flap at the bottom, the dimensions of the top boxing, is used to enclose the Marshall springs unit. Sew the IB cover, welt, IB top and side boxings and IB backing together. It will look like a large, boxed envelope. The front seams of the boxed back will be sewn so they are not visible. The IB cover and IB boxings will be sewn face to face. The rear $^1/_2''$ seams on the top and sides have to be exposed. These $^1/_2''$ seams are used to tack the cushion back onto the frame. These seams are made by sewing the IB boxing and IB backing wrong sides together.

Step 6

After the cushion back is sewn, a burlap strip (pull strip) is sewn to the bottom of the IB backing. It is the width of the IB backing and the length needed to reach the rear seat rail where it is tacked.

Step 7

Now you are ready to stuff the Marshall unit into the cushion back. We highly recommend that you have a professional upholsterer do this process. To do it right requires a special stuffing machine.

Step 8

The burlap flap at the bottom of the IB backing is hand sewed closed so the Marshall spring unit will not fall out.

Repairing a Platform Rocker Back

The back on a platform rocker and some other boxed backs are made with a similar construction. The back of the chair is like an attached cushion. Many of these backs have a spring cushion unit which is similar in construction to the Marshall spring unit, except that the crossties holding the springs together are spring wire (Fig. 12–10). They are mounted together so that the springs cannot be separated. This spring construction has a harder feel than Marshall springs. The edge wire and cross wires also have a tendency to break, at the joinings and between them. Sometimes the coils themselves are broken. If this is the case in your project, either replace the whole unit if possible or add a piece of polyurethane foam at least 1" bigger than the spring cushion unit. If you wrap the chair with cotton, you

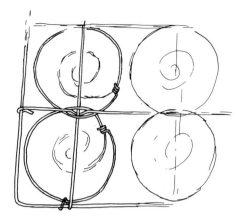

Fig. 12–10 Spring unit found in platform rockers—and in some other types of chairs—has spring wire crossties.

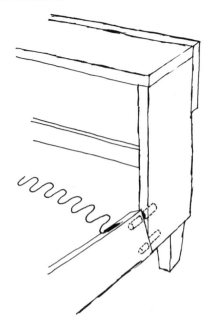

Fig. 12–12 Twisted seat rail in a No-Sag spring construction needs repair.

could make the foam the same size as the spring cushion unit.

The casing in the platform rocker is similar to the boxed casing for the Marshall spring back, except that there is no boxing. The boxing and the face of the back are all one piece, with pleats in the top corners (Fig. 12–11).

Repairing No-Sag Springs

No-Sag or Zig-Zag springs are the modern version used instead of coil springs. There is a discussion of No-Sag springs, No-Sag clips, helicals, crossties and related supplies in Chapter 3. This section is mainly concerned with No-Sag spring repairs.

There are several different ways that a No-Sag spring foundation could break. The No-Sag clips could break off or become loose. Maybe the wrong nail was used, especially in any previous repair jobs. The clip may not have been put on correctly.

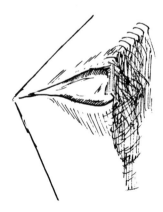

Fig. 12–11 Pleat is found on the top of platform rocker back.

The seat or back may have received a lot of use or abuse. Sometimes the No-Sag springs themselves snap in half. There is constant tension and pressure on the springs. No-Sag springs have inadequate resiliency compared to the coil springs. However, the clips and springs may be in perfect shape. You may only have to add helicals, No-Sag rubber bands or crosstying.

In a No-Sag seat construction, another repair job might be in the frame of the chair. In a seat, No-Sag springs run from front to back. Sometimes, from the pressure of a person sitting in the seat, the back and front rails are twisted. The clips are nailed on top of the seat rails, so the bottom of the rails twist upward, forcing the dowels out (Fig. 12–12). To repair twisted seat rails, you should detach the No-Sag springs on one end, releasing the tension. Clean, glue and reclamp the dowels. Then put your springs back in place.

Repairing a No-Sag spring construction may require several consecutive steps.

Step 1: Determine the Length

In reupholstering, there is always evidence of the length of the spring. If there is at least one good spring anchored on the seat or back (whichever you are repairing first), then that spring would be your guide. Count the number of turns, i.e., zigzags, to determine the length of the new springs. If all the springs are broken, you can still count the number of turns by starting at one side of the frame, counting the turns up to the broken turn, then continuing

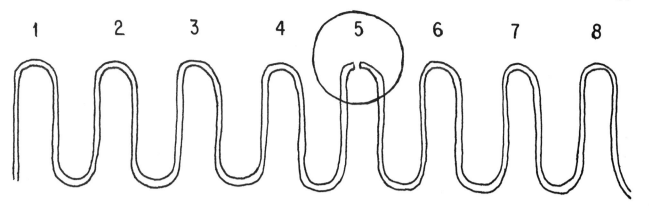

Fig. 12–13 How to determine the length of a new No-Sag spring.

to the other side of the frame. Always count the top or bottom turns, not both (Fig. 12–13). Do not complicate matters by trying to measure the length of the springs with a tape measure.

Step 2: Repair the Frame

After you release the tension on the springs, do any frame repair that is necessary. Take the nail out that holds the spring in place. Unhook each spring, one at a time. Then you can do your frame repair work.

Step 3: Renail Clips to the Frame

If you put a new board in to replace split or warped wood, then place the old board alongside the new board, marking the center hole of each clip (Fig. 12–14). If the board is in good shape, not warped or split, you can use the old holes. We recommend that you use stronghold screw nails instead of common nails. Stronghold screw nails are tempered or hardened. They are less apt to bend than a common nail when driven into hardwood. The stronghold screw nails are also a little longer than the standard nails used by factories.

Follow the design of the chair when renailing. If the old clips were nailed on the top board, nail the new clips to the top board. Nail them where they were originally. Do not change them.

Step 4: Install Helicals or Rubber Bands or Crosstie

Helicals, rubber bands and crosstying serve the same function. They prevent the springs from tipping sidewise; distribute the sitter's weight, so that two or three springs do not carry the whole burden; prevent the burlap from sagging between the rows of springs; and they make the No-Sag spring unit feel as close to coil springs as possible.

Helicals are small springs with hooks on both ends. You usually find two helicals for each pair of No-Sag springs (Fig. 12–15). After the helicals are hooked on, the clips are squeezed closed with

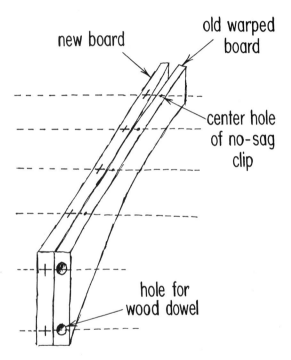

Fig. 12–14 + represents the markings for the center hole of each clip (*on top*) and for the dowel holes (*on the side*).

pliers. At the frame, a stronghold screw nail with a big head is driven into the frame, anchoring the helical.

Tough rubber bands for upholstery are $2^{1}/_{2}$" or $4^{1}/_{2}$" in circumference and $^{1}/_{2}$" wide. Please do not use any conventional rubber bands! Slip the upholstery rubber bands over a loop of each adjacent No-Sag spring (Fig. 12–16). The number of rubber bands used follows the same setup as helicals, two rubber bands between each length of No-Sag spring. The rubber bands can be put on horizontally or at an angle, as shown at *1* and *2* in Figure 12–16.

Crosstying involves using spring twine. No-Sag

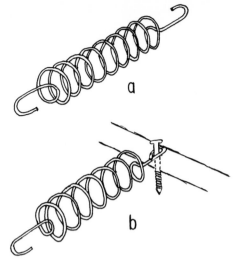

Fig. 12–15 Installing helicals. *a*. Helical is a small spring with a hook on each end. *b*. Hook is anchored around a stronghold screw nail driven into the frame, then end is closed with pliers.

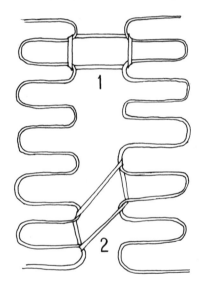

Fig. 12–16 Tough upholstery rubber bands can be slipped on two No-Sag springs horizontally (1) or at an angle (2).

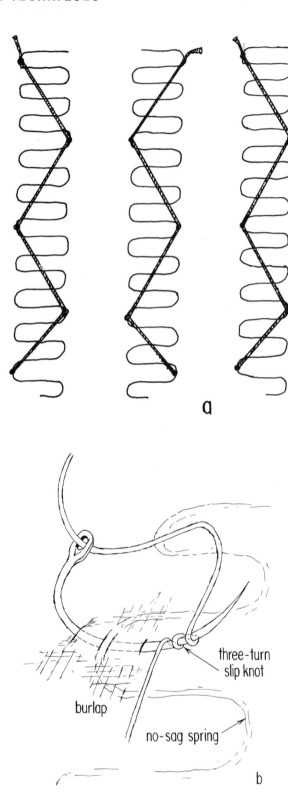

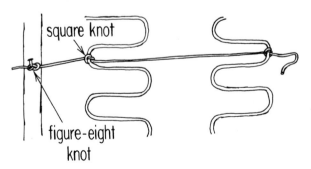

Fig. 12–17 Crosstie No-Sag springs with figure-eight knots and square knots.

Fig. 12–18 Stitched-on-burlap method. *a*. Stitch burlap to No-Sag springs with a zigzag pattern (for clarity, the burlap is not shown). *b*. Three-turn slip knot is used to attach the burlap to the No-Sag spring.

spring typing is similar to tying coil springs. You use a figure-eight knot as a starting and finishing knot and a regular knot at each spring (Fig. 12–17).

Stitched-on-Burlap Method

Instead of using helicals, rubber bands, or cross-tying to keep the No-Sag springs from shifting and to help them work as one unit, you can stitch the 10-oz. burlap to the springs. Then you can anchor the springs in place using stitching twine to hand sew the springs onto the burlap. Instead of crosstying from side to side of a back, you will be stitching from front to back (do not use this method for the seat). The biggest advantage of the stitch-on-burlap method is that the back has a much softer feel without the added use of heavy helicals, rubber bands or spring twine.

Start on the bottom of the back. Make an upholsterer's slip knot at the first zigzag on the spring. Stitch every turn opposite from where you were, so that the stitching is zigzaged (Fig. 12–18a). Stitch and knot a three-turn slip knot (Fig. 12–18b).

Start to take the stitch with a curved needle, putting the needle in under the burlap. Take the string from the first knot, and wrap it around the needle three times, stretching the string to the point of the needle. Now pull the needle through the burlap, finishing the knot, and stitch.

Continue to the end of the spring, finishing off with the same three-turn slip knot. Stitch and knot the remaining springs.

Chapter 13

The Old and New Stuffing

The main function of stuffing is to cover the springs and give the chair a comfortable feel. A neat, professional stuffed chair also has eye appeal.

The main point to remember is to never throw out the old stuffing. The stuffing gives a chair or couch shape and design. It takes a skilled craftsman to know how much or how little stuffing to use and where to put it. Even if it smells, it can be deodorized with a sanitizing spray. Always remove the stuffing gently, noting where it belongs on the chair and which end is the front. Always add to stuffing. Rarely will you take away from it. If the top layer of cotton felt is bumpy, you will want to peel off enough to get to the smooth layer. If someone previously reupholstered the chair, left the old upholstery cover on and put another layer of cotton on top, resulting in an overpadded chair, than the top layer may be discarded.

In Chapter 3 you will find detailed descriptions of the different types of stuffing you might find in your chair. This chapter is concerned with the reupholstery process of putting on the old and new stuffing.

Sterilizing Sprays

Bacteria build up on any organic object, especially under humid conditions. Bacteria and objectionable odors on upholstered furniture need to be sanitized and deodorized. We recommend that every chair or couch be sterilized with a sanitizing deodorant spray approved by your state and stocked by your professional upholsterer. There are several trade names for sterilizing sprays. Each spray has its own inert and active ingredients that are approved by your state. Hospitals use sterilizing sprays on sickroom equipment, plastic mattress covers and mattresses.

The average chair needs 4 ounces of sterilizing spray; the average couch, 8 ounces. We recommend that you spray the surface of your upholstered furniture until it feels wet to the touch. Sterilize before you take any of the old upholstery cover off. Let the chair sit overnight to dry before removing the cover. The spray will have soaked through to the stuffing. We suggest that you bring an empty refillable plastic bottle with a spray head to your local upholsterer and have it filled with the antibacterial deodorant spray that he uses.

The First Layer

After the old upholstery cover is removed gently so as not to disturb the stuffing, the stuffing itself should be removed and gently set aside. When the webbing is repaired, the springs are retied and the 10-oz. burlap is tacked on, then you are ready to rebuild or reupholster your seat or back. The first step is to carefully put the stuffing back on the chair as it originally was. Sometimes the stuffing will actually separate into two distinct layers.

The first layer of stuffing is the layer closest to the springs. It is the first layer of stuffing to be placed back on the rebuilt seat, back or arms. The first layer, which acts as an insulator so you do not feel the springs, is usually coarse and resilient (bouncy). Some first layers, like sisal, tow, moss and hand-picked hair, tend to pack or mat down. Even when it is packed down, it still acts as a good insulator. So do not try to revitalize it. The stuffing fits the shape of the chair, so leave it alone. If it is damaged or very uneven, it should be picked by hand until it becomes fluffy. Redistribute the tow, moss, hair or sisal evenly over the whole area of the seat or back.

To eliminate the loose fibers of tow, moss and hair shifting around, you will have to sew them in

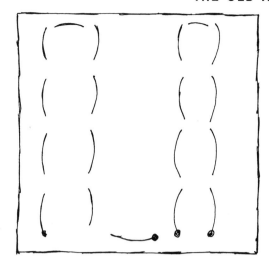

Fig. 13–1 Loose fibers of tow, moss and hair should be sewed down to the burlap so they don't shift.

The Second Layer

The second layer of stuffing is directly under the upholstery cover. This stuffing is soft and comfortable to touch and to sit on. Ninety-five percent of all second layers of stuffing are made from cotton felt. When you take the old cotton felt off, you may notice that it is packed down. It usually is not really hard and it retains the shape of the chair. Place the second layer of stuffing on as it originally was. If the old felt is smooth and evenly distributed, then we recommend that you always add a fresh, new half to full layer of cotton felt to give the chair a fresh new look and feel. Even if your chair has only foam rubber over springs, add new cotton felt—it will add years of life to the foam. The sunlight cannot penetrate the foam and rot it. This new layer of cotton felt should always be shaped to the seat or back of the chair.

If the cotton is badly damaged, measure the amount (the thickness) of the cotton that the chair had. Peel off adequate cotton to reach a smooth surface. Then add the necessary extra layers of new cotton to reach the original thickness, always shaping the cotton to the seat or back.

Sometimes polyurethane foam or foam rubber is used as a top layer of stuffing. You may find 1″ foam on the seat and 1″ or 2″ foam on the back, either alone (as in the case of some kitchen or dining room chairs) or with sisal, tow or rubberized hair underneath.

place (Fig. 13–1). You will need a 6″ curved needle and flax or nylon stitching twine. Knot a long strand of stitching twine and sew running stitches 1″ or 2″ apart. Do not pull the twine tightly. Follow Figure 13–1, making sure that you have knots at both ends of a length of stitching twine. It is not necessary to sew down sisal, or pads of stuffing like polyurethane foam, foam rubber or rubberized hair. These last three stuffings are springy and resilient. They do not mat or pack down. They simply rest on the burlap-covered springs.

Chapter 14

Machine Sewing

In Chapter 3, there is a detailed discussion of the differences between home and industrial sewing machines. Sewing machine threads are discussed there, too. If you have real trouble getting your home machine to sew through heavy upholstery fabric, don't hesitate to purchase this service from your local professional upholsterer, tailor, seamstress or laundry.

This chapter is concerned with the techniques of machine sewing seams, curves, corners, welt and pull strips. You will know which fabric pieces have to be machine sewn by noting where the old upholstery cover had machine sewing.

Before You Begin

Using Old Fabric Pieces as Patterns

Every piece that will be machine sewn has a distinctive shape or measurement. Usually, a welt is also sewn in. Examples of the old upholstery piece used as a pattern are a shaped IB (overstuffed chair), a T cushion, a square cushion or an arm boxing. A pattern is not needed when the fabric piece is tacked on all four sides and pulled into shape by hand. Examples are a seat with no cushion or a pull-over back or arm.

The new fabric piece is shaped like the old one by putting both face down or face up or, if you need one right and one left piece, the new fabric is face down and the old is face up. Then, and only then, are you ready to sew.

Magic $1/2''$ Sew Line

Half-inch seams are the standard seams in upholstery sewing. If you lack the eye to gauge $1/2''$ in a sew line, then mark your sewing machine with masking tape $1/2''$ to the right of the needle. This $1/2''$

is critical where exact measurements are needed, as in making a tailored fitted arm boxing.

Curved Seams and Corners

If you are familiar with machine sewing, you know that it helps to clip the $1/2''$ seam when the fabric must follow a curve. In upholstery, clipping the $1/2''$ seam is not necessary on curved seams when the welt is made on the bias, but is necessary if welt is on the vertical or horizontal edges of the fabric. Bias-cut welt can be stretched, shaped and flattened while sewing without any clipping.

Remember, if you have to sew the welt around a curve and it is not cut on a bias, the smaller the curve, the closer together you make the cuts. You can make the cuts as close as $1/2''$ apart or as much as $1^1/2''$ or $2''$ apart. The purpose is to let the welt follow the curve of the pattern and lie flat. If the welt and boxing do not lie flat, snip them. Cut both the welt and boxing at the same time. Normally, you will just cut the welt and boxing to get your fabric to lie flat.

Always clip to within $1/16''$ of the seam line. You do not want to cut open any part of the sew line, leaving a hole. Never clip the main fabric piece, i.e., the top or bottom of the cushion, the IB cover or the arm cover—only the welt and boxing sides.

When you reach a corner and want to make a 90° turn, then you make a cut in the welt and boxing $1/2''$ from the edge of the fabric. When you are sewing a rectangular piece of goods and the corners do not line up automatically, you have to make them line up. After you sew a few inches past one corner, hold the ends of the two fabric pieces together at the next corner with one hand. Machine sew up to the next corner, making sure the fabric pieces are stretched slightly so that the next corners will meet.

Then, to turn 90°, make a cut in the welt and boxing $1/2''$ from the edge of the fabric. Machine sew the corner and proceed to sew as mentioned above.

Making and Using Welt

As mentioned in Chapter 3, welt is a cotton or paper cording about $1/4''$ in diameter covered with fabric $1\frac{1}{2}''$ wide by the length needed to do the whole chair. Before you take the chair apart, when you do all the measuring for new fabric pieces, you also want to measure how much welt you will need for the whole chair. All the welt you will need is not always showing! Welt may be hidden where the back of the chair goes into the seat or where the bottom of the arms go in the seat. Push your hand in the hidden spots and estimate how much welt is needed but does not show. You could also push a tape measure or yardstick in to give you the number of inches hidden in each section. Write down the total number of inches needed.

There are two ways to cut the welt fabric. Either you can cut with the thread, making the $1\frac{1}{2}''$ strips vertically or horizontally on the fabric, or you can cut your fabric on the bias. Bias welt has more elasticity. However, if you have several strips of fabric running in the same vertical or horizontal direction, instead of one big block of fabric, you may want to cut the strips on the vertical or horizontal threads. Always cut the welt fabric either vertically or horizontally; never use a combination. When you cut your welt on the straight edge with strips of varying lengths, always join the seam by machine sewing on the bias (Fig. 14–1).

Cutting and Sewing Welt on the Bias

Whenever possible, cut your welt fabric on the bias. The welt will stretch, making curves and straight edges easier to shape. Also, the threads of the fabric will not unravel.

We have found an easy, fast way to make welt on the bias. Some couches need up to $1000''$ of welt strip. The best way to avoid sewing lots of little strips together is to create a cylinder and cut one long $1\frac{1}{2}''$ strip (Fig. 14–2, steps *1* through *6*).

Step 1
Refer to the Welt Chart in Chapter 7. One column tells you how large a fabric square you will need to make the length of welt needed (second column). Both measurements are expressed in inches. Example: If you need $756''$ of welt, a moderate amount, use a piece of fabric 1 yard square or $36''$ by $36''$. Set your ruler on diagonal corners of the square. Mark with chalk, as shown, and cut.

Step 2
Lay the two triangles face to face as shown in the diagram. The bottom X is laid on top of the top X. Sew the first seam across the top.

Step 3
Fold each half into a triangle. Sew sides *a* and *b* together.

Step 4
Sew the second seam along the base of the two triangles so that the fabric forms a cylinder. Make sure both seams are on the outside.

Step 5
Lay the cylinder flat on the table so you can see the V seam.

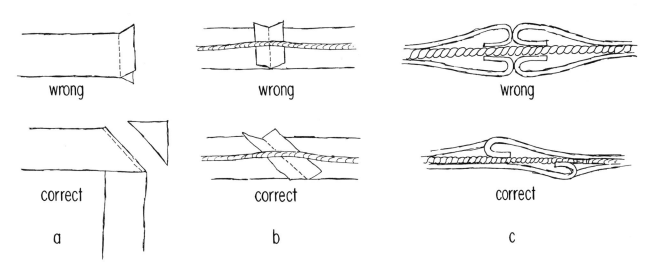

wrong   wrong   wrong

correct   correct   correct

a   b   c

Fig. 14–1 Making welt. *a.* Join welt strips on the bias, not vertically. *b.* The correct way has a stronger joint, especially with heavy material. *c.* The wrong way gives you a bulky four layers of fabric. The correct way gives you a thinner three layers of fabric.

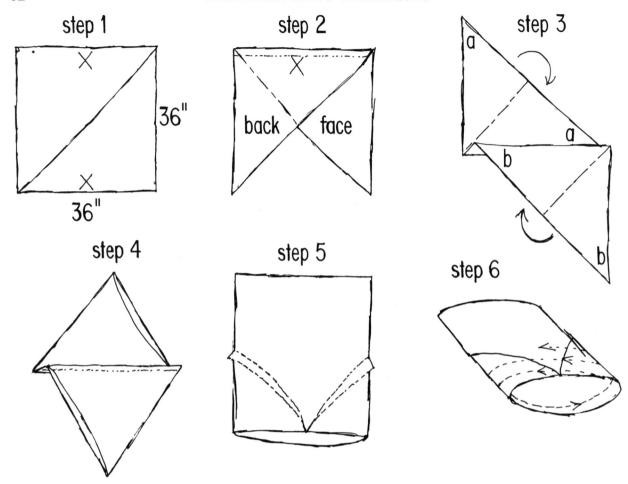

Fig. 14–2 The steps in cutting welt.

Step 6

Start cutting the cylinder from 0″ up to 1¹/₂″ and keep cutting, around and around the cylinder. Make yourself a paper gauge 1¹/₂″ by 1¹/₂″. Check at intervals to see if you are cutting accurately. It is not critical to get the strip to be exactly 1¹/₂″ wide. Trim off the starting piece, less than 1¹/₂″ wide.

Make the final adjustment, if necessary. Place the welt cording on the wrong side of the fabric. Fold the fabric in half and sew right alongside the welt cording. If you are using a home sewing machine, use a zipper foot. Your local professional upholsterer will use a special welt foot.

After the welt cording is sewn into the welt fabric strip, measure to see that the seam is ¹/₂″ wide. Trim where necessary.

Sewing Welt to Fabric Pieces

Here, for example, you want to see a strip of welt between the cushion boxing and the top of the cushion. The seam of the welt should be ¹/₂″ from the edges of the fabric. When you sew the three pieces

of goods together, you are actually sewing over the same welt seam line (Fig. 14–3).

Turning Corners

Stop the sewing machine when you are about 2″ from the corner, with the needle down so the fabric will not shift. A ¹/₂″ from the corner notch (on the boxing), make a cut within ¹/₁₆″ of the seam. Cut the boxing the same as the welt. Sew up to the cut. Leave the needle in the machine. Lift up the pressure foot and turn the corner. Make sure the welt is where it belongs—¹/₂″ in from the edge of the fabrics. Continue sewing the same way to the next corner, holding with one hand the corner notch of the boxing at the corner of the top of the cushion.

Joining Welt Ends

Cut the welt so that the ends overlap about an inch (Fig. 14–4a). Open up each side of the welt about 2″ to allow a little working room. *If the fabric is not bulky or heavy,* cut the welt cording so that the cording butts, i.e., the ends touch head-on. Cut

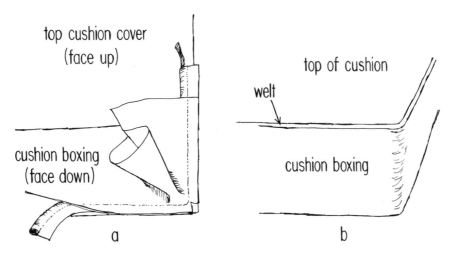

top cushion cover
(face up)

cushion boxing
(face down)

a

welt

top of cushion

cushion boxing

b

Fig. 14–3 Sewing welt to fabric pieces. *a.* Sew welt to the cushion boxing and cushion top. *b.* Finished cushion with welt on the edges.

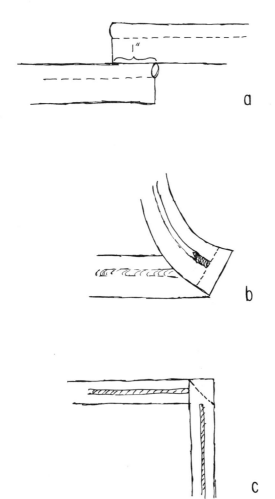

1″

a

b

c

Fig. 14–4 Joining welt ends. *a.* Cut the welt so the ends overlap an inch. *b.* Light fabric can be closed vertically. *c.* Bulky fabric should be closed on the diagonal.

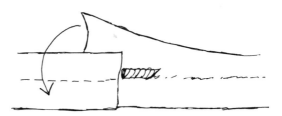

Fig. 14–5 When joining vinyl-covered welt, no cross (vertical) seam is sewed.

just the paper or cotton welt cording, not the welt fabric cover. The cording will be recessed ¹/₂″ from the end of the fabric. You are ready to join the fabric strip. Place the fabric face to face and sew a ¹/₂″ seam. Now close the welt up (Fig. 14–4*b*). Finish sewing the boxing, welt and cushion top together.

If the fabric is bulky, join the welt fabric on the bias so that the bulk is evenly distributed on both sides of the seam (Fig. 14–4*c*).

Vinyl Plastic or Leather. Welt ends for plastic or leather are joined a little differently. Overlap 1″ and cut for the exact measurements. On one side of the welt only, open up the stitches about 1¹/₂″. Cut out an inch of the paper or cotton welt cording. Slide the extra welt fabric right up against the opposite welt cording. Press in place so it is tight. Sew the joined ends in place (Fig. 14–5). Never fold plastic or leather, or you will have a large bump on your welt.

Pull Strips

The purpose of a pull strip is stated in its name. Pull strips are used to pull the bottoms of the IAs and IB fabric pieces taut, so they can be tacked on the seat rail. Pull strips are not visible. They start 1″ or 2″ below the seat level, so as not to be seen. You could end up using a yard or more of expensive upholstery fabric. The professional upholsterer has heavy, tough scraps of upholstery fabric that he uses for pull strips. The home craftsman can use decking fabric, burlap or maybe even the scraps of the old upholstery cover that are still tough and not worn. Burlap and decking fabric are considerably less expensive than upholstery fabric. Study the old pull strips. You can determine the length of the new pull strip by measuring the old one.

If the IB or IA has a curve to it, make ¹/₂″-deep pleats about every 4″ (Fig. 14–6). Sew the pleats in the pull strip before or after you sew the strip onto the IB or IA.

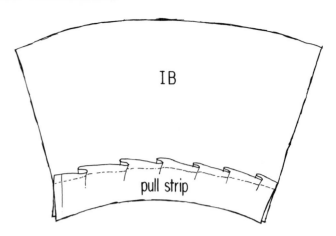

Fig. 14–6 Sew ¹/₂″ pleats in a pull-strip attached to an IB or IA fabric piece.

Chapter 15

Putting on Reupholstery Fabric

The Professional Look

When you finish putting on your reupholstery cover, your chair will have a tailored look with straight welt, no wrinkles and no pulls. From the center of the chair to the right and from the center to the left, you should see the same thing in reverse. Pleats should be the same depth and height on both sides. When you pinch the fabric in any location on the chair, you should not be able to lift up material. If you can, then the fabric has to be tightened.

You can determine the feel of the finished product with your fingertips. Start at the center of the chair, working to the left and then to the right; make sure that the stuffing is evenly distributed and not lumpy. If you feel any holes or bumps, redistribute the cotton stuffing to eliminate them. Use an ice-pick or stuffing regulator. If there is a hollow spot in the stuffing, move the cotton from a high spot to the hollow spot. The stuffing regulator is poked through the fabric by twisting it around.

You should have very little occasion to use a stuffing regulator on the body of the chair. The regulator is primarily used around pleats and corners. Only cotton stuffing can be regulated, not polyurethane foam or foam rubber.

The professional-looking reupholstered chair also has all the fabric pieces facing the same direction (*see* Figs. 5–3 and 7–18).

Packing and Pintacking

Pintacking is the most important process in putting on the new upholstery cover. Pintacking means driving tacks in halfway, so they can be knocked out if necessary. Pintacking is a way of controlling the fit of the fabric on the chair for each individual fabric piece. The inside pieces on the whole chair—

the IAs, IB, IWs and seat—should be pintacked. Once all the inside pieces are pintacked, they should be inspected to see that the welt, seams and thread of the fabric are tacked on straight. Each fabric piece should also fit snugly.

If you are reupholstering an overstuffed chair, you can readjust the pintacked IB and IAs if the cushion fits too snugly or too loosely on the deck (seat). If the cushion is a little too tight, then the bottom of the arms and back can be pulled tighter to loosen up the openings. If the pillow is too small for the deck, the bottom of the arms and back can be loosened to close the openings.

All pintacks should be about 1″ apart. After you inspect the work you have done and are satisfied with the results, drive in all the pintacks.

The actual process of pintacking involves packing down the section of the chair you are working on. We'll use the seat as an example. After you put four pintacks in your fabric piece—one on each side, like a cross—then you are ready to pintack the remainder of the seat. Pack the fabric down with your right hand while pounding, smoothing and pulling the fabric with your left hand to make the fabric as taut and wrinkle-free as possible. When the fabric feels taut enough, then you pick up the hammer and pintack.

Using Your Muscles

The average beginner is using a set of muscles that usually do not get a workout. You have to exert these muscles in your arms to get a tight, professional look. The fabric pieces that should fit most snugly are the inside pieces—the IB, IAs and seat.

In the seat without a cushion and the IB, you will put quite a bit of effort into compressing the springs to get a definite shape. Use your judgment as to what the shape of the seat, IB and IAs should be.

For example, in the introductory chair at the beginning of the book, the seat without a cushion has a "crown" shape to it.

Tacking vs. Stapling

Stapling with a hand gun is faster than pintacking and then driving the tacks in. We recommend that you pintack all the fitted inside pieces, e.g., the IAs, IB and seat. You can make adjustments with pintacks; it is difficult to remove staples in order to make changes. The outside pieces, which are rectangular in shape with little or no padding underneath, are not pulled and packed down. Once these pieces are centered, they can be easily stapled. On the top of the OAs and OB, you can staple the tacking strip as close to the top as possible. The bottoms are also stapled, while the sides are usually hand sewed.

Major Upholstery Cuts

Sloppy corner cuts and folds can ruin an otherwise professional-looking chair. Cuts are made around legs and posts—arm posts, wing posts, center of the back, back slats—any place where a board gets in the way of your pulling the fabric. These cuts allow the fabric to be fitted snugly around any post or rail.

Study your old fabric pieces to see which cuts to use, how deep and at what angle into the fabric to make them. It is always best to make small cuts. Keep trying to snugly fit a piece of fabric around a board. Undercutting several times leaves room for adjustments. Overcutting can mean a mistake that will be hard to correct.

There are five major cuts used in upholstery. The first three—45° cut, Y cut and the wide Y cut—are folded and tacked down. The last two cuts, the square cut and the V cut, are sewn.

45° Cut

Common 45° cuts are used on the corner legs and any other corner board (Fig. 15–1). You use the 45° cut for cambric, as well as for the fabric pieces. To make an accurate 45° cut, the fabric should already have been pintacked on all four sides to within 4″ of the leg. The fabric almost automatically folds itself up against the leg. Cut 45° into the leg. Then, fold each cut under and fit it to the leg. Pull down neatly and tack under.

Y Cut

Common Y cuts are done on any middle board (Fig. 15–1). The fabric should be smooth and tight,

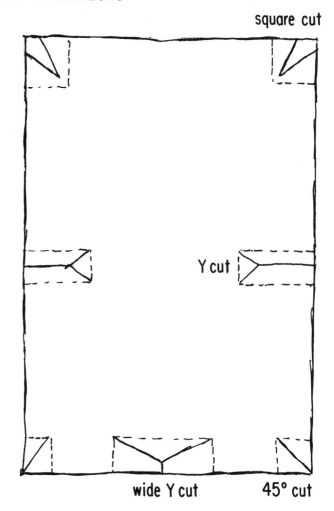

Fig. 15–1 Cuts are made in the fabric any time a post, leg or other board gets in the way of pulling the fabric through. Cuts enable you to make neat corners and to get rid of excess fabric.

with the fold right up against the leg or post. The legs of the Y are usually the width of the wood: If the post is 1″ wide, make the legs of the Y 1″; if the wood is 2″ wide, make the legs of the Y 2″. Fold the top of the Y underneath the center of the leg. Fold the other pieces to the left and right of the board and tack down.

Wide Y Cut

Wide Y cuts are rare, used on an inside board 3″ or 4″ wide (Fig. 15–1). Wide Y cuts are folded and tacked down the same way as a regular Y cut.

Square Cut

Square cuts are used on spring-edge seats. Square cuts are very common cuts. The seats of chairs that have a square cushion use square cuts. Most seats are $3^1/_2$″ to $4^1/_2$″ wide. Study the old pat-

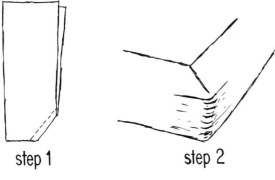

step 1   step 2

Fig. 15–2 Square cuts are used on the front corners of spring-edge seats.

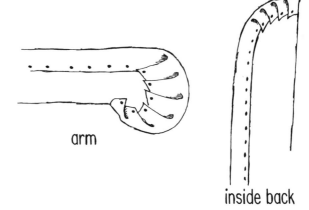

arm

inside back

Fig. 15–3 Pleats in the fabric piece help to make a smooth curve.

tern for the depth of the cut. Sew the cut edges together with a $\frac{1}{2}''$ seam (Fig. 15–2). Sewed square cuts enable the fabric to make a 90° turn.

V Cut

V cuts are used in making a hard edge (instead of using burlap fox edging), and you'll encounter them rarely. Instead of using two pieces of fabric joined together to shape around a corner, you make a V cut. Sew the two ends of the cut with a $\frac{1}{2}''$ seam.

An experienced upholsterer has almost X-ray eyes. He can see where a hidden post is located and, from experience, knows how deep it is. The beginner will have to study the boards that interfere with his fabric being pulled snugly. He can estimate the dimensions of a board with his hand or use a tape measure or ruler. Above all, he will study the old pattern to determine how deep and wide his cuts are.

Pleats

Pleats are made any place where there is excess fabric. Folds should be evenly spaced out and all run in the same direction. Two examples are pleats made around an arm or back. Several folds are made to allow the fabric to lie flat while taking the excess out and going around a curve (Fig. 15–3).

Double Welt and Gimp

The purpose of gimp or double welt is to hide the heads of the upholstery tacks where the fabric is tacked right up against show wood. Scroll gimp, or double welt covered with the same fabric as the chair, also adds to the attractiveness of the chair. Gimp is used on antiques. Double welt is the mod-

ern version used on colonial furniture and other styles with exposed wood.

The process of applying gimp or double welt is simple. You can work right off the roll. It is not necessary to measure and cut each strip as you need it. With white glue, glue the back of the gimp welt, about one foot at a time. Spread the glue out with the spout on the container then glue down the center of the gimp or double welt. With number 3 tacks for gimp and number 6 tacks for double welt, pintack every 5″ to 6″ for straight strips and as close as an inch around sharp curves and corners. *Never* stretch gimp or double welt when pintacking. When the glue dries, it shrinks and will pop off the chair if it is stretched. Just press the gimp or double welt down gently.

Trial Sample. Always test to see if the glue sticks to the fabric you are working with. It sticks to tapestry and velvets very well, not too well to nylon and not at all to Herculon. If the glued gimp or double welt does not stick to your fabric, use gimp tacks or small $\frac{1}{8}''$ staples that would fit in a regular staple gun. Most modern factories use staples.

As a trick to hide the staples, you can enamel paint the heads of the staples the same color as your fabric or a dominant color in the print. Staples should be painted a day before you are ready to use them. Stretch a piece of string between two points with the staples hanging in the middle. Spray paint the staples.

Ornamental Nails

The purpose of ornamental nails is the same as double welt and gimp, i.e., to hide the heads of upholstery tacks where the fabric is tacked right up against show wood. The head of an ornamental nail is $1/2''$ in diameter. When you want to count the number of nails you need, figure two to the inch in order to touch each other. There are times where you may want the ornamental nails to be an inch apart. An example would be around the legs of a wing chair, where there is no place that the fabric can be anchored tightly. Ornamental nails will anchor it.

Ornamental nails are found especially on old leather or plastic-covered chairs. Ornamental nails have either plastic or brass heads. They are used on the top, sides and perhaps the bottom of the OAs and OB instead of hand sewing.

Decorative Buttons

Decorative buttons are found on the IB of a tufted or shallow imitation tufted-back chair or couch. Once in a great while, you will find decorative buttons on cushions. The most popular diameter sizes are 22 mm—approximately $1/2''$—or 36 mm—$7/8''$. Other size buttons exist, but they are not used very often. The best custom-made buttons are those made using the professional upholsterer's button-making machine, with the special dies that are good for heavy upholstery fabric. The charge per button should be minimal, so do not hesitate to get the best for the finishing touch.

Attaching Buttons to the Chair

The tools and supplies needed to attach decorative buttons to the chair are a 10" straight needle with one point (or two), stitching twine and custom-made buttons. You should add buttons as soon as the IB is tacked on. Do not put any stuffing or upholstery cover on the OB. The IB cover will be tacked on and only burlap is exposed on the back of the IB.

Step 1

Mark the front of the IB where you want the buttons with small Xs or crosses with chalk. Measure and study the old IB cover for hints. Make several 18" lengths of stitching twine, as many as you have buttons. Put the stitching twine through the loop in the button and place the two ends of the twine together, holding them up so the button drops down.

Step 2

Take the straight needle and put both ends of the twine in the eye of the needle. Pull the twine in at least 3". Stick the needle through a chalked X or cross on the IB. Pull the needle through to the back of the IB. With the two ends of the twine, make an upholsterer's slip knot.

Step 3

Place a piece of cotton about the size of a golf ball inside the slip knot you just made, as shown. Pull the knot tightly up against the cotton. The cotton acts as a backup plate so the knot will not pull through to the front. Repeat for each button.

Step 4

When you finish tying all the buttons, adjust them. Make them tighter or looser by adjusting the slip knots. When you are satisfied with the depth of every button, tie two regular knots at the end of each to lock the button in place.

After you finish attaching the buttons, you can continue reupholstering the chair, putting on all the outside pieces.

Hand Sewing

Modern furniture factories do not do any more hand sewing because it requires too much skilled labor. They use $1/2''$-wide metal or double layer cardboard tacking strips with tacks 1" apart. Hand

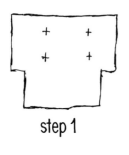

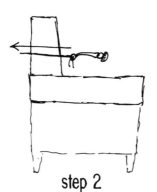

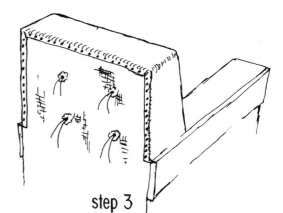

Fig. 15–4 Attaching buttons to a chair.

sewing is better because you can pull the fabric on the right and left, as well as on the top and bottom, giving you a tight fit.

When to Hand Sew

A pleat, seam or any opening over 3″ long should be hand sewn. The most common place for hand sewing is on the sides of the OB of an overstuffed chair. The top of the OB is blind tacked, the bottom is tacked under the chair, and the sides are hand sewed. Another instance is when the OB is curved or has a high crown, making it hard to blind tack; then the top of the OB is also hand sewed.

The OAs and OWs of the wing chair project are done similarly. The tops are blind tacked, the backs are tacked around the back posts and the front is hand sewed.

Any long pleats, 3″ or over, found on the IAs or IB are hand sewed. Any repair work if a seam breaks open, as in a cushion, can be hand sewed. We recommend that the beginner never hand sew leather or vinyl plastic, which will rip too easily and does not respond to hand sewing. If a leather or vinyl plastic cushion needs repairing, let your professional upholsterer repair it for a nominal fee with his heavy-duty sewing machine.

Blind Stitch

The blind stitch lives by its name: The threads are not seen. It is considered "the" upholsterer's hand stitch. If you do a good job, you can use any color thread and it will not show.

Start out with a knot at the end of the thread. The

proper length of the thread should be one and a half times the length to be sewed. Each piece of fabric is turned under ½″ on one side, less on lighter and silky material, then ½″ on the other. The threads are hidden in these bites (Fig. 15–5). The important fact to remember is that the point of the needle should go into the fabric just above the thread when the thread is held horizontally.

Double and Single Sewing

When reupholstering, you can either single or double sew. Double sewing requires the upholsterer to hand sew through four thicknesses of fabric, for example, the outside back, inside back and two thicknesses of welt (Fig. 15–6).

Single sewing involves sewing through only two layers of fabric; in the example given, the IB is tacked down. The top of the OB is blind tacked. On the sides, the welt is tacked. Then the OB is flipped over, with the face of the fabric showing, and ½″ seams are folded and pinned on the sides. The outside back sides are hand sewn to the first layer of welt (Fig. 15–7). Single sewing requires half the effort and half the time used for double sewing.

Reupholstering Loose Wood Panels

Loose wood panels are found at the front of some upholstered arms and IBs. When you pry off the panels with a screwdriver, carefully study how the panels were upholstered.

Step 1
Remove the old fabric and tacks. If you need more stuffing, put a half to a full layer of cotton on top of the wood panel. You should have already made a rough-cut rectangular piece of fabric, allowing at least ½″ to fold under each side of the panel.

Step 2
Lay the fabric face down on the table. Lay the panel with the cotton face down, centering it on the fabric. Tack the bottom, then tack the top. If one side is curved, tack the straight side first. Then tack the curved side. If the top of the panel is round, such as a Lawson arm panel, make one cut where the curve and the straight sides meet. Put several small, equal-size pleats around the curve on the wrong side of the panel so the front side is smooth. Tack each pleat down separately.

Step 3
After the panel is reupholstered, center it on the reupholstered chair. Drive in as many finishing nails as needed, just underneath the fabric. (Finishing nails are nails without heads.) With your

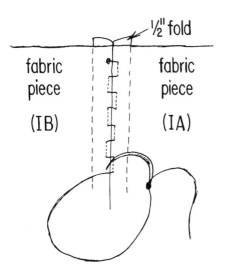

Fig. 15–5 Blind stitch: The small horizontal bites can barely be seen; larger vertical bites are hidden.

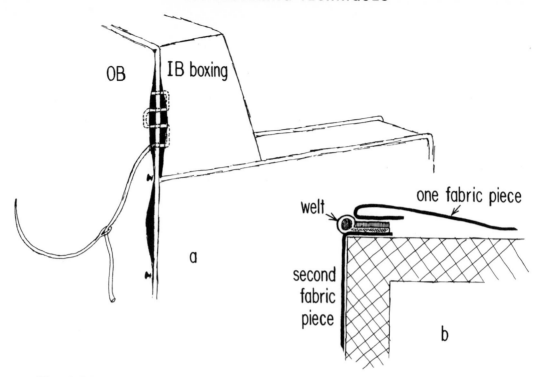

Fig. 15–6 Double sewing. *a*. Double sewing means sewing through two fabric pieces, e.g., the outside back, the inside back boxing and the welt. You are doing two jobs at once: sewing the OB and sewing the IB boxing. Double sewing is more difficult than single sewing. *b*. Top view of double sewing.

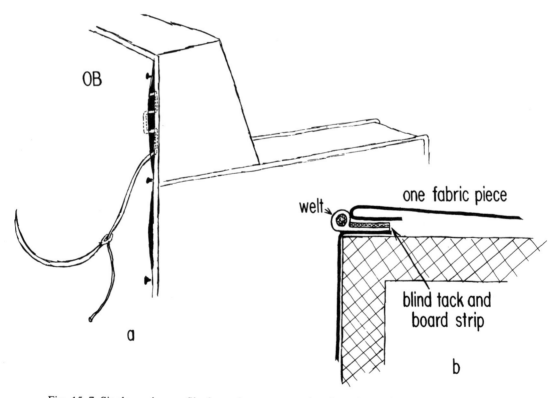

Fig. 15–7 Single sewing. *a*. Single sewing means sewing through one fabric piece and the welt, e.g., the outside back. The IB boxing has already been blind tacked in place. *b*. Top view of single sewing.

stuffing regulator or icepick, lift the fabric up so the nail marks are hidden.

Reupholstering Common Arms, Backs and Seats

Every chair is an individual, with its own uniquely upholstered arms, back and seat. As you take a chair apart, study how it was put together. To give you an idea how several common arms, backs and seats are fitted and tacked on, this section contains brief descriptions. Detailed descriptions of specific chairs are found in the project chapters in Part Three.

Arms

Pullover Arm

The pullover arm consists of two fabric pieces, the IA and the OA (*see* Fig. 19–1). The IA is tacked on the top, where the OA will be attached. The IA is pulled on top of the arm, then down, and tacked under the bottom of the arm. The front and the back are tacked. The OA is blind tacked on top, tacked in place on the bottom and back, and hand sewed in the front (or tacked, if an arm panel is used).

Tailored Arm

The tailored arm has three pieces—the IA, OA where both are the same shape and the top boxing (Fig. 15–8). These three pieces are machine sewn together, pulled over the arm, and tacked at the back and bottom.

Cap Arm

The cap arm also has three pieces. The cap, or top fabric, is tacked on under the cap of the arm or

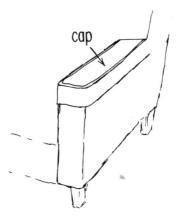

Fig. 15–9 Cap arms vary from chair to chair. Study your cap arm to see how it is made.

on the sides of the arm (Fig. 15–9). The front of the cap can have either two seams, sewn from two square cuts, or it can be pleated. The sides of the arm, the IA and OA, can be either one piece or two pieces. If the cap arm has two side pieces, the IA is wrapped around to the front of the arm. Then an OA is tacked on. If there is one piece, it is wrapped around the IA, front and OA.

All other arms are just slight variations of these three.

Backs

Pullover Back

Most tufted-back, channel-back and wing chairs and antiques have pullover backs. The top of the back is tacked onto the top or back of the back rail, pulled down over the IB and tacked on the seat back

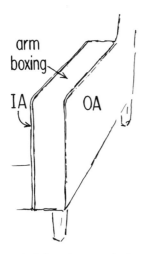

Fig. 15–8 Tailored arm style has an arm boxing between the IA and OA.

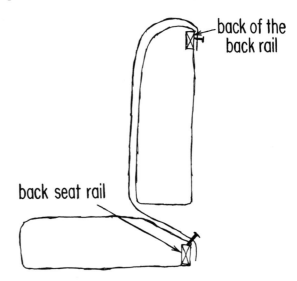

Fig. 15–10 Pullover backs are secured as shown.

rail (Fig. 15–10). The sides are tacked onto the seat, back frame or the back of the arm rail.

Boxed or Lawson Back

Boxed or Lawson backs are found on overstuffed chairs in two variations (*see* Fig. 7–7).

1. The IB is sewn to the IB boxing with a welt in the middle. The whole back is tacked together to the back frame of the chair. The IB boxing could be either one long piece or three separate pieces sewn together, top and two sides.

2. The boxed back consists of an IB, IB boxing and IB border. The IB is sewn to the IB boxing with a welt in the middle. The boxing in this back does not reach the back frame. A border, from 2″ to 3″, is blind tacked in front and tacked down on the edges of the top and side back rails.

Pillow or Colonial Back

The pillow or colonial back usually has a welted knife edge in the center of the cushion (*see* Ch. 20). The front and back of the cushion are cut and sewed the same, with pleats on the top two corners. Pull strips are sewn 4″ into the back of the fabric. The pull strip acts as a border on top and the sides are pulled into the frame. Reupholstering a colonial-back chair is described in great detail in Chapter 20.

Seats

Crowned Hard Edge

The crowned hard-edge seat is called a *crown* seat because the middle is higher than the sides (Fig. 15–11). The upholstery cover is the final seat, with no cushion on top. Some crown seats have seat borders, but most do not. The seat is tacked on all four sides. If the chair has upholstered arms, there could be pull strips on three sides—the back, left and right. The crown seat is tacked on using the "cross system"—pintacking and hand packing the stuffing.

The edge is hard because it is not elastic. It is not a spring edge, with edge wire attached to elastic

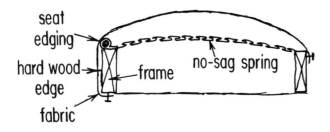

Fig. 15–11 Crowned hard-edge seat has a hard wooden edge and a crown in the middle of the seat.

spring. The edge of the frame in the front of the crowned hard-edge seat is covered with burlaped fox edging or a cotton padded, shaped wooden edge. The springs could be coiled or No-Sag. Antiques, dining and kitchen chairs are a few examples.

Hard Edge with Cushion

An example of a hard edge with a cushion is the wing chair in Chapter 19. The fox edging is hand sewed onto the burlap, covering the hand-tied coil springs. A hard edge with a cushion is flat, not crowned, with a seat-decking construction (Fig. 15–12). The seat fabric piece is in the front, with the decking on top. The cushion rests mostly on top of the decking, which is not visible because it is covered by the cushion. The seat-decking combina-

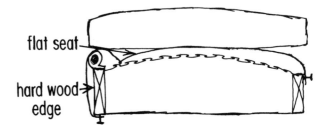

Fig. 15–12 Hard-edge seat with a cushion has an inelastic wood edge and a flat seat to hold a cushion.

tion is machine sewed together, then hand sewed to the burlap and springs at the seam. The seat-decking is tacked on three sides where there are no pull strips, because denim or cotton decking fabric is inexpensive and strong. A seat border may or may not be found on this type of seat construction.

Soft Spring-Edge Seat

An example of a soft spring-edge seat is the overstuffed chair project in Chapter 18. The soft spring-edge seat has an elastic edge wire attached to a spring unit (Fig. 15–13). The individual springs are usually hand tied. The purpose of the edge wire is to hold all the springs at the same level. The springs come right up to the edge of the frame of the seat. The edge wire is on all four sides, not just in the front. A fox edging is hand sewed with stitching twine or hog-ringed onto the edge wire in the front for a soft, curved look and feel.

In the hard edge with a cushion, the springs are inside the frame of the seat. In the spring-edge seat, the springs are even with the outside edge of the seat frame, in the front only. The upholstery cover has a seat-decking combination, with the

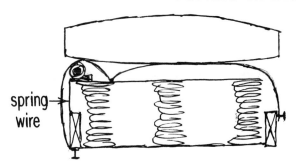

Fig. 15–13 Soft spring-edge seat has an elastic spring wire edge and a flat seat to hold a cushion.

seam hand sewn to the burlap and springs, then tacked down on all four sides, i.e., the same as the hard-edge seat with a cushion.

Making Skirts

Skirts dress up a chair or couch. They cover ordinary legs and give a finished, tailored look. The kick pleat, or inverted V, skirt and the box-pleated skirt are the two most common modern ones. It is a matter of taste which you prefer. If your chair has none and you would like to redesign it with a skirt, go right ahead. If your chair has boxed pleats and you prefer kick pleats, it will be easy to convert. If you are pleased with the way the skirt is designed, reupholster it the same way.

Kick Pleat or Inverted V Skirt

The easiest way to explain how to make a kick-pleated skirt is to follow an example. The seat of this fully reupholstered chair has a 30″ front, 28″ back and two 29″ sides (Fig. 15–14a).

Step 1: Rough-Cut Four Strips of Fabric

In order for the standard skirt to finish 7″ off the floor, each strip (one for the front, one for the back and two for the sides) is cut 8 1/4″ high and 54″ wide. The height of the skirt can be adjusted. If you want to finish off at 9″, add 2″ to the standard height (8 1/4″ + 2″ = 10 1/4″). If you want to finish off at 5″, deduct 2″ (8 1/4″ − 2″ = 6 1/4″).

When you make a kick-pleated skirt for a chair, your measurement chart and cutting diagram will show four strips of fabric 8 1/4″ by 54″, with more for a couch. If the couch has a kick pleat in the center of the front and back, it will require six strips of fabric, 8 1/4″ by 54″.

Step 2: Measure, Cut and Chalk

A very important point to remember is that all chalking is done on the face of the fabric with erasable white chalk. Nothing is more frustrating than

going to the sewing machine to match chalk lines when they are on the wrong side of the fabric!

Start with the front of the skirt, following Figure 15–14b. Take the first 54″ strip. You need a front piece 37″ wide. Measure 37″, cutting and scrapping the remaining 17″. On the face of the 37″ front strip, chalk 1/2″ seam lines on both sides, then mark 3″ in from the sew lines on both sides for the pleat lines.

Take the second 54″ strip, which will be a 48″ side when it is cut (Fig. 15–14b). On this 48″ strip, chalk 1/2″ seam lines on both sides for the sew lines. Then chalk 3″ in from the sew line on both sides for the first pleat lines and 6″ in on both sides for the second pleat lines. Measure, cut and chalk the second side strip, using the first side as a pattern. It is better to do one side at a time, so that you do not waste fabric if you make a mistake.

Now take the fourth 54″ strip, measuring and cutting 35″ for the back piece. Follow Figure 15–14b, using the same instructions for marking as you did for the front. All four skirt pieces are measured, cut and ready to be sewn together.

Step 3: Sew the Four Pieces Together

All pieces should be marked—front, side, top, etc.—on the wrong side of the fabric so that you do not sew any piece upside-down. As a guide, mark each piece as shown in Figure 15–14c.

Pin or staple all four pieces together, double checking that the pieces are in the correct order and in the correct position. Sew 1/2″ seam lines at each joining, giving you a closed circle.

Step 4: Marking the Lining

If the width of the lining is 40″ and all four sides of the skirt add up to 168″ (as in our example, 37″ + 48″ + 35″ + 48″ = 168″), then cut four and a half strips the width of the fabric, which gives you 180″—plenty of room to play with (4 1/2 × 40″ = 180″). Take the four and a half pieces of muslin or other lining material and mark the back of each (Fig. 15–14c). When you pin the muslin, all the seams will be facing the same direction (Fig. 15–14d). Machine sew the seams, leaving one end open. You now have a strip of muslin 176″ wide.

Step 5: Sew Bottom of Lining to Bottom of Skirt

Place the lining and skirt face to face. Starting at the center of the back, sew 1/2″ in on the bottom all the way around, stopping 2″ past the center of the back. This gives you a 2″ overlap (Fig. 15–14e and f). Trim off the remainder of the lining.

Step 6: Sew Top of Skirt to Top of Lining

Fold the skirt so that the faces of both fabrics are exposed and edges of the fabrics meet. Sew the top 1/4″ all the way around (Fig. 15–14g).

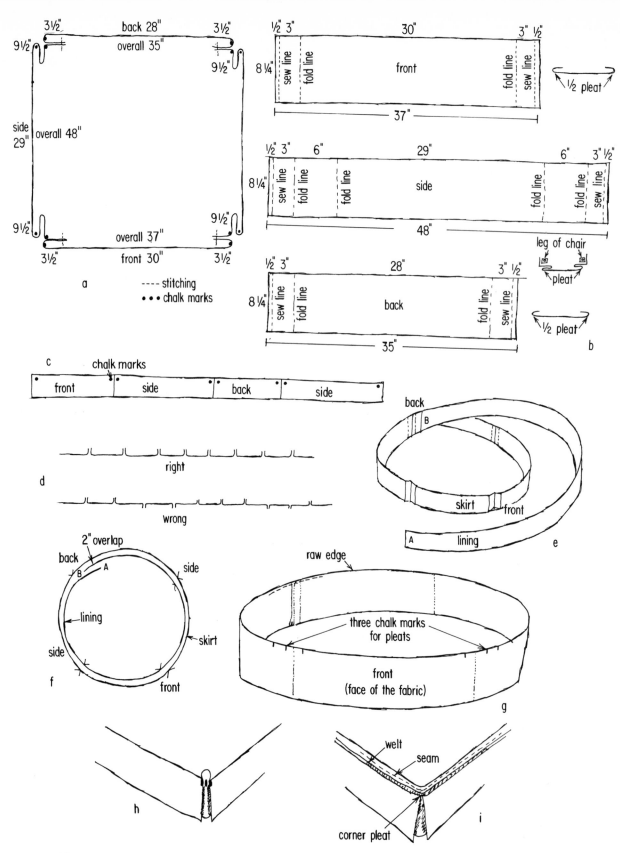

Fig. 15–14 Kick-pleated or inverted V skirt. *a*. Top view of a kick-pleated skirt: skirt cover, 8¼″ high; lining cover, 7¼″ high. *b*. Take each 54″ by 8¼″ strip of skirt fabric and measure, cut and mark two sides, a front and a back as illustrated. *c*. All four sides of the skirt pinned together, with chalk marks indicating "top up." *d*. Top view of the skirt lining shows seams facing correctly. *e*. Sew the bottom of the lining to the bottom of the skirt. *f*. Top view shows the 2″ overlap in the back of the lining. *g*. Sew the top of the lining to the top of the skirt, with both fabrics face out. *h*. Three chalk marks converge to form a corner pleat. *i*. First sew the pleat in place, then sew the welt on top.

Step 7: Marking and Sewing Pleats

For each potential corner of the skirt, there are three chalked lines. The two outside lines come together at the center to form a pleat (Fig. 15–14*h*). With the face of the skirt in front of you, put the needle in the fabrics about 3″ from a potential pleat and ¹/₂″ from the seam. Fold and sew the pleat in place (Fig. 15–14*i*). Sew the remaining three pleats.

Step 8: Press the Pleats

With a steam iron or a wet cloth and iron, press the pleats flat on both sides.

Step 9: Sew on Welt

Sew the welt to the top of the skirt, using a ¹/₂″ seam all the way around. Join the welt at the two open ends. Now you are ready to attach the skirt to the chair.

Step 10: Marking the Chair Corners

For the normal pile rug, the skirt bottom should be ³/₄″ to 1″ from the bottom of the leg. The thicker the rug, the higher the distance.

Place the skirt onto the chair. Take any first corner and put the pleat on the corner, sliding it up and down till you get the position you want. Hold the welt with one hand and gently pull the skirt up with the other hand, exposing the ¹/₂″ seam. Chalk the frame at the bottom of the fabric. Take the skirt off and lay it aside.

Take a ruler and measure the mark from the floor, e.g., 6 ³/₄″. Mark all four legs on all corners, 6 ³/₄″ up. Take a yardstick and draw a line all the way around the chair.

Step 11: Marking and Tacking the Skirt to the Frame

Now mark the center of each pleat on the lining side of the skirt. With the 2″ overlap seam at the back, place the skirt on the chair so the seam line is exposed and resting on the chalk line. The corner marks will also be set in the corner of the chair frame.

Start with one corner. On both sides of the corner, tack 1″ away to hold the skirt in place. Do the same to the other three corners. Starting in the middle of each side, drive in four more tacks to hold the skirt even with the chalk line (more tacks for a couch). Do the remaining three sides the same way.

Step 12: Blind Tacking the Skirt

Take a piece of cardboard tacking strip equal to the distance around the chair. In order to maintain a straight welted edge on the skirt, the easiest way is to tack the blind-tack strip on each corner first, then drive in four more tacks on each side, finishing off with a tack every inch around the skirt. A few pro-fessional tips to remember are: Do not drive the tacks in too hard, but just flush with the fabrics; tacks driven in too hard leave ridges in the top of the skirt. Also, make sure the cardboard tacking strip is always even with the seam.

Step 13: Finishing Touches

For the finishing professional touch, take a wood mallet or hammer and cardboard, then hit the top of the welt down at 3″ from each corner. Thick, stiff fabric, when creased on a fold, may want to stick out. Hitting the welt at the seam should crease the material so it hangs down.

Box-Pleated Skirt

Boxed pleats are found mostly on colonial furniture (*see* Fig. 7–16). The height of the fabric is the same as the inverted V or kick-pleated skirt: 8¹/₄″ finishing off at 7″ plus or minus, depending on the length of the chair's legs and the construction of the chair.

There are three main differences between a box-pleated skirt and a kick-pleated skirt: The fabric is wider for the box-pleated skirt, being twice the perimeter of the chair; the number of pleats in the box-pleated skirt vary, depending on their size and how far apart they are; there is no lining on the box-pleated skirt.

There are two professional methods. One is to tack the pleats on the frame, making one at a time directly on the chair, gauging the width and distance on each pleat. Another way is to gauge and sew the pleats in place on the machine first, then attach them to the chair frame. The example and thirteen steps will be done according to the easier second method. The example is for a colonial chair with 30″ front, 29″ sides and 28″ back.

Step 1: Cut and Sew Fabric Strips

Measure the distance around the chair and multiply by two ($30″ + 29″ + 29″ + 28″ = 116″ \times 2 = 232″$). You can either use four 54″ strips of fabric plus 18″, or sew scraps 8¼″ high together, equaling a little more than 232″. Of course, all the scraps should have the same vertical top and bottom, and horizontal sides. In step 3, you will see how the many seams can be hidden. Now all the pieces are sewn together and you have a strip approximately 232″ wide.

Step 2: Determine Width and Spacing of Pleats

Each pleat can be between 2″ and 4″ wide and 0″ to 2″ from its neighbor, depending on your taste. Also, the depth of each fold in the pleat is usually ³/₄″, as opposed to 3″ in a kick pleat. You might like to take a piece of scrap material long enough to make a set of boxed pleats in the front of the chair. Space them to your taste. Pintack your sample on the couch or chair to see if you like it. Adjust pleats if you wish until you find the sequence you like.

It works out that you use almost the same amount of fabric no matter how wide or how far apart each boxed pleat is. However, if you are short of fabric, then make each boxed pleat closer to 2″ apart. It saves a little fabric.

For the colonial chair example, the pleats will be 1″ apart and 3″ wide.

Step 3: Machine Sewing

Make a gauge with a piece of cardboard, scrap wood or 12″ ruler with masking tape on top, marking a 3″ to 1″ gauge (or the dimensions of your project) to help make even pleats (Fig. 15–15).

On the 232″ strip of fabric, make the first pleat in any direction. With the face of the fabric up, start sewing about 4″ down (a random length, because the first pleat is usually adjusted to approximately 3″ from the last pleat). Turn the fabric under 3/4″. Following Figure 15–16, sew the first 3/4″ plus about 1/2″. Stop machine. Gauge 3″ down from the fold line. Fold under 3/4″ to form the fourth fold. Sew the fourth fold plus 1/2″. You have now completed two full pleats.

It is important to make sure you always sew a seam underneath a pleat, where it will not show. You can do this by making the fold of one side of the pleat longer than 3/4″ inch (in our example, up to 2″ deep), as long as the first fold does not touch the adjacent fold of the pleat.

Step 4: Check Skirt Width

Measure the width of the skirt to see if it is long enough to go around the chair, plus an extra 4″ (116″ + 4″ = 120″). If you need more fabric, add it at this time.

Step 5: Add Welt to the Skirt

You should have 120″ of welt made (for this example). Sew the welt to the top of the skirt using a 1/2″ seam.

Step 6: Close the Skirt

In the corners, pintack the skirt around the chair. Do not stretch it tight. Chalk where the two ends of the welt meet and add two 1/2″ allowances for the seams. Cut off the remainder.

Take the skirt off the chair. Get ready to sew on the machine, making sure that the welt is not twisted. Join the two ends of the welt cording and close up the welt (see Ch. 14).

With the remainder of the unsewed skirt, form one or two pleats to equal the length of the closed welt. Allowing for two 1/2″ seams, cut off the remainder of the skirt. Join the two open ends of the

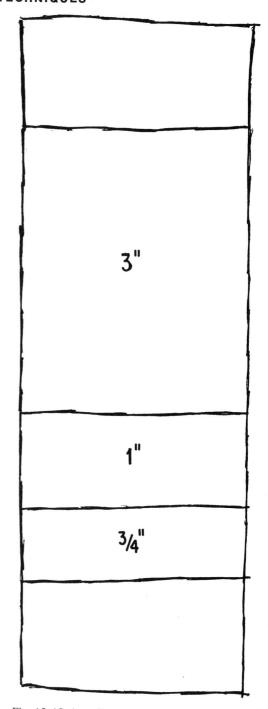

Fig. 15–15 A cardboard or wood gauge will help you make even boxed pleats.

skirt, making a skirt seam. Finish sewing the pleat. Then, sew the welt on top. The last pleat or two will not be the same dimensions, as the others, but should be as close as possible.

Step 7: Hem the Bottom

If the fabric has a tendency to ravel, the bottom of the skirt must be turned over twice for the hem. If the fabric is heavy and rubberized, it can be

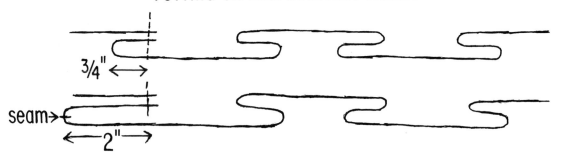

Fig. 15–16 Vary the depth of the pleat as necessary to hide seams.

turned over once, leaving a raw edge. Turn over once 1″, or turn over twice ½″ each turn, so that you finish off at the same dimensions. Turning over a heavy fabric twice gives an unattractive, bulky look. Sew the hem all around the bottom of the skirt.

Step 8: Press the Skirt
Now the skirt is ready to be pressed with a steam iron or regular iron and wet cloth.

Step 9: Attach the Skirt to the Chair
The box-pleated skirt is attached the same way as the kick-pleated skirt. Follow steps 10 through 13 in the previous section. Make sure you balance the skirt so the two front corners of the chair are identical.

Tacking on Cambric

Tacking on cambric is the last step in your re-upholstering project and, fortunately, it is one of the easiest steps. The cambric not only gives the bottom of the chair a finished look, but also acts as a dust cloth, collecting all the cotton fibers, dust and pennies that accumulate over the years.

For the last time, triumphantly turn your chair upside-down. Measure the vertical and horizontal dimensions of the seat bottom for the cambric, allowing ½″ to 1″ extra on all four sides. You will start tacking cambric in the center of the front of the chair. Fold ½″ of the cambric under and drive your first tack in, making sure all folded cambric is within ¼″ of the outside edge of the frame. Stretch your cambric out, pulling on the back. Turn the remainder under. Drive your second tack in. Go to the sides; repeat the same process to the left and right. You now have a cross-shaped pull (Fig. 15–17). Finish tacking the front, both left and right of the center, turning the cambric under. Tack within 3″ of the leg. Go to the back, doing the same. Then do the same to both sides.

Make one 45° cut for a square leg or three cuts for a round leg from the corner of the cambric to the inside corner of each leg (Fig. 15–18). Turn the

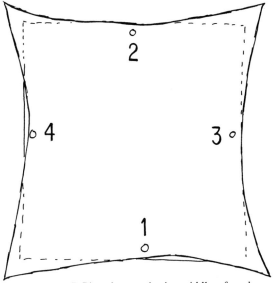

Fig. 15–17 Pintack once in the middle of each side.

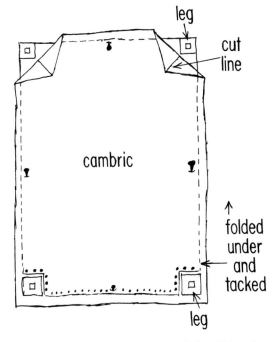

Fig. 15–18 Make 45° cuts at each leg fold and tack in place.

cut(s) under so the cambric is parallel with the edge of the leg. Also, turn the side you are working on under, then finish tacking. Do the same all the way around. You now have a neatly stretched, tacked-on cambric dust cloth.

Making Arm Covers

To save wear and tear on the arms of your chair or couch, you may want to make some arm covers. The welt and front edges of the arms are the first areas to show wear from constant use.

The following steps will help you make professional-looking arm covers.

Step 1: Measure and Rough-Cut Fabric

There are two fabric pieces that make up each arm cover: the shaped front piece and the rectangular top and side piece. The rectangular top and side piece on an overstuffed chair should be about 10″ deep and overhang 3″ or 4″ on each side of the arm. Use your judgment to determine how deep and low you want the arm covers to be—this might depend on how much material you have left. Of course, if you have an old arm cover, you can use it as a guide.

The front of the arm cover should be rough-cut first. Cut a rectangular piece of fabric, equal to the widest point on the front of the arm and the length of the overhanging rectangular piece (Fig. 15–19).

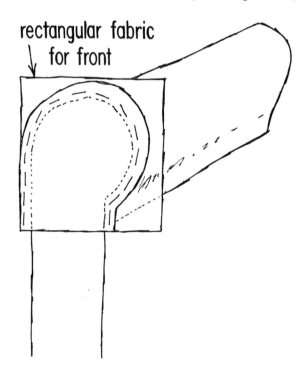

Fig. 15–19 Measure and rough-cut the fabric pieces for an arm cover.

An example would be arm covers for a wing chair: 11″ by 11″ for the top and side piece; 6″ by 6″ for the front. Cut two of each, one for each arm cover.

Step 2: Pin Fabric Pieces on One Arm

Shape the front of the arm cover on the chair. Pin the rough-cut front fabric piece along the outside edge of the arm. Make sure the fabric overhangs the edges at least 1/2″. Lay the top and side piece in place. Stick about four pins in so the front cover is attached to the chair, raising the front arm cover so that it is slightly lower than the top cover.

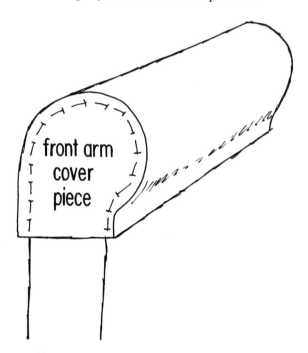

Fig. 15–20 Pin and true-cut the front arm cover piece.

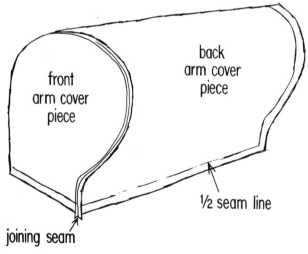

Fig. 15–21 Machine sew the front and back pieces of the arm cover together, face to face.

Notch the center of the two cover pieces and put your first pin in. Stick the pins in, following the edge of the arm. Alongside the first pin, put your second pin in, and follow down to the end of each arm cover piece. Do the same on the opposite sides of the center notches. The pins are your sewing line (Fig. 15–20).

Step 3: True-Cut the Fabric Pieces

On the front piece, take your scissors and cut ½" away from the pins. Trim the bottom. Take all the pins out. Now you have a pattern for the front piece of the opposite arm cover—only in reverse. So lay the shaped front piece on the opposite rough-cut front arm piece, face down, and cut.

Step 4: Machine Sew

Machine sew together the two pieces of each arm cover at the curve seams (Fig. 15–21). Turn the bottom of the arm cover under ½" and machine hem. If the upholstery fabric is thin and might unravel, then fold under ½" twice and sew.

Chapter 16

Upholstered Cushions

Many tailors and seamstresses have a difficult time sewing a perfect upholstery cushion. The most common mistake is sewing a cushion with the corners out of alignment. The trick is to get the corners of the cushion top parallel to the corners of the bottom (Fig. 16–1). Making a perfect cushion is not luck. Even the beginner, making a cushion for the first time, can do a perfect job if he learns a few tricks and carefully follows the slow step-by-step approach.

Before you start to make your cushion, take the time to read through the different steps, several times if necessary, and fully understand how a perfectly fitted cushion is made.

Terminology that we will be using in this chapter pertains to the three common shapes of cushions found in upholstered furniture and the parts of a cushion.

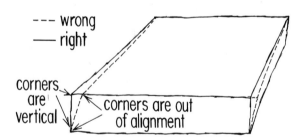

Fig. 16–1 A common problem in reupholstering is encountered when the corners of a cushion are out of alignment.

Cushion Shapes and Parts

There are three basic cushion shapes: the square, the full T and the half T (Fig. 16–2). The square and full-T cushions are found in both chairs and couches. The half-T cushions are located next to the arms of the couch. The half T is reversible and can

Fig. 16–2 The three basic cushion shapes.

be used next to the right or the left arm of the couch. The only difference between sewing a T cushion and a square cushion is that the zipper opening for the former must be extra large in order to stuff in the Ts of foam. The directions in this chapter are applicable to both square and T cushions.

There are three parts to a loose cushion: the top, the bottom and the boxing. The boxing is composed of the front boxing, back zipper boxing, left filler boxing and right filler boxing (Fig. 16–3).

Making a Cushion Cover

These are the seven basic steps to follow for making a perfectly fitted cushion.

Step 1: Measure and Cut the Top

There are a few tips to remember before you start to measure and cut the fabric. The lengthwise grain of the fabric runs from the front to the back of the cushion. Any pattern in your fabric must be in the center of the cushion and lined up with the IB, seat, and any boxings, borders or skirt. Stripes in your cushion should follow the same rule. The stripe that starts at the top of the chair should run continuously to the bottom.

There are two ways to arrive at the shape of the cushion top. The easiest way is to use the old chair cushion as a pattern. This method is especially good if the old cushion fits snugly in the chair. Take apart

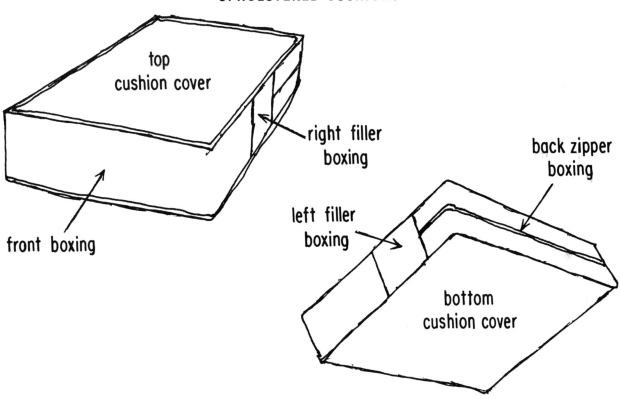

Fig. 16–3 The parts of a cushion.

the old cushion cover. You will only need to use the top of the old cover as a pattern. Throw the other pieces away. Fold the top of the old cover in half from front to back, putting right sides together. Smooth the fabric flat and staple the edges to insure an exact pattern. Fold the new fabric in half, with the middle of the center stripe or pattern (if there is one) on the center fold. Lay the folded old cover on top of the folded new fabric cover. Staple and cut the new fabric. Open up the new fabric, removing all the staples. You now have a fitted top for the cushion.

The second method for arriving at the shape of the cushion top should be used when the cushion does not fit properly or if the chair or couch does not have any cushions available. You are starting from scratch. You will be making a pattern for the exact shape of the cushion.

Rough-cut the top and bottom of the cushion. The rough-cut cushion, top and bottom, is two rectangular pieces of fabric the dimensions of the cushion at its widest points, length and width. Few cushions are perfect rectangles for one of several reasons: the back of the cushion may be smaller than the front; the IB always sticks out—bellies out—so wedges are sometimes needed in the back of the cushion (Fig. 16–4); the T deviates from a

perfect rectangle; some cushions have curvatures on the sides.

Now measure the width of the seat at the front. Mark the center with white chalk or straight pins

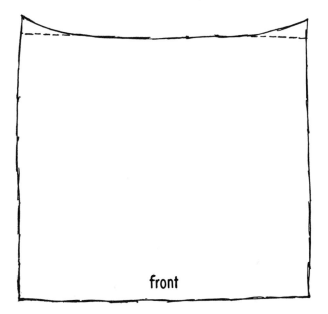

Fig. 16–4 Wedges are sometimes needed in the back of the cushion because the IB "bellies out," leaving a distinctive shape.

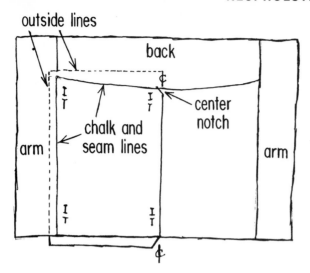

Fig. 16–5 Determining the shape of the cushion. The chalk lines are the sewing lines.

right on top of the front edge—roughly about an inch long. Measure the back, finding the center, chalking or pinning the bottom of the IB an inch long. Notch the center of the rough-cut cushion fabric at the front and back. Place the new rough-cut cushion top with the front notch on the front chalk line of the seat. Let the fabric overhang $1/2''$. Pin at the center notch. Line up the back notch with the back chalk line. Smooth the fabric from front to back and pin it into the deck at the back notch. Make sure that the threads of the fabric are straight. Stick several pins down the center line of the deck to keep the fabric straight (Fig. 16–5).

On *one* half of the cushion top only, smooth the fabric out in front and pin it so that the edge of the fabric is extended from the seat edge $1/2''$. Do the same for the back, smoothing the fabric out, pushing it under the IB and pinning it about 2″ from the end (Fig. 16–5). Smooth the side out and under the arm and pin about 1″ from the edge.

To establish the sewing line on the back of the cushion, take a 4″ pointed chalk, standing it up vertically and as far back as it can go (touching the IB). Mark the seat fabric, following the shape of the IB and IA. If the front has a straight edge, chalk an inch on the side and center. Take a straight edge, a ruler or yardstick, and connect the two lines to give the front sew line. To do this, put a ruler up against the front edge of the seat vertically and mark $1/2''$ in on the seat cover. If the front is curved, figure out where the front sewing line should be and chalk it.

Take the pins out and move the chalked pattern from the seat-decking section of the chair. Fold the fabric in half with the chalk side up. Pin the halves

together. Cut $1/2''$ outside that line. Do not cut on the chalk line. The chalk line is your sewing line.

Step 2: Cut the Cushion Bottom

Remembering to match stripes, center patterns and position the lengthwise grain of the fabric running from front to back, place the opened, true-cut top of the cushion face down on the rough-cut bottom of the cushion, which is face up. The top is a pattern for the bottom. Staple or pin the two pieces together and cut. With plastic, always remember to staple within $1/2''$ of the edges because plastic will show holes.

Step 3: Cut Wedges to Preserve the Rectangle

Wedges at the corner of a rectangular or T cushion compensate for the crown of 4″ on the sides and 5″ in the middle. If you stuffed a piece of foam into a rectangular boxed cushion cover, the cushion would have a tendency to look like the one in Figure 16–6. By cutting off wedges at the corners of the top and bottom of the cushion cover, you can resquare the cushion.

For the average 22″-square cushion, cut wedges as illustrated in Figure 16–6. At each corner of the top and bottom, measure and mark between $1/8''$ and $1/4''$. Measure and mark from 4″ to $4 1/2''$ down on the adjacent side. Draw a connecting line between the two points. Measure and mark all four corners of both the bottom and top. If the cushion is a T, mark only the square sides. Cut the wedges.

Now the top and bottom of the cushion are completed. Lay them aside. You will be making the third most important part of the cushion, the boxing.

Step 4: Measure and Cut the Boxing

The boxing gives the cushion its depth. Most foam rubber or polyurethane foam will be 4″ to 5″ crown: 4″ at the boxing and 5″ at the center to give a crown effect. The crown, with an extra inch in the middle, gives a more comfortable feel. The width of the boxing for all four sides will be $4 1/2''$ to allow for two $1/2''$ seams for the top and bottom. This makes the actual width of the boxing $3 1/2''$, $1/2''$ smaller than the 4″ foam sides. The foam will fit snugly in the cushion cover, giving a fitted, tailored look. If you have 4″ flat foam, then the boxing is exactly the same. For 3″ foam, cut the boxing $3 1/2''$. When sewn up, the boxing will be $2 1/2''$. You will always want a closed boxing $1/2''$ smaller than the sides. Below are directions for making the four parts of the boxing.

Front Boxing: The front boxing extends along the sides of the cushion. Cut a strip of upholstery

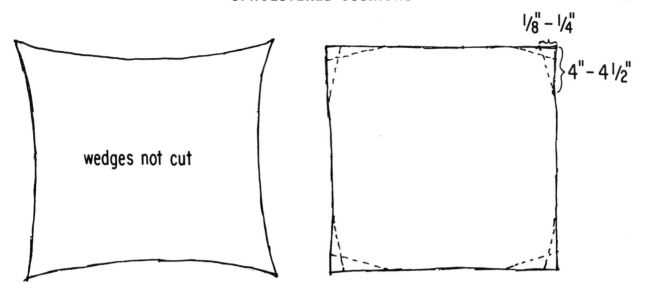

Fig. 16–6 Cut wedges to preserve the rectangular shape of the cushion.

fabric 54″ wide and 4½″ high. The front and sides of the cushion may sometimes be longer than 54″, but the front boxing is a good start. Mark the boxing face down (Front CU BX) so you know which edge is the top of the fabric. Fold the 54″ strip in half, notching the top and bottom centers.

Now place the front boxing on the top cushion cover with right sides together and center notches corresponding. Make ¼″ cuts on the boxing ½″ from the end of the front of the cushion cover (Fig. 16–7a). These marks act as a ruler and also allow you to turn the corner when you sew the boxing and cushion top together.

On one side of the boxing, turn the corner, using up the rest of the 54″-long boxing. Mark the top

cushion cover ½″ from the end of the boxing. Do the same for the opposite side (Fig. 16–7b). These markings are important to help you figure out how much filler boxing is needed, if the front and sides of the cushion require more than 54″.

Back Zipper Boxing: The back zipper boxing is made from two strips of fabric with the zipper sewn in the middle. Cut two 3″-wide strips of fabric the length of the opening for the zipper. For a square or rectangular cushion, the zipper opening will be the length of the back of the cushion. For a T cushion, the zipper opening will be the length of the back of the cushion plus 4″ on each side, e.g., $4″ + 22″ + 4″ = 30″$.

Turn under ¾″ on one side of one 3″ strip. Place

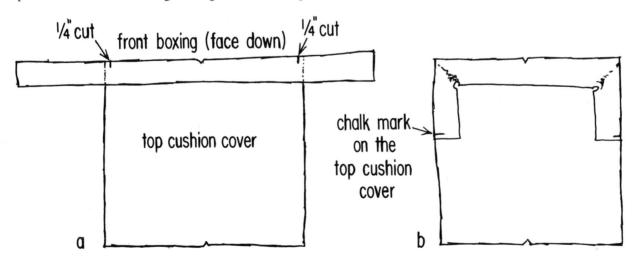

Fig. 16–7 Front boxing. *a.* Mark the front cushion boxing with ¼″ cuts. *b.* Mark the top cushion cover with chalk.

the fold in the center of the zipper. Pin or baste in place and sew. Take the other 3″ strip. Turn one side ³/₄″ in, placing the fold right up against the other goods, i.e., the center of the zipper, then sew (Fig. 16–8a). Notice that the zipper boxing is now 4¹/₂″ wide, the same as the front boxing. Always use a heavy upholstery zipper, as described in Chapter 3. A dress zipper is not strong enough.

Notch the center of the zipper boxing. Place the center notch of the zipper boxing on the notch of the cushion top. Make your ¹/₄″ cuts at each end of the zipper boxing, ¹/₂″ from the corners of the cushion

top in order for the boxing to turn the corners (Fig. 16–8b). Mark the cushion top ¹/₂″ in from each end of the zipper boxing.

Now your cushion top has four marks. Each boxing has two ¹/₄″ slits (Fig. 16–9). You are ready to make the filler boxings.

Left and Right Filler Boxings: A filler boxing is a strip of fabric that goes between the front boxing and the back zipper boxing. A filler boxing on each side will close up the boxing to form a complete circle. Not every cushion needs filler boxings. The front and side 54″-strip boxing may be sufficient.

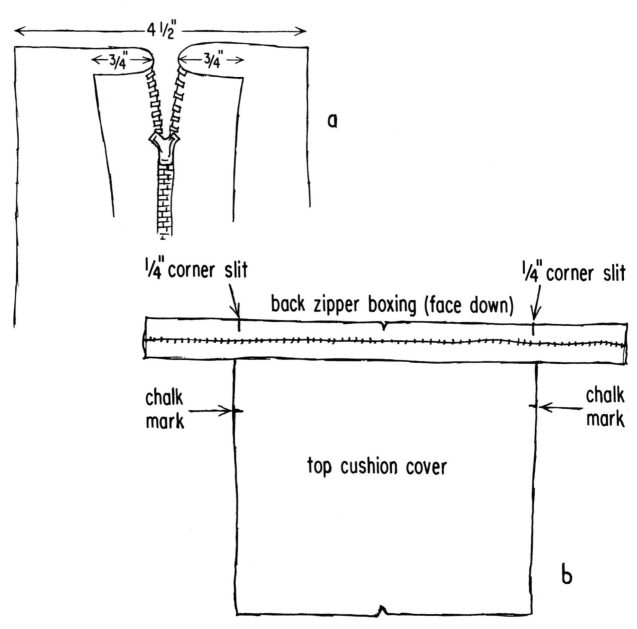

Fig. 16–8 Zipper boxing. *a.* Sew the zipper to the back zipper boxing. *b.* Make ¹/₄″ slits on the back zipper boxing and chalk mark the top cushion cover.

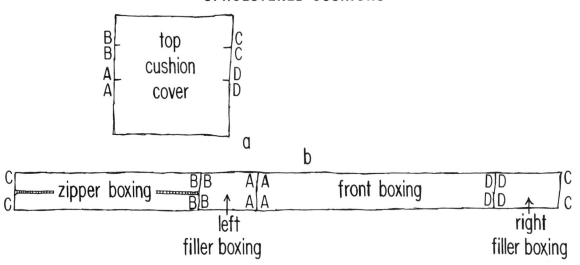

Fig. 16–9 Boxing assembly. *a.* The four marks on the top cushion cover give you the measurements for the filler boxings. *b.* Sew the four parts of the boxing together. Join C to C to form a circle.

But in many cases fillers are needed. So measure between marks A and B, then C and D, in Figure 16–9*a*, to get the length of the filler boxings. For the example shown, cut two filler boxings $1/2'' + 5'' + 1/2'' = 6''$ long, by $4^1/2''$ wide.

You should already have made up enough welt for the top and bottom edges of the cushion.

Step 5: Assemble the Boxings

With $1/2''$ seams, face to face, sew the four parts of the boxing together so you have a closed circle: front boxing, right filler boxing, back zipper boxing, left filler boxing. Label A, B, C, D on the cushion top and boxings (Fig. 16–9*b*).

Leave the zipper open about $3''$ so you can turn the completely sewn cushion face out. Start at B–B in Figure 16–9. Put the B seam of the boxing on the B mark of the cushion, face to face. Slip the welt in the middle. The edges of the welt, boxing and cushion top should be even. Make sure the welt is $2''$ below the starting point. Sew up to the corner, with the $1/4''$ slit on the boxing at the corner. Make your cut and a 90° turn. Sew to the next corner, making sure the next $1/4''$ cut is $1/2''$ from the corner. To do this, pin the $1/4''$ cut in place, holding the three layers of fabric in place while you are sewing. Turn the corner to match marks C–C and D–D and the $1/4''$ corner cuts. Continue sewing, matching the last corner and $1/4''$ slit and A–A. Stop sewing $2''$ from the starting point. Join the welt. Now the boxing is attached to the top side of the cushion.

There are no markings on the bottom cushion cover or on the bottom of the boxing. Fold each corner of the bottom of the boxing, and make $1/4''$ cuts. The slits will correspond to the corners of the

bottom cushion cover. Sew the bottom cushion cover to the boxing, matching the corners and the $1/4''$ slits.

The T Cushion

The T cushion is measured, marked and cut the same way as the rectangular or square cushion. You have to allow extra filler boxing fabric to go around the additional corners of the T. The markings on the T top cover will be the same as the rectangular cover. The boxing will have six outside $1/4''$ slits at

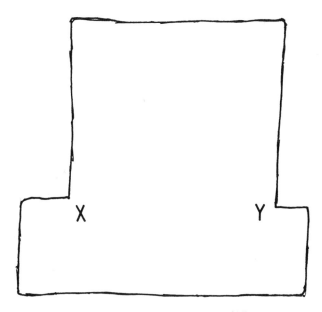

Fig. 16–10 It is not necessary to make $1/4''$ corner slits at the inside corners, *x* and *y*, of the T cushion because the corner does not tend to stretch out.

the corners, instead of four. It is not necessary to make $^1/_4''$ corner slits on the inside cuts, *x* and *y* in Figure 16–10, because the fabric does not have a tendency to stretch. When sewing, match the marks and corners on the cover with the marks and $^1/_4''$ slits on the boxing.

Stuffing a Cushion

Here are some tips that will help you when it comes to stuffing the cushion. Keep the foam compressed when you put it in the cushion case, so as not to put too much pressure on the seams. If the cushion is longer from front to back, make sure it goes into the casing that way. When stuffing the foam in the casing, try to get the selvages (seams) on the boxing side, not on the top or bottom. When you close the zipper, you can work the seam onto the boxing side wherever it is needed. Your goal is to work the corners of the foam into the corners of the cushion cover, with the seams on the sides.

Stuffing foam into a vinyl plastic cushion cover is more difficult than into a cloth cushion cover. Spray the sides and edges of the foam with a silicone spray so that it will almost glide in. Also, purchase four metal air vents from your local upholsterer so that trapped air inside the cushion can escape. In cloth cushion covers, there are hundreds of air holes in the weave of the fabric. In plastic there are none. If trapped air is not allowed to escape through metal vents, then the pressure will eventually split a seam open.

To give full, even corners, we recommend adding a small amount (about a half to a full handful) of cotton or Dacron stuffing to each corner of the cushion. Place the stuffing in the corners of the casing before you put the foam in. This step is not necessary but can be helpful, especially if you are having trouble making good-looking corners.

Sometimes, old foam that is still good needs a lift. For a fresher, fuller feel, wrap a layer of Dacron around the old foam and sew the ends and sides together with nylon upholstery or carpet thread, using a running stitch.

Ninety-nine percent of new cushion stuffing is foam. If you have a casing of down or other feathers, wrap and sew closed in a layer of Dacron, once they are revived (*see* Ch. 3).

Part Three

Reupholstery Projects

Chapter 17

Dining Room and Kitchen Chairs

In Parts One and Two, you have learned how to reupholster according to the slow step-by-step method. You know what supplies are necessary, how to select appropriate fabric for the job at hand, and how each section of a chair is strengthened, refinished and upholstered. Part Three is the action section, where everything you've read will be integrated into practical projects.

A dining room or kitchen chair is probably the first project you'll want to try. Both get plenty of hard use: fabric-covered dining room chairs are easily soiled and hard to clean; plastic-covered kitchen chairs tend to rip on top and along the seams. Or, you may wish to change your decorating scheme.

The Parts

The Seat

There are basically two kinds of seats on dining room and kitchen chairs: the plain pullover seat and the boxed seat (Fig. 17–1). The plain pullover seat requires no sewing. The fabric or vinyl plastic is tacked around all four sides. No pleats are necessary. They stretch out, with any extra bulk hidden right underneath the seat.

The boxed seat looks like a cushion. It has three parts: the top cover, which is the shape of the wood foundation; the side boxing; the welt, which joins the top and the boxing.

The seat usually has a plywood or compressed chipboard base that is screwed into the seat frame. Some older dining room chairs have a webbing-burlap base. Some even have springs, either No-Sag or coil.

The Back

The back of a kitchen or dining room chair is also relatively simple. A wooden frame and cardboard base hold the stuffing. The stuffing looks like cotton at first glance. Actually, it is a paper felt.

There are two ways to reupholster the back.

1. Reupholster as if you were going to do a regular pullover back. The rectangular piece of fabric or vinyl for the IB is pulled and tacked on all four sides. The welt is tacked on top. The OB is blind tacked on top. The ends of the sides are turned under, left and right. The OB is pulled down and tacked on the bottom.

2. The most common back today is an envelope-type back. The IB is shaped to the inside of the back frame. The OB is shaped to the outside of the back frame. The two pieces are joined together with welt between. After the envelop is made, it is slid right over the frame and stuffing, then tacked on the bottom.

Recovering a Chair with Vinyl Plastic

Our project is a kitchen chair covered with vinyl plastic. It has a boxed seat and envelope-type back (Fig. 17–1b). The most important tip to remember is never to railroad plastic. This means never to cut the width of the reupholstery cover piece the length of the fabric. Plastic stretches from left to right, i.e., along the 54″ width of the fabric. Modern vinyl plastic is soft and stretches easily. This is very important when it is time to put the stretched envelope back in place.

Step 1: Examine the Chair

When we examine this chair, we find that there are no broken metal legs or frame parts. If your metal chair is broken where the back and legs are welded together, please do not throw it away. Any local place that does welding will fix it for you—check your Yellow Pages. We notice that the ply-

119

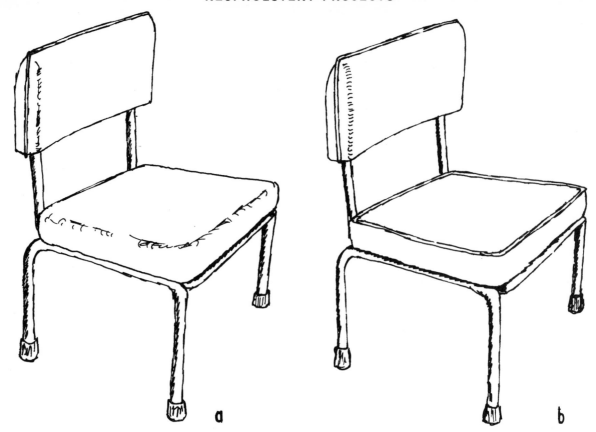

Fig. 17–1 Seat styles. *a*. Plain pullover seat can be found on a kitchen or dining room chair. *b*. Boxed seat with a knife-edge back, the second kind of kitchen or dining room chair style, is the one reupholstered in this chapter.

wood base is split in half, the vinyl is torn at the boxing and the seams.

Step 2: Measurement Chart and Cutting Diagram

First, take all measurements, as shown in Figure 17–2*a*. Use these to make a chart similar to this one, for a set of four kitchen chairs:

	V	H	Welt
(4) seat	18″	18″	
(4) IB	12″	18″	36″
(4) OB	12″	20″	
(4) BX	3″	54″	54″

Once you have accounted for all the fabric required, make a cutting diagram, as shown in Figure 17-2*b*.

Step 3: Take the Chair Apart

Turn the chair upside-down. Remove all screws on the bottom. The legs and back of the chair will come off. If there is a piece of cardboard on the bottom of the seat (similar to cambric), remove it carefully. You may want to reuse it.

Remove the tacks or staples from the disengaged seat cover and the bottom of the back. Slip the back cover off.

Step 4: Sterilize the Stuffing

The stuffing should be sterilized, especially if the old cover had holes in it. Food gets inside and bacteria grow.

Step 5: Repair the Plywood Base

In this project, the plywood base was broken in half. Take a new piece of $^3/_4$″ plywood. Fit the two old pieces together on top of the new, marking all the holes, too. Take out all the T nuts—the metal threads on the inside of the plywood to receive metal bolts (Fig. 17–3). Do this by screwing the bolt into the nut so that the bottom of the bolt is flush with the bottom of the nut. Hit the bolt on the head with a hammer, using medium strength. The nut will come out. Repeat this process until all the nuts are out.

With a saber, band or jig saw, cut out the new piece of plywood. Drill new holes for the T nuts the same size as the old ones. Drive the T nuts in the holes. T nuts have teeth that grip into the wood. File or sand the edges to take off sharp corners.

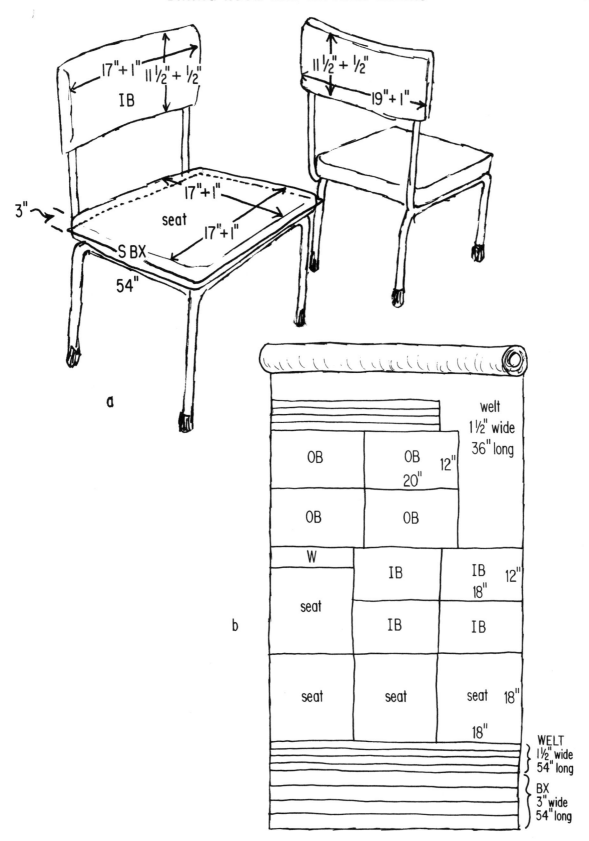

Fig. 17–2 Measurements and layout. *a*. Front and back views supply measurements of the whole kitchen chair. *b*. Cutting diagram provides a fabric layout for four kitchen chairs.

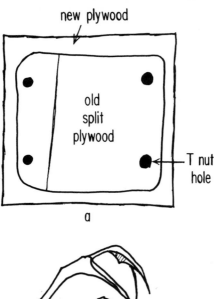

new plywood

old split plywood

T nut hole

a

b

Fig. 17–3 Repairing a plywood base. *a.* Use the old split plywood board as a pattern for the new one. *b.* Enlarged picture of a T nut found in the bottom of a kitchen chair. With prongs protruding underneath and metal threads inside, they come in $^1/_4''$, $^5/_{16}''$ and $^3/_8''$ sizes. The bolt through the metal base of the kitchen chair is screwed into the T nut in the seat.

Step 6: Make a Pattern for the Seat

There are two ways to make the pattern for the seat.

1. Take the old cover and carefully remove the welt and boxing. Press the top with a steam iron, pressing the seams open. Use the old cover as a pattern.

2. Place the wood base on top of the vinyl. Mark the vinyl, following the edge of the wood. Cut $^1/_2''$ outside that line, which will be the sewing line. In this project, we used the wood base as a pattern.

Now center notch the back of the new seat cover. The boxing is a rectangular piece, $3^1/_2''$ wide by $56''$ around. You might foresee a problem since the circumference of the vinyl, according to the cutting diagram, is $54''$, $2''$ short of $56''$. While sewing, the vinyl stretches. You'd be surprised how much extra vinyl we had. We found that the $54''$ strip stretched

to $57''$. We cut off an inch. (We do not recommend that you use vinyl plastic on any chair more complicated than a kitchen chair for the very reason that it stretches so easily.)

Most kitchen and dining room chair seats have a $54''$ perimeter. But if your chair is considerably more than $54''$, then measure the extra piece needed, adding two $^1/_2''$ seam allowances. Center the small piece in the back of the chair. Center notch the small piece. Attach the small piece to the starting side of the $54''$ boxing. Any trimming will be done to the $54''$ piece.

The welt will be the same size as the boxing.

Step 7: Finishing the Seat

Place the foam rubber or polyurethane foam on top of the plywood base. Add a half to a full layer of cotton felt on top. This is recommended, but not necessary. Matching the notches, machine sew the top, welt and boxing together.

Turn the cover inside-out. Lay the cover right on top of the polyfoam, making sure that the cover is not twisted. The shape of the cover should match the shape of the frame (Fig. 17–4).

At one front corner of the chair seat, pull the boxing around to the bottom. Pintack in place at the bottom of the boxing. At the opposite front corner, making sure you do not move the fabric out of position, do the same thing (Fig. 17–5). Make sure the bulky seams lie on the boxing side, not on top of the seat.

Pull over the boxing in the back of the seat and pintack the back corners just as you did the front. Go to the center of the seat in the back. Pull down the boxing until the sew line to the bottom is $1^1/_2''$, in this project. You can get your measurement from the height of the old seat cover before it is removed or you can study the removed seat cover to see where the old crease line is located. Every inch to the left and right of the center, pintack underneath the chair, pulling the vinyl down just as you did at the starting center point (Fig. 17–6). The back will overlap about $1''$. Do not fold plastic. Leave the ends of the overlap raw.

Check to make sure that the height is the same all the way around from the seam to the bottom of the seat, in this case $1^1/_2''$. If it is not, adjust and re-pintack, check, then drive in all the tacks.

If you want to, you can staple or tack the cardboard back on the bottom of the chair. It is not necessary.

Step 8: Make a Pattern for the Back

Cut the stitches of the old back cover and take out the welt. With a steam iron, press the IB and OB. Fold the IB in half. Center notch on top. Do the

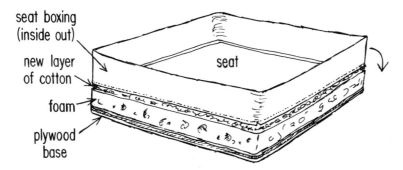

Fig. 17–4 Carefully position the seat and seat boxing on top of the new cotton, foam and plywood base.

Fig. 17–5 Pintack the two front corners to the plywood base to square the fabric on the wood.

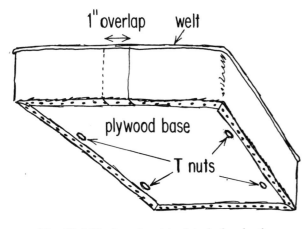

Fig. 17–6 The boxed seat is pintacked under the plywood base on all four sides.

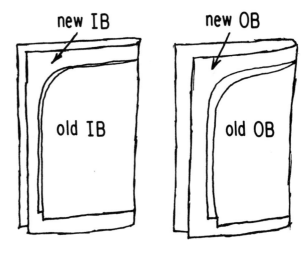

Fig. 17–7 Make the new IBs and OBs, using old ones as patterns.

same to the old OB cover. Lay the old OB and IB covers on top of the new rough-cut IB and OB covers (Fig. 17–7). Staple in place and cut, making sure you center notch the new covers.

Measure the welt. In this project, the welt is 52″ long. Fold the welt in half and center notch. Take the new OB, welt and IB, lining up and matching the center notches. Now you are ready to sew.

Step 9: Sew the Back

At the sewing machine, insert your needle at the center notch. Start sewing one side until you reach the bottom of the back. Start at the center again and finish sewing the rest of the back.

Step 10: Put on the Back Cover

To make it easier to slide the cover on the back, spray the inside of the cover very lightly with silicon. You can purchase a silicon spray in a hardware or paint store.

Turn the back cover face out. Gently pull the cover over the chair's back frame. Pull hard on the welt on one side of the back cover, then pintack on the bottom. Pull hard on the welt on the other side. Pintack on the bottom.

If you are reupholstering a whole set of kitchen or dining room chairs, you will probably want to do all the cutting and sewing at the same time to save steps. However, you may want to reupholster the first chair from start to finish to minimize any mistakes. Your newly reupholstered kitchen or dining room furniture should withstand many, many years of crumbs, spills and wear.

Metal Office Chairs

The seat of a metal office chair is measured, cut and sewn the same way as the dining room or kitchen chair. It usually has a boxed seat. The back is upholstered similarly to the seat.

All the pieces unscrew and come apart. There is no tacking or stapling involved. The only tools needed are a screwdriver and hammer. There are metal-pronged teeth that bite into the plastic, holding it in place (Fig. 17–8).

Remember that your chair "talks" to you. Study

Fig. 17–9 A highchair is reupholstered in a similar manner to a kitchen or dining room chair.

it carefully and you'll find this is one of the easiest chairs to reupholster.

Highchairs

Most highchairs are covered with cheap plastic. The plastic was melted and compressed at the seams, instead of being sewn tightly. You reupholster it exactly the same way as the kitchen chair (Fig. 17–9). The seat and back unscrew and are easily removed from the frame. If you decide to reupholster your baby's highchair with the tough, high-quality vinyl plastic available now, it will last many more years and babies.

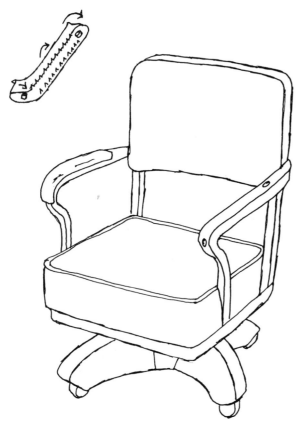

Fig. 17–8 The typical metal office chair has four removable vinyl pieces: seat, back and two arms. Toothlike prongs hold the vinyl on the frame.

Chapter 18

Overstuffed Chairs

Introduction

Every home has an overstuffed chair or couch. It is the most used, indispensable and loved piece of furniture. Your family may be hesitant to part with an old friend, a comfortable, relaxing overstuffed chair. Your project may be to reupholster your sturdy, favorite, but threadbare couch or chair. Maybe you have added a family room for your energy-charged kids to occupy and you are ready to fix up the living room with a semiformal decor to add a touch of elegance to your life.

An overstuffed chair is a comfortable, relaxing chair that has springs on the seat and sometimes in the inside back, a cushion on the seat and occasionally on the inside back. The top edge of the cushion is 16″ to 18″ off the floor, making it harder to get out of—if you really want to—than the dining room chair. It is a very inviting chair to relax in after a long, hectic day. It comes in many shapes, styles and sizes.

Our Project and Your Overstuffed Chair

In this important chapter, there will be a description of the slow step-by-step method of reupholstering in great detail. All the tips and tricks of doing a professional-looking job will be integrated in this discussion. We will not just tell you how to tie springs, tack on fabric and leave you to devising your own plans from scratch. We want to let you see how a chair similar to yours is reupholstered from start to finish. We want to introduce the first, second, third and last sections of our project so that you can plan your procedures.

You will want to consult the many how-to steps in Parts One and Two. We advise you to study Chapter 15, carefully. If the back, arms or seat vary from our example, then you can determine your own comprehensive steps from this chapter.

This project chapter is concerned with an overstuffed chair. If your project is a couch, remember that it is just an expanded chair with a double or triple-width seat, inside and outside back and two or more cushions. Also, the projects dealing with the wing chair, colonial chair, convertible hide-a-bed, channel-back chair, tufted chair and recliner are basically overstuffed chair projects. Study this chapter carefully and you will be greatly rewarded when you tackle any other projects.

Remember that every chair is different. Examine it closely to see how it was put together, what new supplies it needs, where it needs repair, where the individual fabric pieces were tacked, and other pertinent information. Take frequent notes whenever you feel the need, especially if you plan to stretch the work on your project over several weekends.

Never strip the whole chair in one operation unless the frame needs extensive repair. It is much better to do one section at a time. Your memory is fresh and your notes are clear. Reupholstering a deceptively "difficult" piece of furniture becomes easier and more fun. An amazingly professional-looking chair or couch will be your greatest reward.

Reupholstering an Overstuffed Chair
The Preliminaries
Step 1: Sterilize the Chair
Sterilize the chair with an upholsterer's sterilizing solution to kill bacteria growth and unpleasant odors. Spray the outside of the whole chair until it feels wet to your touch.

Step 2: Examine the Chair

The next step in any project is to examine it very closely. The frame on most overstuffed chairs, fortunately, remains rigid over the years. But some chair frames are poorly assembled from the start. A chair can also get plenty of abuse from day to day. Sometimes when a person is ready to relax, he drops heavily into a chair. This may be a healthy response after a hard day's work, but it's bad for the chair. Sitting down hard on a chair pushes the back backward. Getting in and out of a chair will push the arms in and out.

To test whether the chair frame is loose, face the chair and push the arms in and out, then the back of the chair forward and backward. The dowels holding the different pieces of the frame together could be broken or loose. Also test for looseness on the diagonal, pushing the back corner of the chair away and the opposite front corner toward you.

Look underneath for sagging webbing and loose or broken springs. By examining a chair, you are sizing up just how big and what kind of job lies ahead.

Our overstuffed chair frame is as rigid as it could be. (The frame in the next project chapter, the overstuffed wing chair, is exactly the opposite.) There are no sagging webbing strips or loose springs. The chair is at least twenty years old, so we realize that the springs should be completely retied.

Step 3: Measurement Chart and Cutting Diagram

Measure the chair, remembering to add ½″ on each end for machine-sewn edges and 1″ on each end for tacked-on edges. For example, if the deck is 25½″ (V) by 30″ (H), sewed in the front and tacked

on the back and two sides, the measurements will be 27″ (V) by 32″ (H).

You may want to review Chapter 7 to get accurate dimensions. Make a similar measurement chart and cutting diagram for your chair (Fig. 18–1). They are your guides for the next step. The cutting diagram also tells you exactly how much fabric you will need to purchase.

Step 4: Chalk and Cut the Fabric

All pieces that will be rectangular in shape do not require old cover pieces for patterns. The irregular-shaped front arm boxings and the IB do. These pieces should be rough-cut now, then true-cut later in the reupholstering process. Label the backs of all fabric pieces.

Step 5: Take the Chair Apart

Turn the chair upside-down. Take the tacks out all the way around. Remove the cambric and the bottom of the upholstery covers, i.e., the seat, arms and back. Cut the stitches on the sides of the OB. If there are no stitches, then the OB sides are held together with a metal or cardboard tacking strip. Pry off the metal tacking strips and throw them away. (You will be hand sewing the new OB sides on for a neater, easier job.) Loosen the tacks and any sewing stitches on both OAs.

Now all the tacks and stitches are removed from the OAs and OB, so that each piece can be flipped over the arm or back. Take the ripping chisel and finish removing the OAs and OB, old cardboard tacking strips and all. Label the old covers and put them aside for future reference.

Now that all the outside pieces are off, i.e., the OB and both OAs, you are ready to tackle one section of the chair at a time; first, the seat; second, the

		V	H	Welt
	Seat	14″	30″	
	S BD	4″	27″	27″
	Deck	27″	32″	
	IB	27″	27″	90″
	B BX	4″	54″	
	B BD	3″	54″	54″
	OB	27″	27″	90″
(L,R)	IA	27″	29″	80″
(L,R)	OA	15″	29″	
(L,R)	A BX	18″	5″	
(2)	CU	23″	23″	200″
	CU BX	4½″	54″ + ⎰ 4½″ ⎱ 4½″	
	(4 pcs)			
	Skirt	8¼″	54″	120″
	(4 pcs)			

661″ (36″ square
bias welt)

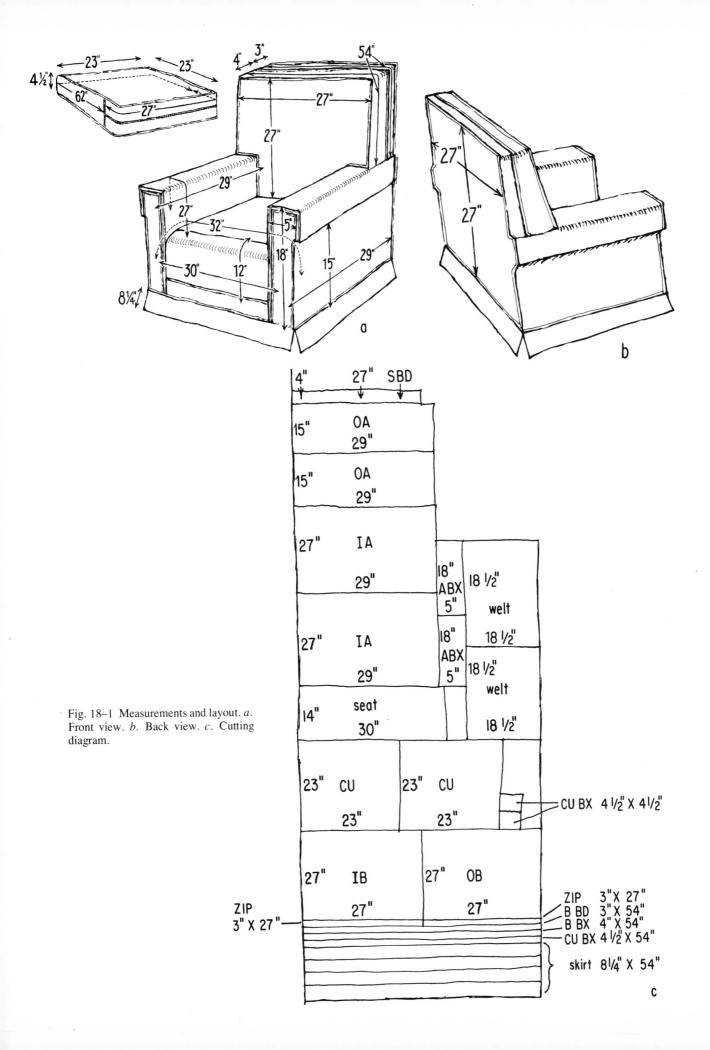

Fig. 18–1 Measurements and layout. *a.* Front view. *b.* Back view. *c.* Cutting diagram.

first IA; third, the other IA; fourth, the IB; then you can close up the chair by tacking on all the outside pieces.

The Seat

Step 6: Expose the Seat

With the chair still upside-down, remove the tacks holding the bottom of the IAs and IB, as well as the seat-decking combination. Then turn the chair right-side-up. Take the bottom of each IA and pintack it to the IA rail at the seat level. Do the same on the IB. This method is used when the IB and IAs do not need any frame repair (Fig. 18–2).

The purpose of this procedure is to expose the seat edges without disturbing the stuffing of the IAs and IB while you work on the seat. When a chair is upholstered, the bottom of the IAs and IB are almost always tacked on top of the seat or decking edges. Remember, you are going to reupholster this chair the easy way, one section at a time. The first section to be reupholstered is always the seat.

Now, all the edges of the seat-decking combination are exposed and all old tacks removed.

Step 7: Take off the Seat-Decking Assembly

Lift the decking fabric forward, so that the $1/2''$ seam that holds the seat and decking together is exposed. Cut the hand stitches that hold the seat-deck-

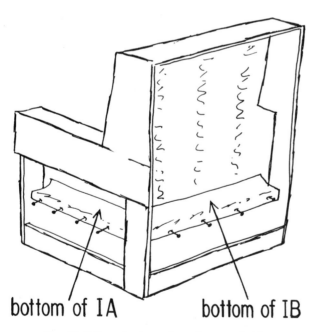

bottom of IA   **bottom of IB**

Fig. 18–2 In order to work on the seat decking without disturbing the back or arms, pintack the bottom of the IAs on the IA rails at seat level and the bottom of the IB on the IB rail at seat level. The IAs and IB were originally tacked on the sides and back of the decking.

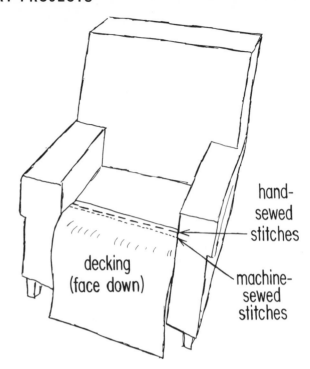

hand-sewed stitches

decking (face down)

machine-sewed stitches

Fig. 18–3 To remove the seat-decking assembly, cut the hand stitches that hold it to the burlap and springs.

ing seam to the burlap and springs (Fig. 18–3). The seat-decking assembly can now be removed from the body of the chair.

Step 8: Remove Stuffing, Burlap and Edging

Take off the front seat stuffing (remember that the seat is in the front of the chair, the decking is the surface the cushion rests on.) Gently lay the stuffing aside and remove the stuffing underneath the deck, then lay it aside.

Now the light 10-oz. burlap and fox edging is exposed. The fox edging in our chair is made of paper and clipped to the chair with hog rings. Remove the fox edging by cutting the hog rings or twisting them off with a pair of pliers. Buy a new burlap-covered fox edging strip the length of the old. Set it aside. Then go all the way around, taking the tacks off the burlap. Remove the burlap. Now you can see the springs.

The coil springs will come either wired together in a unit or they will come individually tied with spring twine. In the second case, leave all the spring twine intact if it is not broken. New spring twine will be tied on top in step 10 to give added strength.

Step 9: Repair Webbing or Heavy Burlap

Turn the chair upside-down. Retighten any old webbing or put on new webbing or 17-oz. burlap.

In our project, the 17-oz. burlap just needed to be restretched and retacked.

Nail on steel webbing, from front to back over every row of coil springs, for added strength (not necessary, but recommended).

Step 10: Retie the Seat Springs

Turn the chair right-side-up. In our overstuffed chair, there are metal fasteners that hold the springs in their proper position to the 17-oz. burlap. If these fasteners should break or if new 17-oz. burlap or webbing is needed, the springs should be sewn in place to the webbing or burlap.

This particular chair has an edge wire so that the front coils, when anchored to the edge wire, keep the seat a square shape. If the clips holding the springs to the edge wire are loose, they should be reclamped with sturdy pliers.

Retie the springs, leaving in the old spring twine. If the old twine is rotten, remove one row from front to back so you have the other two rows to copy. Cut all the rotten twine and retie the rest of the coils. Make sure that the front coils are even with the edge of the frame, not pulled inward too far.

Step 11: Add Burlap and Fox Edging

Measure, cut and tack on the 10-oz. burlap, pleating the corners neatly so the springs are not exposed. This is the foundation for the stuffing.

Now it is time to hand sew the fox edging to the edge wire. If all goes well and the edge wire is even with the edge of the seat rail, the front of the fox edging should be sewed on $1/4''$ ahead of the edge wire, i.e., the fox edging extends $1/4''$ over the edge wire. Hand sew the fox edging to the burlap and springs as explained in Chapter 11.

Step 12: Cut the Seat and Deck

If you are working on this project over several days, make sketches to help you get the feel of how a seat-decking combination is constructed. Take out all the seams and study the cuts and sewing lines. But it is not necessary to use the old seat and decking as a pattern. It will not be tailor fitted.

Take your rough-cut rectangular seat upholstery piece. Measure your edge wire from left to right, for example, 22''. Add $1/2''$ on each side for seam allowance (23''). Take the seat fabric (14'' by 30''), fold it in half and center notch top and bottom. Each half measures 14'' by 15''. Measure about $3^{1}/_{2}''$ from each corner (between 3'' and 4'' for most chairs).

Cut out a $3^{1}/_{2}''$ by $3^{1}/_{2}''$ square from the outside corners of each layer of fabric. Cut one layer at a time in order to cut perfectly matched halves. Open the seat fabric up. Fold the two $3^{1}/_{2}''$ cuts face to face so that the corner of the square forms a diago-

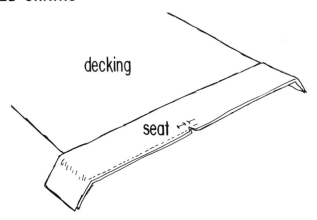

Fig. 18–4 Starting at the center and sewing one half of the seat-decking assembly at a time insures proper centering.

nal to the bottom of the seat. Do the same on the opposite side.

Step 13: Sew Decking and Seat Fabric

The decking has already been cut. Fold the decking in half and center notch the front and back. Put the top of the seat and decking face to face and pin the center notches together. Go to the sewing machine. Start the needle $1/2''$ from the edge and right at the notch. Continue sewing this half of the seat until both fabric pieces are sewed together. Cut the thread. Sew the other half, starting at the center notch. This method of sewing is the easiest way to insure that the seat and decking fabric pieces are sewed center to center without a lot of unnecessary pinning (Fig. 18–4).

Step 14: Sew Seat-Decking Seam to Burlap

Mark the center of the burlap between the front of the arms at the top of the seat (see Fig. 18–3). Take the seat-decking and fold the decking back so the $1/2''$ seam is exposed. Lay the seat on top of the burlaped fox edging, so the side seams are even with the edge wire. If this is done right, the notch will fold right on the center line.

Making sure that the seat is even with the front of the fox edging, take upholsterer's skewers or safety pins and put three to five into the fabric and the burlap. Be sure that the burlap is stretched out, left to right, with no wrinkles.

Take your curved needle; the thread should be one and a half times as long as the width of the seat. At the starting end, you should catch the edge wire, burlap, seat and decking. Pull the thread through and make an upholsterer's slip knot. Give it a good pull and tighten it up. Use the overthrow stitch or hem stitch, making sure you bite the coil spring when you go past it. Sew to the end. Finish off with a three-turn slip knot.

Put the decking back in the finished position. Re-examine the seat, making sure that it fits properly on the edge wire. Now is the time to adjust the seat if it does not fit properly.

Step 15: Stuff and Pintack the Seat

If the seat fits right, lift it up and replace the stuffing just as you found it. Add a new half to full layer of cotton felt on top to give it new life. Put the seat down. The first pintack should be positioned so that the center notch of the seat is on top of the center mark of the frame. Pintack across, to left and right of the center tack.

Step 16: Finish the Seat-Decking Assembly

At the corner of the seat rail, chalk a dot where the arm and the top of the seat rail meet. At this location there is a tacking board, usually $7/8''$ wide, that prevents the fabric from being pulled through. On the seat cover, make a 45° cut about $7/8''$ in, toward the dot on the frame. Do the other side the same way (Fig. 18–5).

Pull the seat cover down the through the seat rail. Finish tacking the ends of the front.

Pull the decking over the seat so the burlap is exposed. Take the deck stuffing and lay it in place, making sure the stuffing is level and it goes over the edge wire on the sides of the deck. Lay on an extra half to full layer of new cotton stuffing.

Take the decking and flip it back, making sure all the stuffing is pushed right up against the seam so you do not feel the edge wire. Push the decking under the IB and under the arms.

Make a mark at the center back of the frame. The center notch on the back of the decking should meet this center mark. Pull the slack out of the decking, back and sides. Pintack at $1''$ intervals. If you pintack any further apart, you'll see the tack pulls. Inspect your work. If needed, make small cuts in the rear corners so the decking fabric stretches out. When you are satisfied with your work, drive the tacks home.

Inside Arms

Step 17: Putting on the IA

Reupholster one IA at a time so that you always have one arm to study as a guide. Take all the tacks out of the old IA cover. Gently remove the IA, being careful not to disturb the stuffing. Notch the center of the top of the IA. You will notch the three layers of fabric: the IA, the welt and the arm boxing. Cut out the stitches in the IA and arm boxing, separating them. Now you can use the old IA cover and the old arm boxing cover as patterns. Notch the top, bottom and two sides for easy fitting later (Fig. 18–6). Press them both first with a wet rag and iron or a steam iron.

Place the two new rough-cut covers face to face. Lay one of the old IA covers on top of the new IA covers. Staple or pin together. Cut, shaping the new IA covers, making sure you transfer all the notches. At this time you should also make the cuts at the back end of the IA covers. The IA covers have to be slit in order to be pulled around the bottom back rail

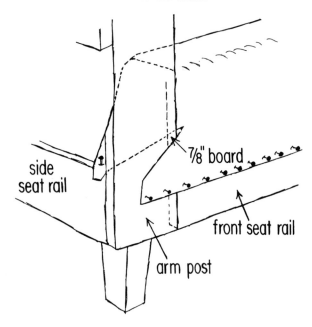

Fig. 18–5 Make a 45° cut where the seat meets the arm post so the seat fabric can be pulled through.

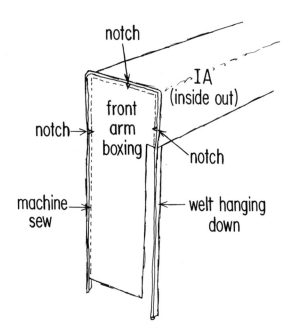

Fig. 18–6 Sew the IA to the front arm boxing, matching the notches.

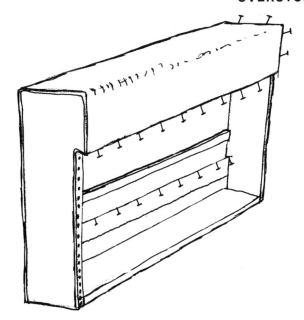

Fig. 18–7 Pintack the IA and check for pulls before driving tacks in.

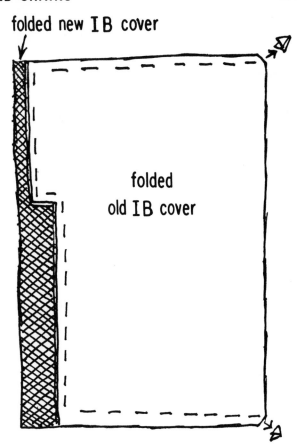

Fig. 18–8 Shape the new IB cover from the old IB cover.

of the chair. Make the new slits about an inch shorter than the cuts. It is better to undercut than overcut.

Make the two new arm boxings the same way, cutting all the notches.

Step 18: Sew the IA to the Arm Boxing

Place the IA and arm boxing face to face with the welt between (Fig. 18–6). Match the notches. First sew to the left of the center notch, then to the right.

Add a pull strip to the bottom of the IA.

Step 19: Tacking on the IA

Put a half to full layer of new cotton stuffing over the old IA stuffing. Lay the newly sewn IA and arm boxing in place and pintack (Fig. 18–7).

Pull first from front to back. Then go underneath and tack from front to back also. Then pull the IA pull strip and pintack. Examine your work. If there are no unsightly pulls, drive the tacks all the way in. Also, tack on the arm boxing's outside edges, making sure that the welt is not overpulled or underpulled. The welt should be in line with the corner of the board (Fig. 18–7). Tack the loose welt on the edges of the OA.

Step 20: Reupholster the Other IA

Do the other IA and arm boxing the same way, using the newly reupholstered arm as a guide. Repeat steps 17–19.

The Inside Back

Step 21: Shaping the New IB Cover

If the old IB is well fitted, remove the sewed, shaped IB cover. Gently separate the boxings and the welt from the old IB cover. Press the covers with a steam iron so that all the $1/2''$ seams lie flat. Fold the old IB cover in half and staple the ends so that the vertical sides of the back and the arm cut-outs are even. Press again. Pressing flattens it out into one piece of goods. Center notch at the top right and bottom right corners (Fig. 18–8).

Take your rough-cut new IB cover. Fold it in half. Square the new fabric, i.e., stretch the new fabric on the bias so the fold is square to the top and bottom of a table or carpenter's square. Between the time the fabric is manufactured and the time you are ready to use it, it can be stretched out of shape. Lay the old IB cover on top of the new IB cover, stapling the sides together. Center notch the new IB, so you can line up the new IB and top back boxing.

Step 22: Cut and Sew the Back Boxings

In our project there is no back border. The back boxing comes in three pieces: the top, left side and right side. The top boxing should be from left to right, the exact measurements of the top of the IB, allowing for two $1/2''$ seams on the sides. Center notch the top back boxing on the top and bottom. Sew the side boxings in place. To get the correct measurements for the side boxings, allow 1/2" for the seam and below the top of the arm. Then you can attach decking or other scrap fabric to the bottom of the side boxings as pull strips, to be tacked to the wood frame. Pin the center notches of the IB and back boxing together, face to face.

Step 23: Sew the IB and Back Boxings

Before you sew the IB and back boxings together, sew a pull strip to the bottom of the IB (Fig. 18–9). Your welt should already be made. Fold the welt in half and notch.

Put all three center notches together: IB, welt and back boxing. Carefully place the sewing machine needle through all three layers without shifting them.

Before you start sewing, pin one end of the IB cover and one end of the top boxing together with the welt sticking out. If the IB is long, add a second pin halfway. Now you are ready to sew. Put your hand where the second pin is. Put the welt between the two layers of fabric and pull where the second pin is. Sew up to the second pin, then remove it. Grab the pin in the corner. Repeat the operation. Sew to about 1" from the corner. Stop the machine. Take the pin out. Cut the welt to within 1/16" of the seam in order to make a 90° turn. Carefully sew right up to the cut. Turn the fabrics 90°. Continue sewing, 6" at a time. There is no need to rush.

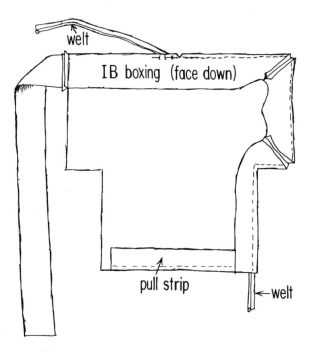

Fig. 18–9 Sew the IB and IB boxings together, one half at a time, starting at the center.

When you get to the next corner, cut the welt in order to make another 90° turn. Continue sewing down to the bottom of the IB, making the last 90° turn. Cut the thread.

Now you can sew the other half of the IB, welt and back boxing. Turn in reverse. If the top boxing was on top, the IB cover will be on top, i.e., facing you. Place the machine needle about 1" in from the center, sewing over the preceding starting stitch. Sew the second half of the IB and back boxing the same way you sewed the first side.

Examine all your sewing to see that you did not leave a hole or bury the welt in any place. The reason you sew half of the back at a time is to insure correct fit. You will get a nice square back as your finished product (Fig. 18–9).

Step 24: Tack on the IB

Mark the center of the frame at the top and bottom of the OB. Provided the IB looks good and needs no rapair work, you can put a half to a full layer of cotton on the IB to give a soft, full look and feel. Sometimes you can use a half layer of cotton added to the old cotton on the back boxings.

Lay the chair on its back so you are working with gravity. Turn the IB inside-out. The boxing will be standing up. Gently work the boxing over where it belongs. Pull the boxing over all the way around.

Pintack the seam in the first corner. Go to the opposite corner and do the same thing. Use your hand or a wedge tool to push the bottom and sides of the IB and pull them through to the outside back. Look at the old IB cover to see where any cuts were made. Make the cuts the same way.

Put the chair on its feet. Pull the pull strip attached to the IB. Pintack it across where the old IB was tacked, on top of the seat decking.

Step 25: Tack on the Back Boxings

As an example, the back boxings will finish at 6" width from the welt sewing line to the back edge of the frame. Start at the center. Pintack here first. Work from the center of the frame to the corners, one side at a time, pintacking at 1" intervals.

Place your straight-edge yardstick on the front of the welt. Make your welt as straight and parallel to the yardstick as possible. Release or pull the fabric a little bit, depending on what the yardstick tells you (Fig. 18–10).

Now remove the old pintacks on the IB bottom pull strip. Pull the IB pull strip down so the welt is parallel and straight to the yardstick.

Start working on the sides. Pull the pull strip on the side bottom end of the side back boxing. Take the slack out of the boxing. Pintack. Do the same to the opposite side. Spot check for true fit by check-

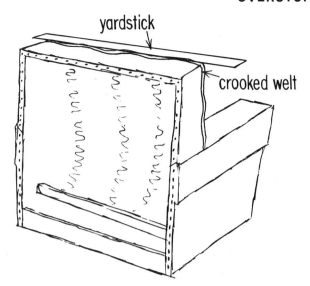

Fig. 18–10 Make sure the welt on the IB is not crooked by checking with a yardstick.

ing the horizontal measurements of the side back boxings. Example: If the one side back boxing measures 8″, make sure the other side back boxing measures 8″ (Fig. 18–11). Also, measure the base of the IB welt on the seat line. From front to back and left to right should be the same distance.

If your chair has buttons, put them on at this time. Take one more look to see if the cover is straight and balanced.

All the inside reupholstery pieces are on now. You are ready to fit and make the cushion, then put your outside pieces on.

The Cushion
Step 26: Fit and Make the Cushion
Follow Chapter 16 for this important step. Place the finished, fitted cushion in the chair. If there are holes between the cushion and the arms or back, or if the cushion fits too snugly, make the necessary adjustments in your pintacked back and arms. When no adjustments are needed, drive all the pintacks home.

The Outside Pieces
Step 27: Tack on the OA
The OAs are already cut. Take one OA and lay it face down over the top of the IA. Center it so you have at least 1″ in the front, 1″ in the back and ½″ on the top to turn under for blind tacking. At the top of the OA, put one tack each on the front and back tacking boards. Tack the OA on the horizontal tacking board with tacks about 4″ apart (*see* Fig. 7–11). Drive the tacks in.

Tack your ½″ blind-tack strip. Put a tack in the

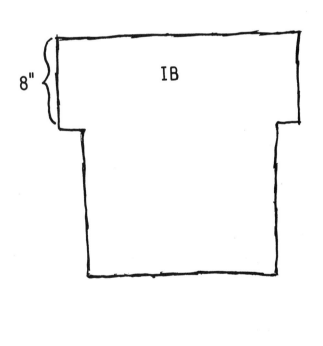

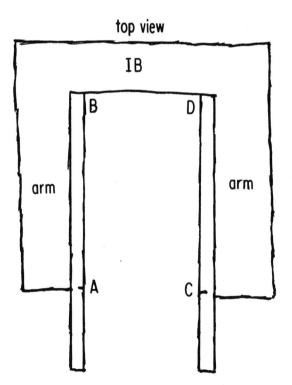

Fig. 18–11 To be sure the IB is tacked on evenly and neatly, the distance from A to B should equal the distance from C to D.

front and back, stretching it out. Tack the blind-tack strip every inch with number 6 tacks. Pull the cover over. Maintain the inch in the front so that the fabric remains straight. Put one pintack at the bottom about 4″ from each end, making sure the OA is taut. Give it a 45° cut at the corner of the legs. Pintack the corners in place.

Turn the front of the OA under to make it even with the welt. Put a few pintacks on top about every 4″ to hold it in place. Turn under, even with the bottom of the chair. Fold the back part of the OA along the angle of the chair over to the OB. Pull the fabric tight. Drive the tacks in. Do the other OA the same way.

Step 28: Tack and Sew the OB

Fold the OB in half and center notch the top and bottom. Some chairs have a welt on the OB. If your chair does, drive in tacks 1½″ apart on the welt. The center line of the welt should be at the edge of the wood, not even with the wood.

Take the OB cover and lay it inside-out over the top back rail. Place the center notch of the OB cover in line with the center notch of the top back boxing and about even with the back welt (*see* Fig. 7–9). Drive in the first tack at the center. Pull to one corner, even with the welt. Drive in a second tack. Go to the opposite corner. Drive in a third tack. Put three more tacks between the center tack and the end tack. Do the same on the opposite side.

Now you are ready for the blind-tack strip. Measure the length of the welt, e.g., 100″. Cut a strip of cardboard blind tack 100″ long. Take one end of the blind-tack strip and put it even with the vertical welt on the OB. Keep the blind-tack tape as high up to the stitch line as possible. Tack it on every inch. You can also stretch the tape out and put the second tack in the opposite corner and cut the tape.

Take the remainder of the cardboard tape. Lay the tape on the vertical edge, tacking down to the bottom and as close to the stitching as possible. Use at least a number 6 tack for blind tacking or ½″ staples for a staple gun.

Find the center of the frame on the bottom. Tack the bottom notch of the OB fabric at the center mark on the frame. Drive a tack in. Start from the center and drive in tacks every inch, stopping 2″ from each end. Turn the end under even with the welt. Tack it under.

Every 5″ or 6″, stretch the OB sidewise and temporarily tack or use upholsterer's skewers with the vertical welt. Now you are ready to blind stitch the sides of the OB. At this time, you can also blind stitch the front of the OAs, removing the pintacks when you finish. The blind stitch is "the" upholsterer's stitch for hand sewing any fabric piece that cannot be tacked or closed any other way. Turn the chair upside down and tack on the cambric (*see* Figs. 15–17 and 15–18).

Chapter 19

Wing Chairs

Introduction

Wing chairs are relaxing overstuffed chairs that you can curl up in for reading a hard-to-put-down novel. Or you can sit back in one and lean your head to one side, using the wings for pillowed support. The larger wing chairs, especially, look regal.

Most contemporary wing chairs were copied from the middle 1700s. In colonial times, the wings had a definite function. A man or woman sat in front of a fireplace, and the wings would catch the heat.

Reupholstering a wing chair only means that you are reupholstering an overstuffed chair with wings. If your project is a wing chair, you will need an extra yard of fabric to reupholster the wings. If a comparable sized overstuffed chair took 5 yards of fabric, you'd need 6 yards of fabric to do this job.

This project chapter differs from the previous one in several ways: There is a detailed description of how to reupholster wings; the frame needs extensive repair and the chair must be taken apart completely; the seat springs are coil springs and the back springs are No-Sag springs.

Reupholstering a Wing Chair

The Preliminaries

Step 1: Sterilize the Chair
Step 2: Examine the Chair

Our wing chair project was picked up at a local Salvation Army store by an enthusiast, after she kept her eyes and ears open for months (Fig. 19–1).

Take a firm grip on the chair. Notice that the frame is completely loose. The chair was probably in a room where there was no moisture. The glue in the doweled joints dried out. The springs feel loose, so you can assume that they need retying. The evidence of a yellow tag attached to the cambric shows that the chair has been reupholstered at least once. The chair is probably 35 or 40 years old.

Step 3: Measurement Chart and Cutting Diagram

When you complete your measurement chart, make a cutting diagram for the wing chair (Fig. 19–2).

Fig. 19–1 Wing chair: the frame needs extensive repair.

Deck	27″–29″ (use decking)	Welt
Seat	12″–27″	
IB	36″–27″	
OB	34″–27″	90″
IA	22″–27″	
AP	20″–5″	
OA	16″–27″	
IW	21″–15″	25″
OW	19″–12″	
CU	22″–23″	180″
CU BX	4½″–54″ + 8″/23″–26″	
AC	top: 10½″ + 1″	
	front: 6″–6″	

                                                    _____
                                                    295″
                                            (23″ square)

Step 4: Measure and Rough-Cut the Fabric

All fabric pieces are tacked and fitted right on the chair. Only the bottom of the IW needs to be cut from the pattern of the old IW cover. Label all the pieces.

Frame Repair

Step 5: Take the Chair Completely Apart

You are probably thinking that we are contradicting ourselves. However, when the frame needs extensive repair, this is the only way. This is where your notes are extremely important. The old fabric pieces and stuffing (kept together as an identifiable unit) should be neatly laid aside. Try to assemble a two-dimensional chair with the wings to the right and left of the IB, seat underneath, arms to the right and left of the seat, and the OB on top of the IB (Fig. 19–3). After you repair the frame, you can pintack the old pieces back in place for a guide, but it is not necessary.

When we took this wing chair apart, we noticed that the original upholstery was hidden under the outside cover and extra layers of stuffing. During World War II when labor was scarce, many upholsterers covered the original worn cover. This wing chair became much too overstuffed and lost most of its charm and grace when it was double uphol-

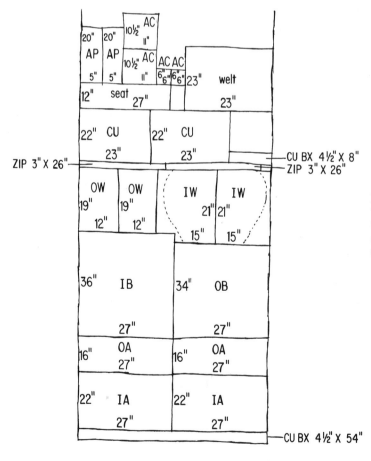

Fig. 19–2 Cutting diagram for wing chair project. To determine the quantity of fabric needed, add measurements in the lefthand column: 4¼ yards.

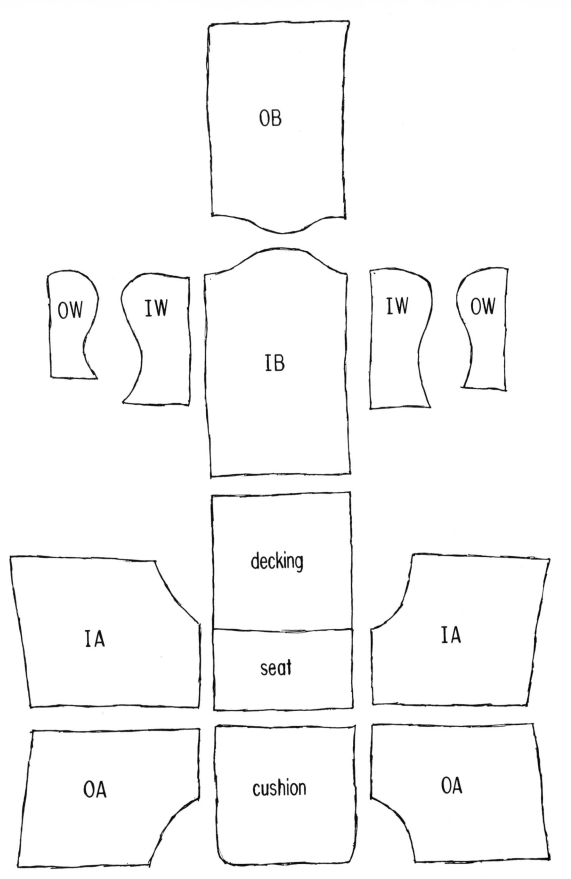

Fig. 19–3 Lay the old fabric cover, stuffing, burlap, webbing, in an orderly fashion on the floor so it will be easier to reassemble after the frame repair. You can also label the pieces of the old fabric cover.

stered. The *original* upholstery cover should always be used as a guide, not the reupholstery covers. Use your judgment concerning how much old stuffing should be thrown away.

In any case, the order of removing the fabric and stuffing is as follows: with the chair upside-down, loosen all four sides of the cambric, seat, OB, OAs and OWs, and remove them all except the seat. With the chair right-side-up, take off the IB, IWs, IAs and, last, the seat. Lay the fabric pieces and several layers of stuffing aside, as described above.

Take the springs out. In this case the seat springs are coil and the back springs are No-Sag. Before you remove the seat springs, mark the frame where the spring twine is attached for easy reference when you go to put the springs together. Remove the seat springs as a tied unit. The No-Sag spring clips stay on when the frame comes apart, the springs come off. Loosen the part that holds the springs (two nails) and leave on the one nail that fastens the clip to the frame.

Step 6: Knock the Frame Apart

Refer to Chapter 9 for instructions on knocking the frame apart. Remember to number the joints 1–1, 2–2, 3–3 as specified in this section, so you can put all the pieces in the frame "puzzle" back together with little effort (*see* Figs. 9–3 to 9–5).

Step 7: Repairing, Regluing and Reclamping

Do any necessary repair to broken or split boards, legs or dowels. Reglue and reclamp only four joints at a time to insure correct setting. The joints should be really tight. Allow at least one hour for each gluing and clamping session.

The Foundation

Step 8: Tack on Webbing or Burlap

In this project, the chair needed a new foundation. Heavy 17-oz. burlap was the choice. The chair is turned upside-down and the burlap tacked on.

Step 9: Resew and Retie Seat Springs

With your 6″ curved needle or 10″ straight needle and some stitching twine, sew the seat springs in place on the webbing or burlap. On top of the springs, cross-tie eight ways.

Step 10: Cover the Springs with Burlap

Cover the springs with 10-oz. burlap and, in the front of the seat, sew on the fox edging.

Step 11: Tack on Steel Webbing

This is an optional step, but we recommend it. Turn the chair upside-down. Tack on three strips of steel webbing from front to back over each row of coils. Use four strips if the chair has four rows of coils. The bottom of the seat will never cave in.

The Seat and Arms

Step 12: Restuff the Seat

Restuffing any section of the chair should be done immediately before putting on the reupholstery cover for that section. Now you are ready to place the old stuffing back on the seat. Also, add a half to a full layer of fresh cotton felt.

Step 13: Put on the New Seat Cover

The seat cover in the wing chair is attached similar to the overstuffed chair (Fig. 19–4). Study the old upholstery cover and review Chapter 15 for this and the following steps.

Step 14: Reupholster the IAs

Reupholster one IA at a time. Tack on the webbing and 10-oz. burlap combination, 17-oz. burlap or cardboard, as it originally was. In our project,

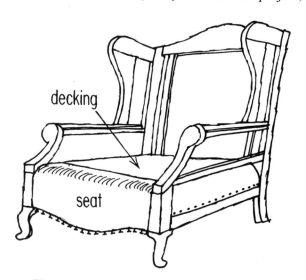

Fig. 19–4 Tack on the new reupholstery seat cover.

Fig. 19–5 Tack on the IAs.

the foundation of the arms was cardboard. Put on the old stuffing and add a half to a full layer of new cotton felt. Recover one IA (Fig. 19–5). Follow the same steps for the opposite IA.

The IWs and IB

Step 15: True-Cut the IWs

The main difference between reupholstering an overstuffed chair and a wing chair is, of course, the wings. The IWs are reupholstered similar to the IAs. There is a webbing and 10-oz. burlap, 17-oz. burlap or cardboard foundation, and stuffing. The only difference is that the IW is *shaped* on the bottom where a welt is sewn.

To shape the new IWs, take one of the old IWs. Cut the stitches that hold the welt and IW together. Press the IW flat. Lay the two rough-cut new IW covers face to face, both tops up. Lay the pressed old IW cover on top of the new IW covers, face or wrong side down (Fig. 19–6).

Cut out the bottom of the new IW covers to match the old cover. Sew new welt to the new IW covers to resemble the old welted IW cover. Now you are ready to put the IW covers on the chair.

Step 16: Pintack the IW Covers

Follow the sequence shown in Figure 19–7, along with the text. Lay the cover on the wing. Center it. The first tack goes in the welt at the end, where it meets the IA. The second tack goes in the other end of the bottom of the welt, after the welt is pulled through the slats.

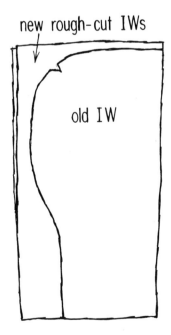

Fig. 19–6 True-cut fabric covers for the IWs.

Pull the middle center of the top of the IW cover over to the top of the OW frame. Pintack here. There are no pintacks on the bottom of the IW. The IW covers will be sewn after all the tacking is done. Pintack first to the left, then to the right, of the center. Pull the fabric with one hand to get all the slack (wrinkles) out and pintack with the other.

Study the old IW cover. Note that there is a V cut on the top back corner where the IW meets the top back rail (Fig. 19–7a and c). Pintack the middle wedge part of the cut to the top back rail in the immediate vicinity. Take the top part of the cut and bring it to the back part of the wing. Pintack it down. Take the bottom of the cut and pull it through the slat, then pintack from the welt up.

Come around to the front, pulling horizontally. Pintack around to the OW. Pintack from the center, up and down.

Now you are ready to pintack the curve. The easy way to pintack a curve, which we are sure you will be most interested in, is to keep subdividing (Fig. 19–7d and e). Pull the fabric with one hand and pintack with the other.

Do the opposite IW cover the same way. Now both IWs are pintacked on the chair (Fig. 19–7e). Hand sew the bottom of the IWs (Fig. 19–7f).

Step 17: Put Springs on the Back Frame

Lay the chair on its back. Fasten the springs back on the No-Sag clips, using new nails a little longer than the old ones to hold the springs down. If you are going to renail in the same holes, use stronghold screw nails. You can purchase these at your local upholsterer's shop.

The procedure of putting the springs back into the clips is to first nail the No-Sag springs on the lower back rail. Then, with your right hand, hold the top end of the spring. With your left hand, push down the belly of the spring, flattening it out. Give the spring a slight pull with your left hand to hook it onto the top clip. Nail the spring clip closed. Do the same to the other two or three springs. Now all your springs are in place.

Step 18: Tack on New Burlap

Tack 10-oz. burlap over the No-Sag springs. Use the stitched-on-burlap system as a substitute for crosstying to keep the springs from shifting to the right or to the left (Fig. 19–8).

Step 19: Prepare the IB Frame and Cover

Take the old IB stuffing and lay it on the way it was originally placed. Add a half to a full layer of new cotton felt. Chalk mark the center of the chair frame on the OB top rail and on the bottom back rail. Also, chalk the center of the rear seat rail.

Sew a pull strip on the new IB cover, the same as

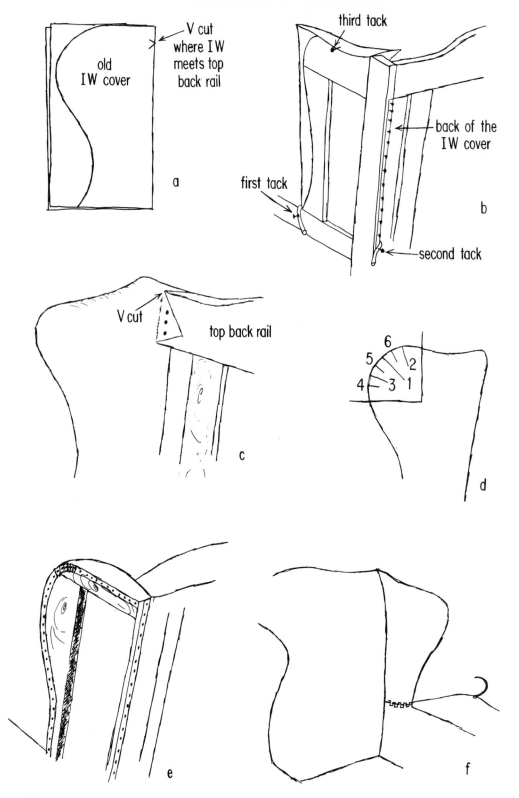

Fig. 19–7 Reupholstering IWs. *a.* Make a V cut at the top back rail so you can pull the IW cover through. *b.* Pintack the IW cover in place. *c.* Part of the V cut of the IW cover tacked on top back rail. *d.* Pintack the curve of the IW cover, subdividing as illustrated. *e.* The fabric along the curve has a pleated effect. *f.* Hand sew the bottom of the IW covers, using the upholsterer's blind stitch.

Fig. 19–8 Use the stitched-on-burlap method as a substitute for crosstying.

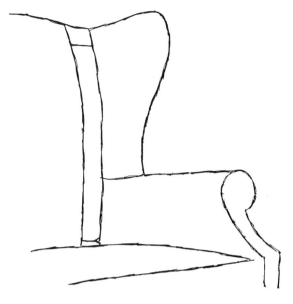

Fig. 19–9 Make the V cut around each IB side rail in order to pull the fabric through neatly.

the old pull strip. Fold the IB cover in half and notch the center of its top and bottom.

Step 20: Start the Cross on the IB

Start at the top of the chair. Pintack the center notch of the fabric on top of the chalked center of the top back rail, pulling the fabric over the top edge 1″. Now stuff the bottom part of the fabric and pull strip through the opening below the lower back rail, pulling it tight.

Stand the chair on its legs. Grab the pull strip at the notch in the center, lining it up with the chalked mark on the rear seat rail and here put the first pintack for the bottom of the IB. It is very important that you make sure the IB cover is pulled tight before pintacking.

Step 21: Finish the IB Corners

Make V cuts around each IB side rail in order to pull the fabric through neatly. Push the three parts of the V into place (Fig. 19–9).

Step 22: Pintack the IB Cover

Tack the center on both sides to form a cross. Pintack the top, bottom and sides of the IB cover, constantly pulling out the slack. Make sure the three wedges of the V cut are turned under, pulled tight and pintacked in place.

Step 23: Measure and Make the Cushion

Follow Chapter 16 for detailed instructions on making the best-fitting and best-looking cushion possible.

Step 24: Drive Your Pintacks Home

Set the finished cushion in the chair. Check to see that it fits snugly, but not too tight. If there are any holes between the IB or the IAs and the cushion, then make adjustments by knocking out your pintacks, pulling and retacking. When you are satisfied with your job, release your excess energy and drive those tacks home.

The OWs, OAs and OB

Step 25: Tack on Welt

Start at the front edge of the bottom of the OW frame, about 1″ into the OA frame. Tack the welt in place. On the straight edge, drive the tacks in every 2″. On the curved edge, add tacks closer together. Make sure the center of the welt is even with the edge of the wood. Tack the welt all around the top edges of the OW, OB and opposite OW frames and down to the opposite arm board (Fig. 19–10).

Step 26: Put on the OW Covers

The OW cover is tacked in the back on the back post. In the front, it is hand sewn (Fig. 19–11). The bottom of the OW is tacked to the top of the arm tack board.

Take the OW covers, which will be rough cut. Lay an OW cover on the frame of the OW, top up. Start on the top, allowing about 1″ above the welt and 1″ on the front of the wing. Place a few pintacks about 2″ or 3″ apart, along where the welt was tacked. When this is in place, pintack the back of the OW cover to the back post about every inch.

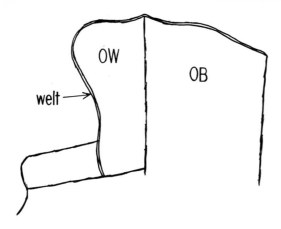

Fig. 19–10 Welt goes from the bottom of the OW, over the top of the OB, down to the bottom of the other OW.

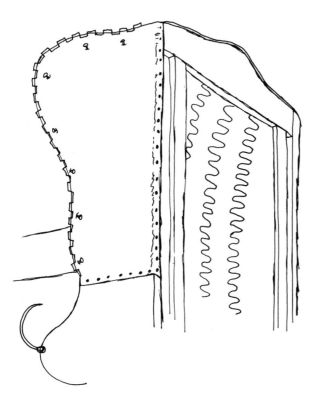

Fig. 19–11 Tack and hand sew the OW covers.

With your scissors, cut a good ¹/₂″ above the welt, from the top of the arm to the top of the OB frame. Gently tack one pintack at a time, turning the fabric under ¹/₂″ so it is even with the sew line of the welt. Continue around the whole welt, pintacking every inch or so.

At this point, it is best to hand sew the OW cover through the welt to the IW cover. Sew blind stitches about ³/₈″ to 1″ apart. Sew the whole length of the welt from start to finish.

At this time, any wrinkles can be pulled out by

adjusting the pintacks. Adjust either by pulling toward the back of the chair or by pulling straight down.

When you are satisfied with the job, drive the tacks in. Do the other OW cover the same way.

Step 27: Start Tacking the OA Cover

Turn the OA cover face down, with the top up. Lay the OA cover over the OA frame so that the top of the fabric is even where the IA is tacked. Center the OA left and right, by eye. This should give you an inch overhang on each side. Tack the OA on every 3″ or 4″ so the edge of the fabric is even with the arm board tacking strip (Fig. 19–12). This procedure gives straight edges. Now tack on the cardboard blind-tack strip on the same top edge of the OA.

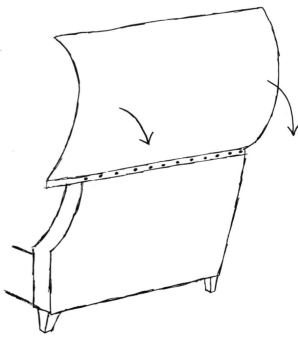

Fig. 19–12 Blind tack the top of the OA.

Pull the OA over and down. Pintack the bottom of the OA first in the center, then once on the right edge and once on the left edge.

Step 28: Tack on OA Welt

Tack the welt on the front edge of the OA, putting tacks 1″ apart.

Step 29: Make the Cuts on the OA Covers

Study the cuts of the old OA cover. The bottom corners have to be cut 45° to the top of the leg (Fig. 19–13). Pull the fabric tight to make accurate cuts. Fold corners *1* and *2* under. Pintack the corners in place at both legs.

Step 30: Tack the OA Sides

Fold the front under, probably about 1″, and pintack on top. Now pull the back part of the OA, tak-

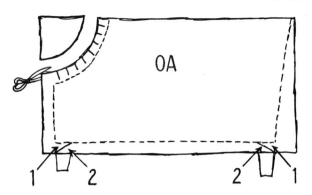

Fig. 19–13 Make 45° cuts at the legs and at the curved edge on the front of the arm.

blind tack every inch with the cardboard tacking strip (Fig. 19–14). Flip the OB over. Pull on the bottom. Pintack in the center, left and right, in front of the legs. Make the necessary 45° cuts at the leg. Turn the corners under and pintack. Fold the sides of the OB under and pintack. The side openings will be sewn later (*See* Fig. 19–15).

ing the slack out of the fabric. Drive the tacks in the back of the arm every inch.

Step 31: Tack the OA Curved Edges

Trim the curved edge of the OA to within $1/2''$ of the welt seam (*See* Fig. 19–13). Make slits $1''$ apart, a little less than $1/2''$ in from the edge of the fabric. Fold and pintack. This edge will be sewn after the other OA and OB edges to be sewn are completed.

Do the other OA the same way, repeating steps 27 through 31.

Step 32: Tack on the OB Cover

You will use the same procedure as for the OA covers, except that the OB cover is hand sewed on both sides. Flip the OB over the top of the chair so that the top of the wrong side of the fabric is even with the edge of the welt. Tack the top of the OB even with the edge of the welt every $3''$ or $4''$. Then

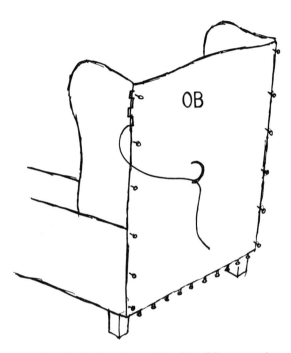

Fig. 19–15 Pintack the sides of the OB cover and tack the bottom. Later, hand sew the sides.

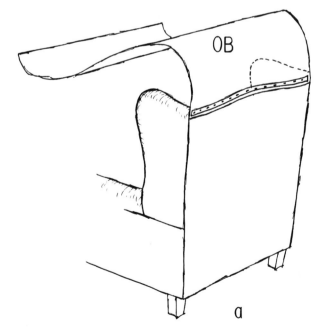

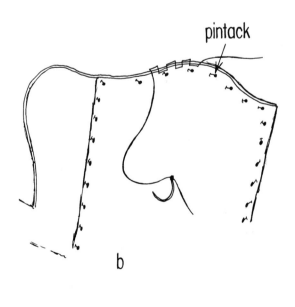

Fig. 19–14 The OB cover. *a.* Blind tack the top of the OB cover. *b.* If the curved top of the OB makes it too difficult to blind tack, you can hand sew the top, starting in the middle of the high crown.

Step 33: Add Cambric

Turn the chair upside-down and tack the bottom of the OA covers and OB, driving the tacks in. Now the bottom of the chair is ready for cambric. Measure, cut and tack on the cambric.

Step 34: Hand Sew the Open Edges

Put the chair on its legs. Using the upholsterer's blind stitch, hand sew the pintacked edges of the OAs and OB (Fig. 19–15). With a steamer or steam iron, steam any areas that are wrinkled, or that might be improved by minimal shrinkage, to give a finished professional look.

Step 35: Finishing the Arm Front

Take a piece of cotton, 1″ by 20″. Twist like a loose rope. Tack the cotton in the center of the front of the arm frame, tacking 3″ apart, with one tack on each side of the cotton.

Following the steps in Figure 19–16, fold the inside edge of the arm panel fabric piece under ¹/₂″. Pintack every 2″, even with the edge of the wood (arm post) up to the curve. Rough-cut the arm panel ¹/₂″ larger than needed.

Turn the outside edge of the arm panel under ¹/₂″ and pintack up to the curve. At the curve, draw a chalk line about ¹/₂″ in from the edge of the wood. Turn your fabric piece under to meet that line. Pintack in place. When the panel looks good to the eye, drive in brass-headed nails, either next to each other or 1″ apart. Remove any pintacks that are not covered by brass-headed nails.

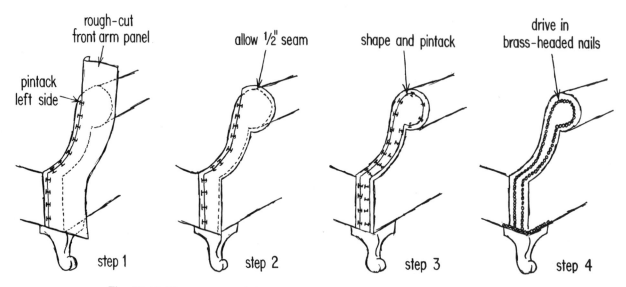

Fig. 19–16 Measure, cut and shape the front arm panel, then nail, directly on the chair.

Chapter 20

Colonial Chairs

Introduction

Colonial furniture is one of the most popular styles. Colonial chairs and couches are designed for comfort. A colonial couch is large and can seat several people. It fits perfectly with the informal decor of many modern homes. If you have a colonial chair or couch that you'd like to reupholster, do not hesitate. Once you understand how to reupholster the average overstuffed chair in the first project chapter and the wing chair in the second project chapter, you have a good foundation for reupholstering a colonial chair.

The only difference between the colonial chair and the wing chair is the IB. The wing chair has a pullover back. The colonial chair has a pillow back (Fig. 20–1). The pillow back looks like an attached

Fig. 20–1 Colonial chair project explains how to reupholster a pillow back.

cushion or like a large, attached throw pillow with buttons. The attached pillow has a knife edge. There are two pieces of fabric, the front and back, with the welt between. There is no boxing.

The front part of the IB is shaped according to the chair, where the wings and IAs give the back a distinctive shape. The back fabric piece of the IB has the same exact shape as the front of the IB, only in reverse.

The colonial pillow back has four separate pull strips to attach it to the chair. On the bottom is the standard pull strip. On the top, the pull strip acts as a pullover back. The $1/2''$ seam that joins the pillow back and the top pull strip is blind tacked on a strip of wood attached to the frame for this purpose. A layer of cotton is laid on top of the seam and top back frame. The pull strip is pulled over and acts as a border. The two side pull strips are pulled through the slats. They are not visible in the finished product. Their purpose is also to anchor the pillow in place.

The instructions in this chapter will help you make the colonial pillow back. Follow the initial steps in Chapter 18. When you are ready to do the colonial back, follow this step-by-step approach. Then you can complete the chair by referring back to Chapter 18.

Reupholstering a Colonial Pillow Back

Step 1: Label Pieces and Number Seams

The most important step in reupholstering a colonial pillow back is labeling all the IB fabric pieces, numbering all the seams and notching them.

The average one-pillow colonial chair has six IB fabric pieces and eight machine-sewn seams. A three-pillow colonial couch would have eighteen IB

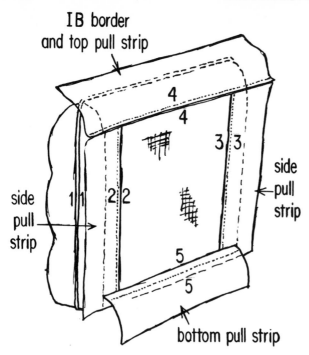

Fig. 20–2 Number all the seams to avoid confusion.

fabric pieces and twenty-four seams. These are just the fabric pieces for the IB. Imagine how many fabric pieces there are for the whole colonial couch!

Do not confuse yourself needlessly. Wherever there is a seam that connects two pieces of fabric, number both sides with the same number: 1–1, 2–2, etc. (Fig. 20–2). Make your numbers with a good magic marker that will not be erased while pressing with a hot steam iron.

Step 2: Separate and Press Fabric Pieces

Separate all the seams of the old IB pillows. They will be the patterns for the new pillows. Press out all the seams. Straighten out any curved sides that were originally straight: You can tell which sides were straight by either the pattern, stripe or thread of the goods. Fabric pieces can be easily straightened out by pinning them to the ends of a square table or board, just as you would a needlepoint.

Step 3: Measure, Cut, Notch and Pleat

Roll out the new fabric. Lay the old pieces of the back on top of the new fabric, like a puzzle. Remember to match any stripes, patterns or plaids. (We highly recommend that your first project be a solid-color fabric.) You can pin each piece in position, then cut. It is not necessary to number the new seams if you keep the old and new fabric pieces together until you are ready to sew. However, label

all new fabric pieces with chalk in case they get separated from the old patterns.

Fold the IB front and back pieces, and center notch on top. Measure and cut the welt needed for each pillow, adding an extra few inches. Fold the welt in half and center notch. Then it is easy to match the starting point for sewing the front and back of the IB and welt together.

The square cuts at the top of the IB covers will be the same as the old pattern. When the edges of each square cut are sewed together, the result is a pleat (Fig. 20–3). These pleats give the top of the pillows a curved look. Sew all the necessary pleats.

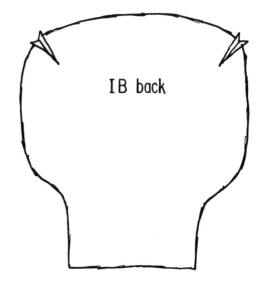

Fig. 20–3 Front view of the IB. As you face the chair, you can see the two top corner pleats.

Step 4: Sew on the Pull Strips

First, sew the top and two side pull strips together. You may be thinking, "How do I know where to attach the pull strips to the pillow back?" Study the old IB back cover (see Fig. 20–2). Do you see where the former seams were that attached the pull strips to the pillow? Measure the distance from the old seam lines to the edges of the fabric. Chalk the sew lines of the new back IB cover, using this information. The chalk lines will be 1/2″ closer to the edges of the fabric. Sew the correctly placed pull strips (by number and label) to the new back IB cover, using 1/2″ seams. The edges of the pull strips will be up against the chalked lines on the IB back cover. The bottom pull strip will be sewed to the bottom of the IB back cover. The chalk lines are usually 3″ or 4″ from the edges of the back of the IB.

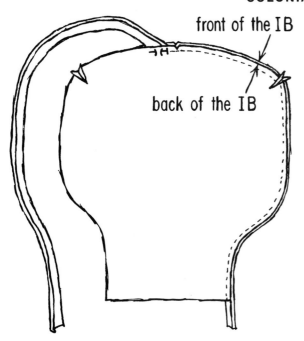

front of the IB

back of the IB

Fig. 20–4 Sew the IB front and back together with welt in the middle.

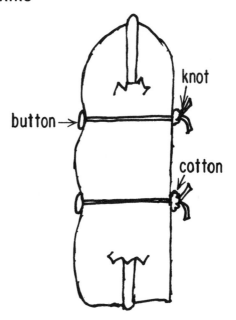

button →

knot

cotton

Fig. 20–5 A see-through look at how buttons are attached to the IB.

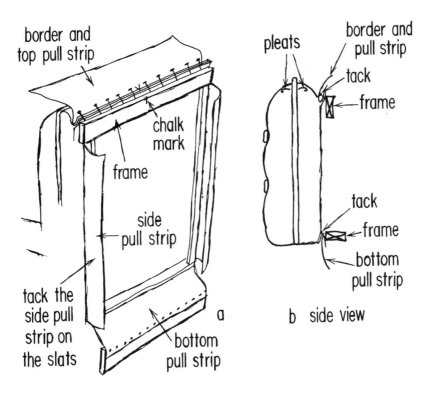

border and top pull strip

chalk mark

frame

side pull strip

tack the side pull strip on the slats

bottom pull strip

a

pleats

border and pull strip

tack

frame

tack

frame

bottom pull strip

b side view

Fig. 20–6 Attaching a pillow back. *a.* Tacking the pillow back on the chair. *b.* Side view of pillow back tacked onto frame.

Step 5: Sew the Pillow Back

Place the front and the back of the IB face to face, top up, with the welt in the middle (Fig. 20–4). Start sewing at the center notch. Sew down one side to the bottom. Turn the fabric around. Start 1″ before the center notch, sewing over your first starting point. Sew to the bottom of the opposite side.

Stuff the foam in the cushion. The old foam will be shaped to the cushion. Stuff a little bit of loose cotton in the corners to give the cushion a full look, covering the foam with a layer of Dacron if needed.

Step 6: Close Up the Cushion

Pin or staple the bottom of the cushion closed. Machine sew ¹/₂″ from the bottom. Make sure you get somebody else to hold the pillow back while you sew or you will be wrestling your way through the seam.

If you have more than one pillow cushion, repeat steps 4 through 6.

Step 7: Attach Buttons

Colonial chairs and couches always have buttons, usually five or six for each pillow. See the section on attaching buttons in Chapter 15 for instructions (Fig. 20–5).

Step 8: Tack the Pillow on the Chair

Now you are ready to tack each pillow back, one at a time, on the chair (Fig. 20–6). Center the pillow on the chair, or on a given section of a couch. The ¹/₂″ seam that attaches the top pull strip to the top of the pillow is now pintacked to the strip of wood attached to the frame for this purpose. Pintack every 3″ or 4″. Pintack the center of the bottom and two side pull strips. Make sure that the pillow is centered, not slanting. Blind tack the tacked top seam every inch. Finish pintacking the side pull strips that were pulled through the slats and the bottom pull strip. When pintacking, make sure the fabric is pulled tight.

Lay the old stuffing and a half layer of fresh new cotton over the blind-tacked seam and to the back edge of the top back rail. Pull the top pull strip over and pintack like a regular pullover back. When you are satisfied with your job, drive the tacks in. If there is more than one pillow back cushion, tack on the other pillow backs in this same fashion.

The inside pieces of the colonial chair or couch should be finished at this point. Follow the Chapters 18 or 19 for completing the cushions and outside fabric pieces. Most colonials have box-pleated skirts.

Chapter 21

Channel-Back Chairs

Introduction

Channel-back chairs are usually slightly or moderately rounded-back chairs (Fig. 21–1). Some channel-back chairs, called barrel backs, are sharply curved as if a vertical half of a barrel were used for the frame of the chair. The channels in curved chairs help ease the fabric cover into the curve.

Channel backs may look hard to reupholster, but they are much simpler to do when you follow our step-by-step approach. There are two types of channel pipes: the straight pipes with the same dimensions on the top and the bottom; the tapered pipes that are smaller on the bottom and larger on top. The basic approach is to take the old channel back off the chair frame, separate the seams and use the old channels as patterns for making new channels.

The only difference between a channel-back chair and any overstuffed chair, with or without a cushion, is the channeled back. This chapter will be concerned with reupholstering the channeled back. If your chair has no cushion, but a crowned seat, follow Chapter 1. If your chair has a cushion, follow Chapter 18. For both types, review Part Two techniques.

Reupholstering a Channeled Back

Step 1: Remove the Channeled Back

When taking the channel back off the chair, mark the top where the seams of each channel touch the frame (Fig. 21–2). By removing the tacks that hold the IB on the frame, you can lift off the stuffed channel back as a unit.

Step 2: Take Apart the Old Channels

Separate the seams of each channel so you have, as an example, four or five channels. Number each channel side (Fig. 21–3). Press all the old channels and burlap or denim backing flat, after you gently remove the old stuffing.

Step 3: Measure and Cut New Channels

Measure the tops of the old channels to get the rough measurement for the top of the rectangular piece of new fabric. To get the height of the new fabric piece, measure the vertical center line of any channel, if all are the same height. If each channel is a different height, use the vertical center line height of the middle channel. Mark and cut your new rectangular fabric pieces, using these measurements. Mark and cut the new burlap or denim backing like the old piece. The upholstery fabric will be

Fig. 21–1 Channel-back chair: Project explains how to reupholster a channeled back.

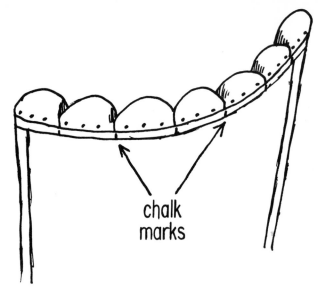

Fig. 21–2 Mark the frame with chalk marks where the seam of each channel touches the frame.

cut into strips. The burlap or denim backing will remain in one piece. Chalk the new backing like the old one is chalked, or where the seams are located (Fig. 21–4).

Lay the old channel patterns on top of the new rectangular fabric so that the pattern or vertical thread is not slanted. Pin and cut. Keep the old and new channel pieces together until you are ready to sew. Separate them one at a time in the sewing process.

Note: Some people feel that they are being smart by fitting the channels together top up, bottom up, and so on (Fig. 21–5). They want to save expensive upholstery fabric from going to waste. Beware. Some fabrics with nap, like crushed velvets, have a different shade when turned upside-down. Many patterns are noticeably different upside-down. Play it safe and follow the correct method.

Step 4: Sew the Channels to the Backing

While you were taking the seams out of the old channels, you probably learned a great deal about how the whole back was sewn together. This next step is to sew the channels to the backing material just like the old backing was. The most common way to sew channel upholstery fabric is as follows: Lay the first and second new channel pieces face to face. With the second channel on top, sew the right sides together. Lay this seam on the first mark on the burlap. Starting on the bottom, sew the $1/2''$ seam on the chalked burlap marking. Sew the sec-

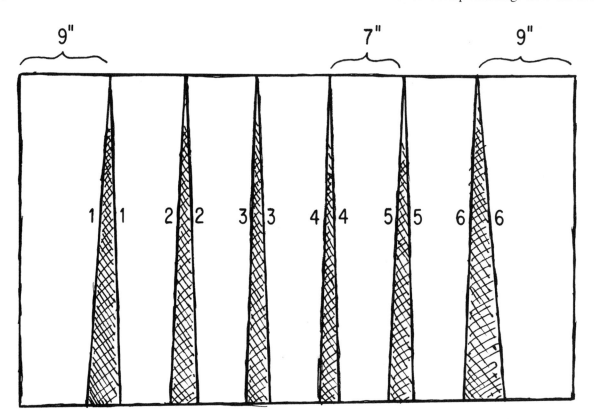

Fig. 21–3 Take apart the old channels and number each channel side. Lay the old channels on top of the new rectangular fabric.

7"

3½"

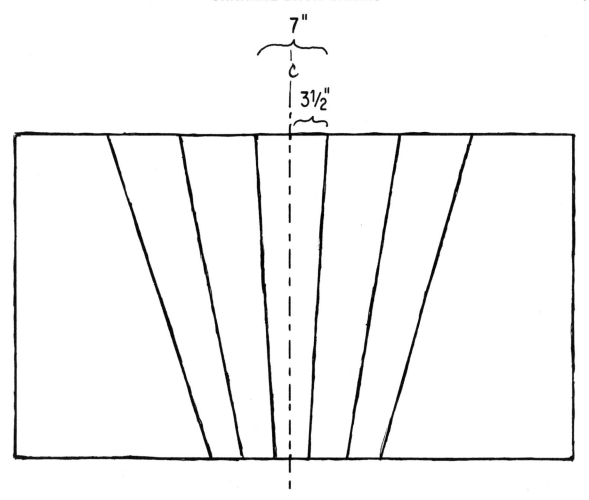

Fig. 21–4 Chalk the new burlap backing where the old seams on the old backing are located. Find the center of the middle channel.

ond and third channel pieces together as described above. Sew this ½″ seam to the second chalk line on the burlap. The first and last seams are left open on the channel back. These pipes will be stuffed on the chair (Fig. 21–6).

Step 5: Sew on a Pull Strip

Not every channel back has a pull strip. If your old channel-back chair cover had a pull strip, sew a pull strip the same size on the new channel back cover. Sew the pull strip onto the bottom of both the fabric cover and backing material. The bottom opening will be closed. If there is no pull strip on the old cover, it is not necessary to machine sew the bottom closed. You will be tacking the bottom closed on the chair. The new channel back is now sewn and ready to stuff.

Step 6: Stuff the Channels

The best channel stuffers are made from tin. For the one-time job, cardboard can be used. To make

your own, cut two strips of cardboard (thin weight is best) about ½″ smaller than the dimensions of the channels (Fig. 21–7).

You will probably use the old shaped cotton from each channel, depending on the condition it is in. Also, use a new half to full layer of cotton felt. The new cotton will be put into the channels so that it can be felt from the outside.

Put the new cotton and old cotton in the home-made cardboard channel stuffers. It will look like a cardboard sandwich with cotton in the middle. Starting at the top, push the channel stuffers and cotton into the first channel, until they are all the way in (Fig. 21–8). Stuff the remaining channels, also called pipes, the same way. Now the back is ready to be tacked on the chair frame.

The purpose of the stuffers is to evenly distribute the stuffing so it is not lumpy in any area of the channel back. If you run into trouble using home-

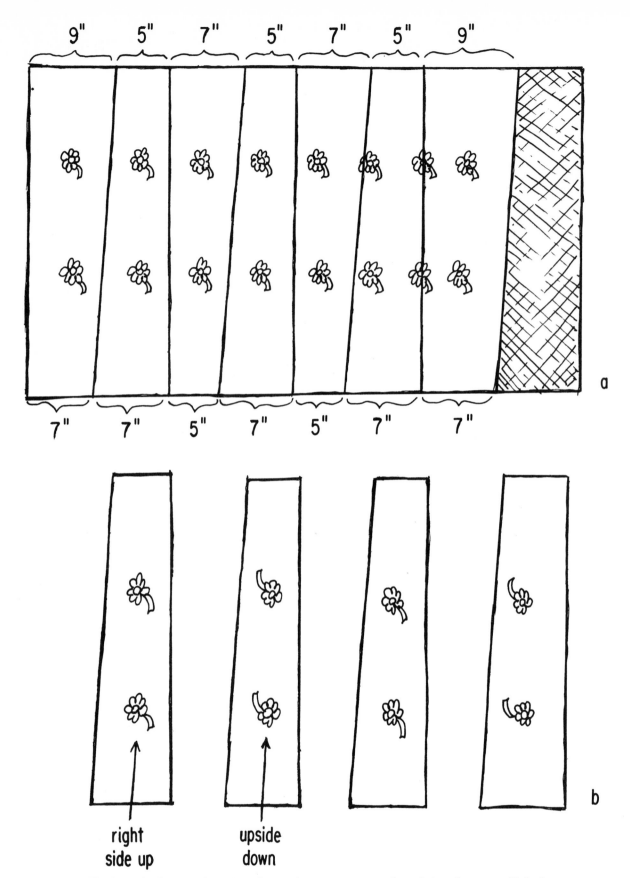

Fig. 21–5 Cutting new channels. *a.* Be careful never to reverse channels in order to save fabric. *b.* The result is an upside-down pattern.

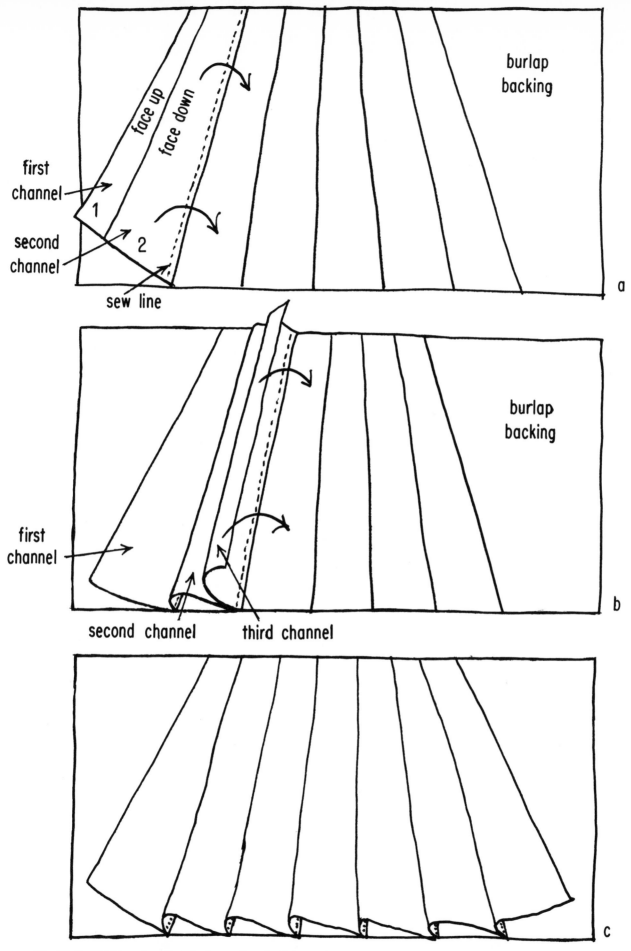

Fig. 21–6 Attaching channels to burlap. *a*. Sew the first two channels together to the burlap backing. Start sewing at the bottom of the back, which is always straight. *b*. Sew the second and third channels together onto the burlap backing. *c*. All the channels are sewn down to the burlap backing. The outside edges of the outside channels are left open.

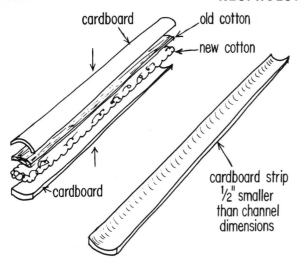

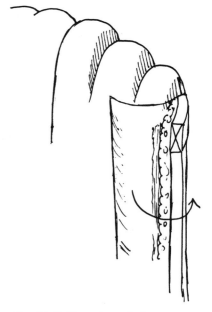

Fig. 21–7 Making your own channel stuffers.

made stuffers, you could ask your local upholsterer to stuff the channels with his professional tin stuffers, for a minimal charge.

Step 7: Close the Channels

Now you are ready to pintack and close the pipes. Do one end at a time. Stretch out the end seam, top and bottom. Lay the old stuffing for this channel, and a half to a full layer of new stuffing, right up against the seam. Take the cover and pull horizontally to the back. Pintack in the center. Pintack the bottom half and then the top half (Fig. 21–9).

The tops of the end pipes are closed just like the

Fig. 21–9 Close the end pipes on top. Wrap the outside edge of the end pipe around the back post and tack.

center pipes. You make a little pleat or two to close up the pipe neatly. Do the opposite end pipe the same way.

Examine the channeled IB to see if it looks good. If you are satisfied with your job, drive in all the tacks. If you are not satisfied, make corrections where they are needed.

Tack between the seams on the bottom, pulling firmly, for the last and final tacking.

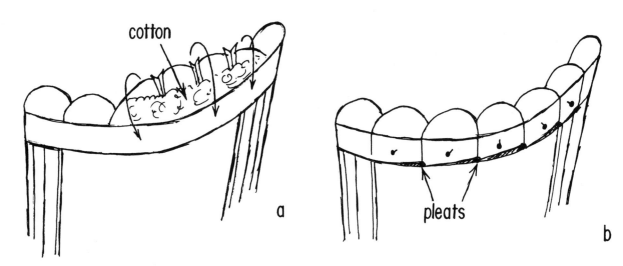

Fig. 21–8 Stuffing channels. *a.* Stuff all the channels. *b.* Pull the tops of the five middle channels over and pintack at the center. Make a pleat at each seam to accommodate excess fabric.

Chapter 22

Tufted-Back Chairs

Introduction

Around the turn of the century, tufting was very fashionable. There was very little plain upholstery work done. Everything was tufted from 1900 until the 1930s, even the upholstery in the horse-drawn buggies and early cars. In the days when labor was cheap, it might take a skilled upholsterer a week to do a hand-tufted sofa back.

Small tufts of hair from the horse's tail were used for the fabric and the stuffing. Cotton mohair was also used extensively.

Today, people still like the elegant tufted look. There are basically two types of tufting done: hand-crafted tufts and machine-sewn tufts. Both types have small, $1/2''$-diameter buttons pulled into the fabric and from button to button there is a pleat. Both tufts come in two designs, the half diamond and the full diamond (Fig. 22–1). The handcrafted tufts have buttons pulled about 2″ deep into the fabric. The pleats start at the center of the button and run diagonal to the next button. The pleats are all turned down so as not to collect dust. The stuffing is

at least 2″ thick, preferably more. There is no machine sewing involved. The machine-sewn tuft has $1/8''$ to $1/4''$ French seams sewn on the chalked design (half or full diamond) on the back of the fabric. The French seams are sewn from button to button instead of pleating.

Tufts have a functional purpose, as well as eye appeal. Tufting makes it easy for the upholstery fabric to follow the curved design of a chair. A chair with an extremely curved back, such as the old barrel-back chairs, pleated from button to button between 3″ and 6″, follows the shape of the back and has enough "give" so the springs compress when you sit in it (Fig. 22–2). The tufted curve makes a very comfortable back. The curved back with no pleats has no "give." When you sit in it, the springs do not compress and it feels like a wooden back. Chairs with horseshoe-shaped backs are tufted. Chairs with slightly or moderately curved backs can be either tufted or channeled. Both methods allow the fabric to easily follow the shape of the chair.

This chapter will describe only the step-by-step

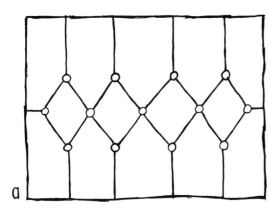
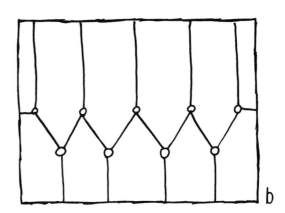

Fig. 22–1 Tufting patterns. *a*. Full-diamond tufted back. *b*. Half-diamond tufted back.

155

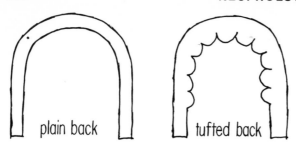

Fig. 22–2 No "give" in an extremely curved back (*left*) conveys the impression of sitting against a wooden back. Tufting a barrel-back chair (*right*) makes it comfortable.

method of reupholstering the back. If your chair has a seat cushion, follow Chapter 18. If your chair has a crown seat, follow Chapter 1 as well as Part Two.

Reupholstering a Tufted Back

Step 1: Examine and Remove the Old Cover

After the OB cover is off and you can see the inside of the IB, you may notice that the burlap on the tufted back is worn out. You will have to replace it. Unless an animal has clawed a couch or chair and done extensive damage, the stuffing will be professionally packed into a definite shape and should not be disturbed.

Carefully remove all the tacks holding the tufted back in place. Cut the buttons off by cutting from the top while pulling the button slightly forward (Fig. 22–3). Gently remove the old cover. It is very important that you do not disturb the stuffing. If you

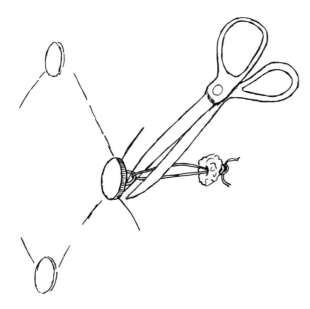

Fig. 22–3 Carefully remove all the old buttons.

do move the stuffing where it indicates the center of a button was sewn, then you are going to have one diamond bigger than another. The shape of the old stuffing also gives you the shape of the tufted back. Do not disturb it.

Step 2: Use the Old Cover as a Pattern

Press the old cover. Straighten it out, squaring it if it was stretched out of shape. It will most likely be a rectangular piece of fabric. There may be penciled markings of the diamonds on the back of the old cover. The most important information that you have on the old cover is the holes where the buttons were.

Make a new rough-cut rectangular piece of fabric at least an inch larger on all four sides than the vertical and horizontal measurements of the old cover. The extra inch on each side allows for pulling and tacking the fabric. Turn the new rough-cut fabric face down. Now you are ready to mark where the buttons and half or full diamonds will be on the new fabric.

There are two ways to chalk or pencil the pattern on the new fabric. The easiest way requires that the fabric be straightened out so that the vertical and horizontal threads are perpendicular to each other. Place the old and new covers face to face, top up. Pin the old cover to the new cover, with the old cover on top. Take a soft marking pencil or pointed chalk. Stick the marker in each buttonhole of the old cover, rotating it to make a mark on the new cover. Mark all the buttonholes. The trick is to keep the two covers rectangular and not slanted. No lines need to be drawn from button to button. The pleats automatically fall into place. The second method is necessary if you cannot straighten the old cover into its true rectangular shape. This method will also determine where to place the buttons. Put the new cover face down. Measure on the old cover the distance between any two buttons on the top horizontal line, e.g., 6″. Measure from the top of the diamond to the bottom of the diamond, taking two or three measurements to get a happy medium. Example: The vertical measurements of three diamonds were $7\frac{3}{4}″$, 8″, and $8\frac{1}{4}″$, with the happy medium being 8″ (Fig. 22–4).

Find out which buttons are in the vertical center of the chair (see markings). Then measure from the top button to the top of the fabric. Example: Between button c and the broken line is $10″ + 1″ = 11″$. Draw your first top horizontal line of buttons (line a in Fig. 22–4). This is to insure that you have enough fabric between the first line of buttons and the top of the fabric. Measure down (8″) and get the second line of buttons from the top. Measure half-

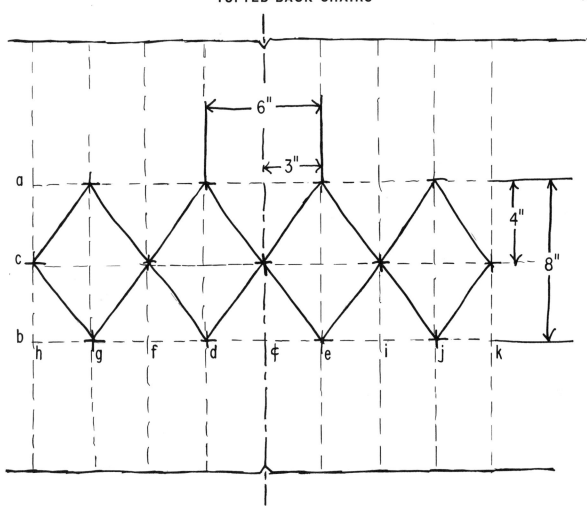

Fig. 22–4 Marking the inside back of a full-diamond tufted back. Draw dotted lines *a* through *k* first. Mark *T* where lines meet to form a diamond. Join the *T*s to form connecting diamonds.

way between the top and bottom lines for the center line. To continue our example, measure 3″ to each side of vertical center, which gives you a 6″ span. Draw these lines. Every 3″ on both sides of these drawn lines, draw more vertical lines.

Now all the vertical and horizontal lines are drawn. To make the diamonds, draw diagonals at the corners and center of each square from the top line to the bottom line, as shown in Figure 22–4. Half diamonds are done very similarly: Figure 22–5 provides a detailed example.

Step 3: Replace Burlap and Stuffing

If you have to replace the 10-oz. burlap and webbing, or the 17-oz. burlap, now is the time to do it. After you tack the burlap on, very carefully replace the old stuffing. Lay the chair on its back. Lay a fresh half to full layer of cotton felt on the whole back. Stick your finger in each recessed hole to show where the buttons will go.

Step 4: Attach New Buttons

All the buttons have been covered. Each is strung up with about a yard of stitching twine, i.e., with two halves folded to make 18″ each. The first button to go in is the top center button. Stick the needle in the face of the fabric so that it comes out on the top center marking. Pull the button through and attach loosely (*see* the section on attaching buttons in Chapter 15). If there is more than one button in the vertical center line, then the second button is right below the first. It is possible to have three or four buttons on the center line. Finish attaching the vertical center buttons. You now have a division of the back—the left side and the right side. Fold the fabric down the center so you can see the second line of vertical buttons on either the left or the right. Starting with the top button, push the needle-twine-button combination in the IB cover, slip knot in the back of the IB and pull the twine loosely so the fab-

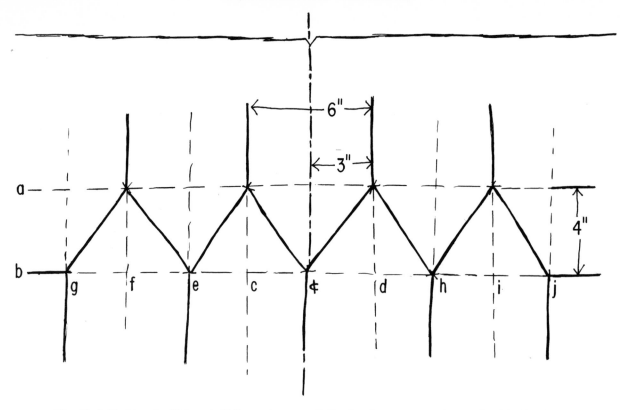

Fig. 22–5 Marking the IB for a half-diamond pattern. Following the same procedure outlined in Fig. 22–4.

ric stays in place. Fold along the second row so you can work on the third row of buttons. Continue this sequence until half of the back is done. Now do the other half the same way. All the buttons are in place.

Step 5: Make the Pleats

Stand the chair on its feet. Pull all the buttons tight. You can aid the tightening process by snugly fitting your finger in the buttonhole while pulling the twine. You are ready to form your pleats. You automatically have pleats in all directions from button to button, but you have to straighten them out sometimes, with a regulator, plain screwdriver and your fingers. Also, make sure the pleats are folded *down* so as not to catch dust (Fig. 22–6).

Start at the top. With your fingers from the top center button to the top of the frame, push the fabric into the cotton-tufted seam. Pintack in the center. Do this to all of the top seams. Go to the bottom of the back. Do the same to the bottom back seams.

Step 6: Pintack the New IB Cover

Return to the top of the tufted back. Make sure there is just enough cotton, without being over-stuffed or understuffed, so that all the top pieces look the same. Also, make sure that the cotton stops at the top of the OB frame. When you blind tack the

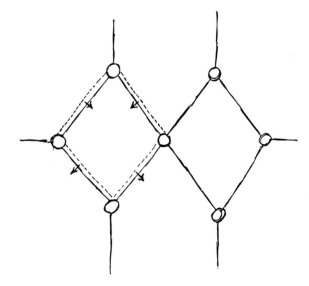

Fig. 22–6 The openings of the pleats should be pointing down so they do not collect dust.

top of the OB cover, you do not want it to be lumpy.

Go to the center of the pipe, i.e., between the seams. Make sure the stuffing is curved and filled out properly. Pintack the center of the pipe. Do this to all the pipes. Then, pulling the fabric, pintack to the left and right of the center of the pipe, making your pintacks 1″ apart. Under each seam is a pleat. Make the pleat so that it falls into the contour of the pipe. When it looks even, go to the bottom of the back and do the same thing. You may have to use a stuffing regulator to balance the stuffing out. If everything looks good, drive the tacks in.

Step 7: Steam the Fabric Tight

If you have a good steam iron or a steamer, steam over the button area and pleats. Press the pleats down flat with a clean screwdriver while steaming. Steaming makes the fabric shrink and fit snugly on the chair. It eliminates any wrinkles or creases.

Tufted Couches

Couches, as well as chairs, are tufted. Today, it is possible to railroad some solid crushed velvets (put the fabric on sideways). The nap of these velvets runs horizontally, the width of the fabric. If the fabric cannot be railroaded, it can be pieced at points where the pleats form. A lot of tufting is done with matelassé fabric—usually a rayon-cotton-nylon mixture. Ask your fabric salesperson for some samples. Certain patterns that are woven into the fabric in matelassé are round, with no distinct top, bottom or sides, and can be railroaded. Your couch back may be up to 6′ long and 36″ wide. The 54″ width of the fabric now becomes the height of the back. The length of the fabric becomes the width of the back.

If your fabric cannot be railroaded, this is what you can do. Mark the diamonds along the whole 54″ width of the fabric. Measure the width of the IB with a cloth tape measure. Slowly and carefully measure across, pushing the tape measure into

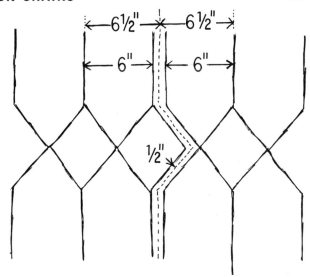

Fig. 22–7 Making a tufted back wide enough for a couch.

every pleat as far as you can. Measure across the widest points on the couch (Fig. 22–7). Then cut another 54″ piece of fabric (or possibly two) the remaining width of the couch, adding the distance of a full diamond so you do not run short of fabric.

Mark the diamond patterns on the second piece of fabric. On the first piece of fabric, cut out ¹/₂″ past the last diamond marking on the 54″ wide fabric (Fig. 22–7). Take the other 54″ wide fabric and cut ¹/₂″ past the markings on the inside of the first diamond. Join the two pieces with ¹/₂″ seams on the sewing machine. Of course, the height of the IB has been carefully measured, as if it were a pullover back. Continue reupholstering the couch as if it were a one-piece tufted chair.

Chapter 23

Convertible Sofas and Recliners

The Convertible Sofa

One piece of furniture that you may have spent a lot of money for is your convertible couch. Convertibles are a fantastic way of converting your den, family room, spare room or living room into a guest room. Many newlyweds who start out with a small apartment, or a small budget for new furniture, make their first double bed a convertible couch. After years of good use, the convertible starts showing wear and tear. It may be too sentimental to throw out. It may be too expensive to replace. Or, it could just be too heavy to move. So the logical conclusion is to reupholster it yourself.

Most convertible couches weigh between 350 and 400 pounds. In the early 1950s, the convertible was made in one piece. Someone must have gotten wiser after many backbreaking trips up and down a flight of stairs. The new breed of convertibles has a removeable back. The back is held in place by bolts and wing nuts, or the use of other methods. Examine the couch closely.

The best way to reupholster a convertible couch is to take the sleeping unit out, i.e., the mattress

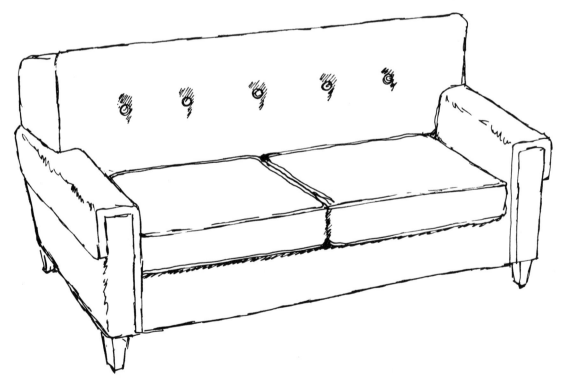

Fig. 23–1 A typical convertible hide-a-bed.

and steel foundation. This method sounds like a lot of work, but in the long run it is easier to reupholster without the unit obstructing your work.

The best part about reupholstering a convertible couch is that the only work involved in the seat is taking the mattress and steel unit out. There is no webbing to tighten, springs to retie or burlap and stuffing to worry about. The mattress and springy steel foundation act as the stuffing and springs. The back springs and stuffing are almost always in excellent shape. All that is needed is to tack on the new reupholstery cover. Each convertible has its own unique arms and back and should be studied carefully.

The following project is a typical modern convertible couch (Fig. 23–1). Putting on this cover is similar to putting on the new cover for an overstuffed chair.

Reupholstering a Convertible Couch

Step 1: Examine the Couch

If it is difficult to open and close the unit, chances are a small spring is unhooked or a steel rivet is broken in the steel unit. The little springs can be hooked in place or the steel rivet hammered back into place. In this project everything was in good shape—the unit, the IB and arms. The upholstery fabric was worn and the cushions needed to be replaced: The foam rubber had disintegrated and was crumbling easily. We decided to replace them with new pieces of high-density polyurethane foam.

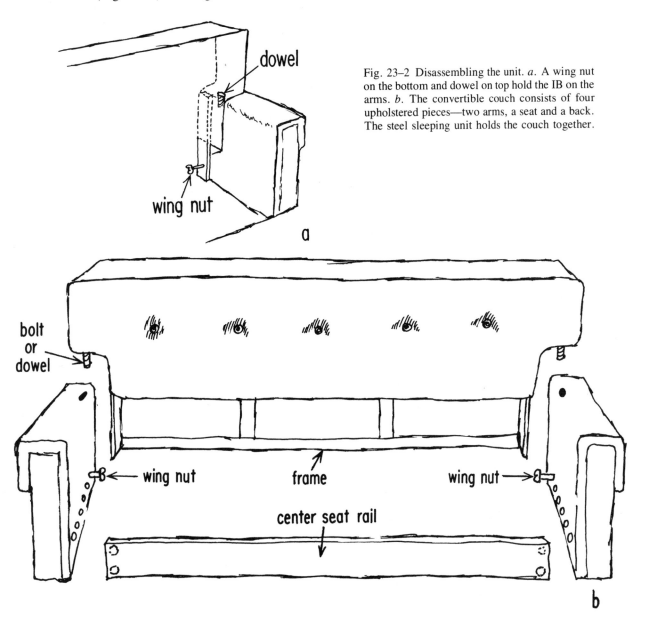

Fig. 23–2 Disassembling the unit. *a.* A wing nut on the bottom and dowel on top hold the IB on the arms. *b.* The convertible couch consists of four upholstered pieces—two arms, a seat and a back. The steel sleeping unit holds the couch together.

Step 2: The Preliminaries

Make a measurement chart and cutting diagram, following the procedures in Chapters 18 and 19 for guidance. Then chalk and rough-cut the fabric pieces.

Step 3: Take the Couch Apart

Remove the IB wing nuts and lift the back off (Fig. 23–2). Set the back aside. Remove the sleeping unit: It is bolted or screwed in the lower part of the front. It is also mounted to the back of the IAs. When you remove the unit, make sure you have someone to help you. You should always put the couch on upholstery horses. Then you can crawl underneath to remove the bolts and screws. It helps to take notes on what you are doing or make a sketch as you go along (Fig. 23–3).

After the unit is removed, the frame is light and easy to work on. There is a rail that holds the two arms and seat together. In most cases, the arms are doweled permanently together. In this couch, the arms and front of the seat separate. This project also has removeable arm and seat panels to be pried out with a screwdriver gently, then reupholstered. They will be nailed back on with finishing nails.

Work on one section at a time, removing the fabric pieces as you do a section. Take one arm cover off and use the other for a guide. Then reupholster the other arm cover. Remove the back cover when you are ready to work on the back.

Step 4: True-Cut and Sew the IB and Boxings

For the IB and IB side boxings, make patterns from the old covers. Fold, center notch, press and lay on the new folded, rough-cut IB and side boxings.

All the other fabric pieces are rectangular. They do not need patterns.

Sew the back boxing and side back boxings together. With the welt between, machine sew the IB to the boxings. Also, sew the IAs to the IA front boxings and IA side boxings. The $3^1/2''$ square cut that is made on each front corner of the seat is machine sewn. Then the seat is sewed to the decking.

Step 5: Replace the Decking

If the decking needs to be replaced, use strong duck fabric as a cover. Duck is similar to a lightweight canvas. It comes in several different colors. Most of the decking on convertibles is gray. Your new decking will consist of two layers of duck with a layer of cotton in the middle (Fig. 23–4b).

Measure the old decking and cut the new 1″ longer on all four sides. Turn three sides under 1″—left, back and right—with a layer of cotton in the middle. Staple it all around. Take your temporarily closed decking to the sewing machine. Sew the three stapled sides $1/2''$ in. The fourth, or front, side of the decking is then sewed to the seat, face to

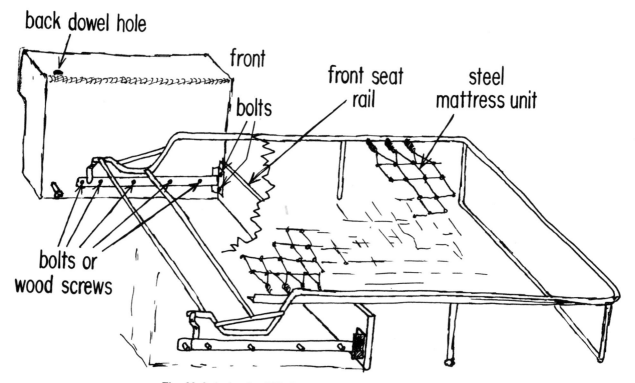

Fig. 23–3 A sketch will help you when you reassemble the unit.

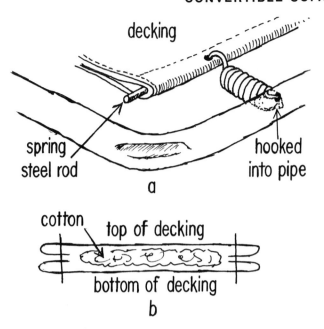

Fig. 23–4 *a*. The steel rod and small springs keep the decking taut. *b*. Side view of the top and bottom of decking, sewed together with cotton in the middle. Vertical lines indicate seam lines.

face. Slide the ⅛″-diameter spring steel rod in the back ½″ seam opening of the decking. This steel rod was removed from the back of the old decking. The purpose of the rod is to hook little springs onto it to keep the decking taut (Fig. 23–4a).

If the decking is in good shape and does not need to be replaced, then just reupholster the front seat rail.

Step 6: Tack on the Fabric Pieces

The first piece to be tacked on is the seat. Then do the two IAs. Screw the steel unit back into the arms (when necessary, as in this project, screw the arms and front of the seat together first). Tack on the OAs. Now you can reupholster and attach the arm and seat panels. As we mentioned earlier, each section of the chair is reupholstered from start to finish, one at a time. Panels are always tacked on last, especially when you can nail on both the arm and seat panels in one step. The basic idea is to completely reupholster the arms and the front of the seat on the upholstery horses and attach the steel unit while everything is on the horses. Put the reupholstered arms, seat and steel unit on the floor. Then set the back of the couch on the horses, so it is easy to work on (Fig. 23–5).

The IB and boxings are tacked on and finished off similar to the back of the overstuffed chair. There is no border. The OB cover is tacked and hand sewed in place. When the back is fully reupholstered, slide it onto the arms, seat and sleeping unit sitting on the floor. Tighten the wing nuts.

Step 7: Make the Cushions

If your couch is not large and there is no dividing line in the middle of the seat, you might consider

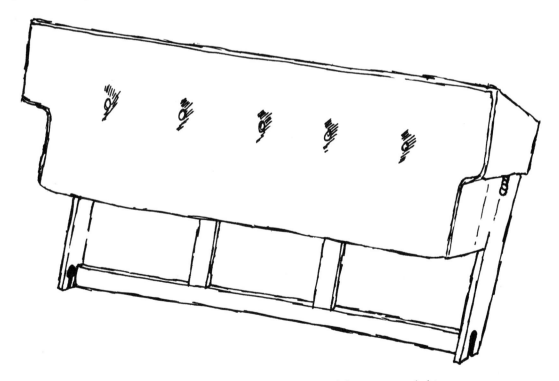

Fig. 23–5 Set the back on upholstery horses so it is easy to reupholster.

using one large cushion. It is more comfortable than two small cushions, especially when you are lying down, since there is no opening under your back.

Recliners

Recliners are similar to convertible hide-a-beds. The chair comes apart into four pieces: the seat; back; the two arms, attached by a cross-piece underneath; and a footrest—some recliners have two footrests (Fig. 23–6). There is the steel unit or mechanism that makes the chair recline. This mechanism has to come out and there is extra hardware that has to be understood. Many people are afraid to tackle a recliner, looking at it as a real mystery. There is no mystery. This section gives you a close look at what a recliner is really like.

The Mechanism

Before you reupholster your recliner, study it very carefully to see if you can take it apart. Look

Fig. 23–6 A recliner disassembles in four sections.

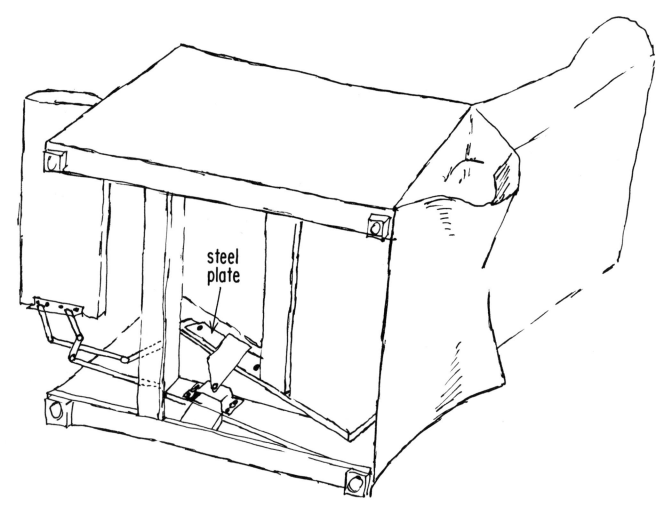

steel
plate

Fig. 23–7 Study the mechanism carefully, taking notes, before you take it apart. Dots indicate bolts holding the mechanism to the chair.

for a plate—usually 2½″ to 3½″ wide by 20″ long. One side of the plate is steel riveted, factory sealed to the mechanism. It cannot be removed. The other side of the plate is screwed to the frame and can be removed.

Turn the chair on its back and take the cambric off. The plate mounts the mechanism or unit onto the chair. Take the three or four wood screws off the frame and the unit comes out. After you take this plate out with the mechanism, then you can unscrew the remaining parts—seat, back, two arms and footrest. Lift the back and seat out first as one section. Then take the back off the seat by unscrewing the two or three bolts on each side (Fig. 23–7). Then reupholster your recliner just as you would a convertible couch or a regular overstuffed chair. Reupholster one section at a time, following the many tips and steps from previous chapters.

Tips for Reupholstering a Recliner

When reupholstering, do not put excess cotton on the sides where the seat and the arms meet, or where the back and the arms meet. Put extra cotton on top of the seat and on top of the back, not on the sides. When your chair reclines, you do not want any friction between the arms and the seat that would keep the chair from working smoothly. Also, before you put the chair back together, put a drop of oil on all the pivot points in the mechanism.

Put the sections of the chair back together in reverse order: Attach the seat to the back, set them between the arms, screw the footrest on and, last but certainly not least, screw the mechanism back in place.

Upholstery Fabric

The average recliner takes between 5 and 6 yards of fabric. Some provincials with show wood on the arms take 4 yards. In these styles, the mechanism is not mounted on the arms. It is mounted on a cross beam between the arms.

We do not recommend that your first recliner be reupholstered with vinyl or plastic. Vinyl stretches easily. It takes an experienced upholsterer, who knows how to work with vinyl, to do a good job. Also, you cannot poke a stuffing regulator into vinyl to move stuffing from an overstuffed to an understuffed area. You will make holes in the vinyl that will rip even larger with a little wear. Any sewing that is done on vinyl must be permanent. If you take out the stitches, you run the risk of ripping it. There are too many other attractive, durable, loosely woven fabrics that do not have these problems. So stay away from vinyl, any type of plastic, imitation leather and leather.

How To Fix a Recliner Mechanism

There is no great mystery to repairing a loose or stubborn recliner. There are only two reasons why a recliner goes back by itself: Check to see if the "friction washers" underneath the screw nuts are tight enough; if the chair mechanism is never oiled, the rivets loosen up and have excess play. Hammer the rivets together, using two hammers or a heavy steel weight and a hammer.

If the recliner is hard to push back, oil all the joints (rivets). Check for any broken rivets that would rub up against the sides of the frame, jamming the chair's movement. Loosen up the nut holding the friction washer that's too tight.

Section-Assembled Chairs and Couches

Some factories make overstuffed chairs and couches in sections. The seat, back and arms come

Fig. 23–8 Section assemblies. (*Above*) section-assembled chair, reupholstered. (*Below*) section-assembled chair, taken apart.

apart (Fig. 23–8). They are reupholstered separately, then screwed back together again. Examine your overstuffed chair very carefully to see if it comes apart. Take notes.

As for any overstuffed chair, take all your fabric measurements first. Take off the cambric and the OB cover. Inside the T of the back are nuts, one on top of each arm, that hold the back down to the arms. A screw or two on each side of the back also holds the back into the arms. Remove these screws. Lift the back up (Fig. 23–9).

In the front of each arm there are two nuts and, in the back of the arm, a wood screw, that have to be removed. When you remove these, the arm and seat come apart.

Section-assembled chairs have the same con-struction as other overstuffed chairs: coil springs, webbing, burlap, stuffing, etc. Reupholster them the same way. When you reassemble the chair, make sure you tighten all the nuts securely. Also, make sure that the arms and seat are even and level.

You will find some antique furniture that is sec-tion assembled. In the victorian lounge chair shown in Figure 23–10, the whole back comes off and the arms come out when the bolts, instead of screws, are removed. Some antique show wood is screwed into the frame. It must be taken out in order to do any reupholstering. These situations are rare, but they exist. We recommend that you examine a piece of furniture very closely before starting to see which parts can be unscrewed and taken apart.

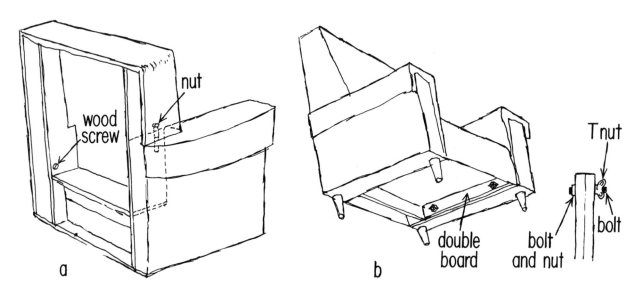

Fig. 23–9 Disassembly process. *a*. Back view: How a section-assembled chair comes apart. *b*. Bottom view: How a section-assembled chair comes apart.

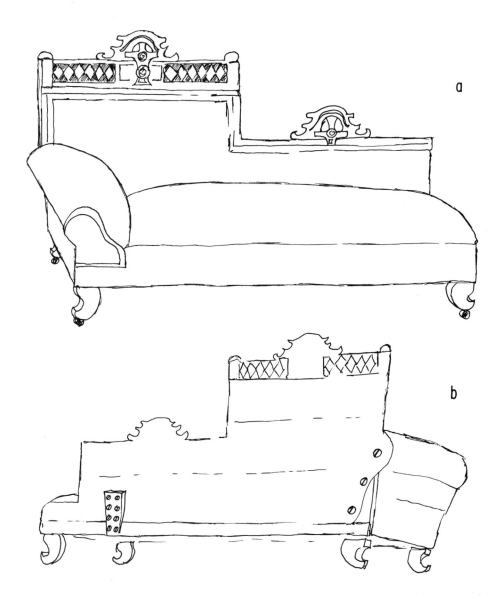

Fig. 23–10 Victorian lounge chair. *a*. Section-assembled antique lounge. *b*. Screws hold the wood frame IB onto the arms and seat.

Chapter 24

Bottomless Rocking Chairs

Introduction

You may be an antique enthusiast who loves to go to antique auctions or browse around flea markets, used furniture shops or antique shops. If you are in the market for a sturdy or not-so-sturdy rocking chair that is repairable and unique, or you already own one, then this chapter can help you upholster it.

Many antique rocking chairs come with a hole in the seat or back, or both. Some have broken caning. If you do not want to go to the expense or time of learning how to cane, and you feel that upholstery would make a more comfortable chair, then build your upholstery seat and back right on top of the old caning—do *not* rip it off. Along with the 17-oz.

burlap and webbing, caning can be part of the foundation of the seat or back. If your rocking chair was already upholstered, then you can reupholster it just as it was originally. Our project is a bottomless and backless rocking chair. The chair consists of a bare frame (Fig. 24–1). Whatever was on the seat and back had been removed. Many rocking chairs are sold bottomless, so that the seller can emphasize the beauty of the wood frame.

Upholstering a Rocking Chair

Step 1: Repair and Refinish the Frame

Move the arms and back of the chair forward and backward to see if the rocker needs any frame repair. In this project, the whole frame is loose and has to be knocked apart (Fig. 24–2). The joints are loose. The frame is wobbly. Some dowels are broken and have to be replaced. So the frame is reglued and reclamped. The wood is refinished.

Fig. 24–1 Bottomless rocking chair before reupholstering.

Fig. 24–2 Parts of the rocking chair—they will be reglued and reclamped for a sturdy frame.

Many old rockers may have a beautiful oak frame under several coats of paint. With a little paint and varnish remover and a little dirty work, you will be amazed at the facelift.

Step 2: Measure and Rough-Cut the Fabric

Measure and rough-cut the fabric for the IB, OB and seat covers. Allow a couple of extra inches on each side for the stuffing buildup. It is better to have a cover that is too large than too small. The edges will be trimmed before the gimp is glued on.

Step 3: Build a Foundation

Stretch woven webbing in two directions for the back and seat openings (or over old caning). Tack the webbing onto the frame $1/2''$ to $3/4''$ past the opening. For added strength, we recommend that you use heavy 17-oz. burlap, instead of the lighter 10-oz. burlap, on top of the webbing. Do not use plywood instead of webbing and burlap to close up the openings. The seat and back would have a harder feel and plywood is not necessarily stronger.

Use whatever stuffing is available. We used a layer of rubberized hair about the dimensions of the burlap. Put a layer of cotton on top, going $1/4''$ past the rubberized hair on all four sides. Instead of rubberized hair, you could use a $1''$ or $2''$ layer of polyurethane foam.

Step 4: Tack on the Covers, Gimp and Cambric

Tack on the IB, OB and seat covers, using the cross system, pintacking, inspecting your work and, finally, driving the tacks home. The covers can be trimmed with a trimming knife if they extend beyond the outside edges where the gimp will fall. Glue and pintack the gimp around the exposed nail edges. When the glue dries, remove the pintacks. Tack the cambric on the bottom of the seat.

Chapter 25

Footstools

Introduction

A matching footstool can make a very comfortable overstuffed chair even more comfortable. What better way to top off your reupholstering talent and knowledge than with a matching footstool?

Footstools come in various sizes and shapes. The most common size is the 22″ by 30″ rectangle. There are also round ones and square ones. Some are very low to the floor, others are higher.

The most popular footstools are the attached-pillow footstool, our first project, and the hard-edge foam footstool, our second project. Neither has any springs. The attached-pillow footstool comes with or without a pleated skirt (Fig. 25–1). The attached pillow is made similar to a colonial chair back. The pillow or cushion is made like a regular boxed cushion (some may only have a knife edge). There is no zipper on the sides. The zipper goes on the bottom (*see* Fig. 25–2) or the opening is hand sewed. The hard-edge foam footstool is a square board with four legs and 4″ foam on top. The cushion boxing is

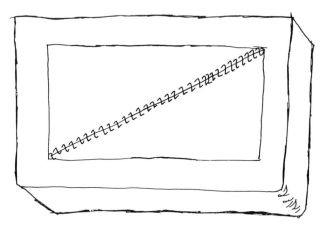

Fig. 25–2 On the face of the bottom of the cushion, draw lines 4″ in from every side.

sewed to the top cover of the footstool. The border is blindtacked approximately three-quarters of the way down.

Other footstools have No-Sag springs. Some have coil springs. Since there are so many styles, we recommend that you study your footstool very carefully. This chapter will give step-by-step instructions on how to do the two most popular types.

Reupholstering an Attached-Pillow Footstool

Step 1: Cut and Mark the Fabric Pieces
Cut the welt, top, bottom and sides of the cushion. On the face of the cushion bottom, draw lines 4″ in from every side (Fig. 25–2).

Step 2: Make the Footstool Boxing
The footstool boxing acts as a pull strip, holding the cushion in place on the footstool. The footstool boxing works very similarly to the boxing for the colonial cushion back. You will be getting two sets

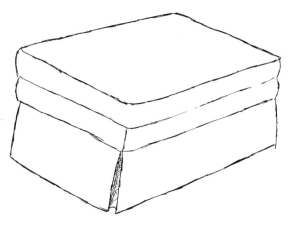

Fig. 25–1 The attached-pillow footstool.

of measurements for the four pieces of the footstool boxing: (1) The two side boxings are each 4″ + height of the footstool boxing + 1″ on the bottom to tack under (for the vertical height) and the horizontal width of the side boxing + two ¹/₂″ seams for joining the front and back boxings; (2) the front and back boxings have the same height measurements, but different width than, the side boxings.

Each top corner of each boxing piece has a 45° cut so that the four boxings will lie flat and neat when joined together. To get the 45° angle, chalk a 4″ square at each corner. Cut on the diagonal, from the inside top to the outside bottom (Fig. 25–3). Then place each boxing piece face to face and sew the angled and straight side seams.

Step 3: Sew the Cushion

Machine sew the boxing onto the 4″ chalk lines of the bottom part of the cushion, face to face. Then sew the top cushion cover to the sides of the cushion (cushion boxing), face to face, with the welt in

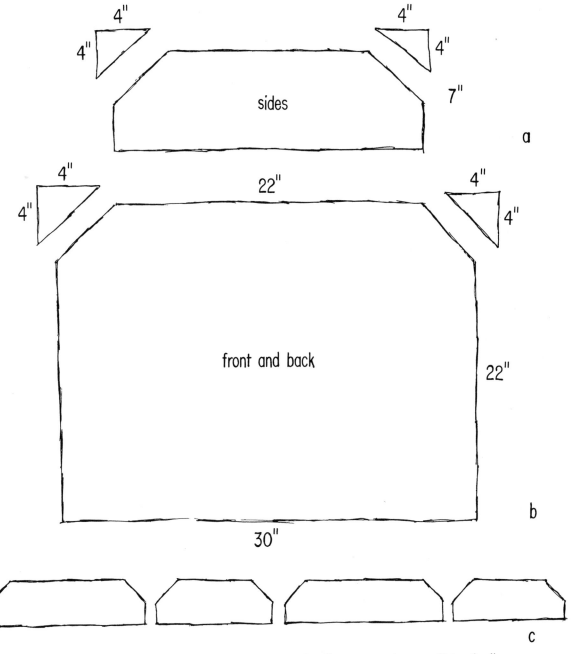

Fig. 25–3 Fitted boxings. *a.* To get the 45° angle, chalk a 4″ square at each corner. Cut on the diagonal. *b.* Follow the same process for the back and front. *c.* Four boxing pieces, side by side.

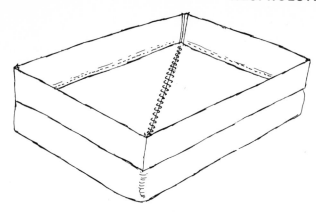

Fig. 25–4 The boxing is attached to the cushion, the foam is stuffed in, then the diagonal cut is hand sewn closed.

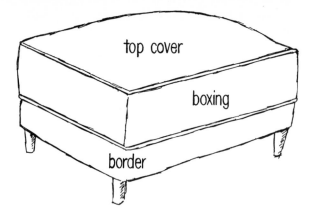

Fig. 25–5 The hard-edge foam footstool.

the middle. Sew the cushion boxing to the bottom of the cushion, face to face, with the pull strips closed inside (Fig. 25–4).

Step 4: Stuff the Cushion

With scissors, cut along the diagonal of the bottom cushion cover, from one corner of the pull strips to the other. With the pull strips on the outside of the cushion, stuff foam in the cushion. Hand sew the diagonal cut closed, using a simple overthrow stitch (Fig. 25–4).

Step 5: Tack the Cushion onto the Frame

Tack a thin layer of cotton around the sides of the frame. Slip the assembled pillow over the footstool frame. Attaching the footstool cover and cambric will be discussed in detail in the next project. Make and attach the skirt using the directions in Chapter 7. Tack on the cambric.

Recovering a Hard-Edge Foam Footstool

Step 1: Mark and Cut the Fabric Pieces

In this project, there is a wood base 6″ high (Fig. 25–5). On top of the wood base is a rectangular, 4″ high piece of foam rubber. The fabric pieces include a top cushion cover, a cushion boxing that finishes off at a measurement half the height of the wood base, and a footstool border that covers the other half of the wood base. When you measure for the fabric covers, remember to add 1″ extra for each tacked seam and ½″ extra for each sewn seam on all sides.

Step 2: Cut New Foam Rubber

In this project, the old foam rubber has lost its buoyancy and rectangular shape and has some holes scratched out by the family cat. It is necessary to cut new foam 1″ larger than the top cover on all four

sides. (Example: If the top cover measures 15″ by 18″, the foam should be cut 17″ by 20″.) Larger foam will fit snugly in the cushion casing, giving a neat, full look.

Step 3: Cut Wedges at the Top Cover Corners

This technique is described in detail in Chapter 16. Without wedges, the cushion will belly at the center of each side (at the top cover). With wedges, the cushion top will look square.

Step 4: Sew the Cover, Welt and Boxing

Sew the four pieces of boxing into a strip. When you sew the boxing to the cushion top, make sure the corner seams of the boxing match the corners of the cushion top. Close up the boxing at the last corner of the cushion top.

To make it easier to match corners, sew each half of the boxing on the cushion top one at a time, i.e., first clockwise from corner 2, then counterclockwise from corner 2, as shown in Figure 25–6.

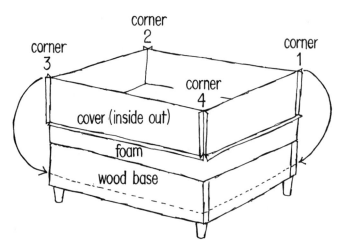

Fig. 25–6 Lay the cover inside-out on top of the foam. Carefully fit the cushion cover over the foam and wood base.

Step 5: Fit the Cushion Cover

Stuff a little cotton on the four side corners of the foam to insure fullness. Place the cushion cover on top of the foam, inside out, so that the corners of the cover meet the corners of the foam (Fig. 25–6). Carefully pull the boxing over the sides of the foam without disturbing the cotton. The fabric will be firm and snug.

Pull and pintack corner *1*, making sure the seam line falls at the corner of the wood base. In the same manner, pull and pintack the diagonal corner *3*, then the remaining two corners. Pull and pintack the remaining sides of the cover so that the cover feels snug and the top welt is pulled straight. When you are satisfied with the fitted look, drive your tacks in.

Step 6: Tack the Border to the Wood Base

Machine sew the remaining welt to the top border, after you have joined the border strips together. The finished border will be half the height of the wood base (Fig. 25–7). If the wood base is 6″, the finished border will measure 3″. Every footstool is different. Use your old fabric pieces as a guide. When you cut the border, allow extra for the sewing and tacking seams.

Measure and mark with chalk 3″ from the bottom on all four sides of the wood base. This step is to insure that the border and its welt are not tacked on the footstool in a zigzag manner.

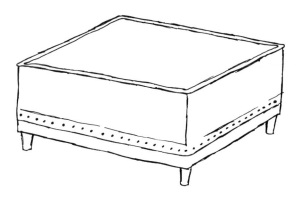

Fig. 25–7 Tack the cushion cover to the wood base.

Blind tack the border with welt on the footstool, using the markings as a top guideline. Make sure you place the vertical seams at the corners of the wood base, in line with the vertical seams of the cushion. The border will overlap at the last corner. Pintack the centers of all four sides on the bottom of the footstool. Tack all four sides down.

Make 45° cuts at the corners of each leg. Fold under the excess fabric and tack the ends in place. If the leg is wide, you can use ornamental nails to hold the fabric down around the legs.

Tack cambric on the bottom of the footstool for the finishing touch.

Glossary

Blind Stitch: The blind stitch provides the appearance of blind tacking, except it is hand sewed to give a finished look.

Blind Tacking: Blind tacking is using a cardboard tacking strip, usually along the welt, to form a neat joint. The result looks like a machine-sewed seam.

Border: A border is between 1½" and 4" wide. It is found at the base of the seat or between the inside back and the outside back.

Boxing: A boxing is a piece of material machine sewed to either the IB, IA or cushion.

Center Notch: Notches you make on center fabric pieces of the chair and sofa, such as the inside back, outside back, seat and cushion, are used to keep the center of the material in the center of the frame.

Cross System: The cross system keeps the fabric lines square on the frame by pintacking the top center, bottom center, and left and right centers.

Crown Seat: A crown seat is higher in the center than on the four sides.

Cutting Diagram: A cutting diagram is a map of all the fabric pieces for the chair or couch, fitted like a jigsaw puzzle in order to use as little fabric as possible.

Deck: The deck is the part of the chair under the seat cushion.

Driving a Tack: Driving a tack is hammering it all the way into the wood.

Edge Roll (Fox Edging): Edge roll is usually made out of burlap-covered twisted paper. It is used mostly as seat edging, but can also be found on arm edges. It keeps loose stuffing, such as hair, moss or tow, from falling out. It also takes away the feel of the sharp edges of the frame.

Edge Wire: A wire that runs on top of the seat coil spring to form the shape of the seat is an edge wire.

Face Down: The wrong side of the fabric is toward you.

Face to Face: The right side of one fabric piece is laid on top of the right side of another fabric piece. Two pieces of fabric are put face to face when they will be machine sewed to make a seam and when they are pinned together to make a left and right facing.

Face Up: The right side of the fabric is toward you.

Hand Packing: Pounding, pulling and smoothing the fabric cover and stuffing, so that the cover fits snugly and smoothly, is hand packing. Loose stuffing, such as hair, tow and moss, are also hand packed and smoothed in place so they are not lumpy.

Hard-Edge Seat: The hard-edge seat is a wooden edge that has no "give."

Left Facing; Right Facing: As you face the inside back of the chair, the right is called the right facing and the left is called the left facing.

Measurement Chart: The measurement chart has all the vertical, horizontal and welt dimensions of the chair or couch. It is used in order to make a cutting diagram.

Nap: The nap is the raised part of the fabric found on velvets. The nap of the fabric usually points toward the bottom of the goods.

Notch: A notch is a saw-tooth cut about ¼" deep made in the fabric to help keep fabric pieces lined up and centered.

Overstuffed Chair: A chair with many layers of stuffing, i.e., hair, cotton and springs in the seat and back, is an overstuffed chair. All living room furniture is overstuffed. The overstuffed chair used throughout this book is a Lawson arm chair.

Panel: A panel is usually made of $1/4''$ plywood. It is shaped, upholstered and nailed on to cover tacks and staples on the side of IB, wing or front of the IA.

Pintacking: Pintacking is hammering a tack one-third to halfway into the wood.

Pleats: Folding fabric in about $1/2''$, repeating as many times as needed, creates pleats. They are used around curves and corners in order to absorb excess fabric.

Pull Strip: Pull strips are strips attached to the inside arm, inside back and seat to save on expensive upholstery fabric. Pull strips are usually made from scrap upholstery fabric or any less expensive heavy material.

Railroading Fabric: When the fabric piece needed for a couch is more than $54''$ wide, cut the width of the fabric *piece* along the length of the fabric.

Rough Cut: Rough cut fabric is a rectangular piece of material that may not be the exact shape needed.

Seam: A seam is the joining of two or more pieces of fabric with a sewing machine or by hand sewing.

Selvage: The selvages are found on both vertical sides of the roll of fabric. They are about $1/2''$ wide and can sometimes be incorporated into your fabric piece.

Sew Line: A sew line is $1/2''$ from the cut edges of the fabric piece; this is your guideline for machine sewing.

Show Wood: Exposed show wood is decorative wood on the arms, back or seat that is refinished and is not upholstered.

Spring-Edge Seat: The soft spring-edge seat has a spring wire that "gives," usually between $1''$ and $4''$.

Stuffing: Stuffing consists of hair, tow, cotton, foam and Dacron, used in a chair or sofa to give it buoyancy, insulate the springs, and give it a soft look and feel.

T Cushion: A chair with arms $4''$ to $6''$ shorter than the seat, from front to back, uses a cushion shaped like the letter T. On a couch, the two end cushions have half-T shapes.

Top, Bottom, Front and Back: As you face the inside back of the chair, each section of the chair and each fabric piece has a top, bottom front and back.

True Cut: True-cut fabric pieces have the exact, fixed dimensions, including the curves. The old fabric piece is used as a pattern for the new true-cut fabric piece.

Tufting: Tufting is pulling the button partway through, usually on the inside back, to give either a full diamond, half diamond or biscuit shape or design.

Welt: Welt is fabric-covered welt cord. Welt gives a finished, tailored look and is used on the cushion, back and many other parts of the chair.

Welt Cording: Welt cording is usually $3/32''$ to $1/4''$ in diameter; it is used for making welt.

Index

Page numbers in **bold** type indicate information in illustrations

Abbreviations
   AP (arm panel), 53
   CU (cushion), 53
   CU BX (cushion boxing), 53
   IA (inside arm), 52
   IB (inside back), 51
   IW (inside wing), 54
   OA (outside arm), 53
   OB (outside back), 52
   OW (outside wing), 54
   Z BX (zipper boxing), 53
Arm board, **66**
Arm covers, **108,** 108–109
Arm panels, 53, **53,** 99
Arms
   boxed, 101, **101**
   cap, 101, **101**
   inside, 52, **52**
   outside, 53, **53**
   pullover, 101
   tailored, 101, **101**
Attachment rails, 65, **66**
Auctions, as source of furniture, **x**

Back border, **51,** 52
Back boxing, 51, **51**
Back panel, 51
Backs
   boxed (Lawson), 102
   channel, 149–154, **150, 151, 152**
   colonial (pillow), 102, 145–148, **146, 147**
   envelope, 122–123
   pullover, **101,** 101–102
   tufted, 155–159
Bar clamps, 19
Barrel-back chairs. *See* Channel-back chairs
Bleach. *See* Wood bleach kit
Blind stitch, 99, **99**
Blind-tack tape, 28
Blind-tacking, 28, **28**

Bottomless rocking chair. *See* Rocking chair
Box-pleated skirt, **55,** 105–107, **106**
Burlap
   foundation, 73, 75
   heavy 17-oz., 27
   light 10-oz., 27–28
   seat edgings, 75–76, **76**
   tacking on, 72
Buttons
   attaching, 98, **98**
   machines that cover, 21, **21**
   marking position of, 98
   sizes of, 98

C clamps, 19, **19**
Cambric
   attaching to chair, **107,** 107–108
   description, 30
Cap arm, 101, **101**
Cardboard tape. *See* Blind-tack tape
Cardboard, upholstery, 27
Chairs. *See also* specific style
   channel back, 149–154
   colonial pillow-back, 145–148
   contents of, **3,** 3–4
   disassembly of, 62–63
   kitchen and dining room, 119–123
   overstuffed, 125–134
   recliner, 164–165
   rocking, 168–169
   section-assembled, 165–166
   tufted-back, 155–159
   wing, 135–144
Chalk, 18
Channel-back chairs
   disassembling old channels in, 149, **150, 151**
   making channel stuffers for, **154**
   measuring and cutting channels for, 149, **150, 151, 152, 153**

Channel-back chairs (*continued*)
    recovering a back for, 149–154
    stuffing channels in, 151–153, **154**
Clamps
    C clamps, 19, **19**
    pipe clamps, 19, **19**
    V clamps, 26
Claw chisel. *See* Tack lifter
Coil springs. *See also* Springs
    double, 24, **24**
    single, **24,** 24–25
Colonial pillow-back chairs
    attaching buttons to, **147,** 148
    fabric pieces for, 146
    making and attaching pull strips to, 145, 146
    numbering seams, **146**
    reupholstering a back for, 145–148, **146, 147**
Convertible sofas
    cushions for, 163–164
    disassembly of unit, **161,** 161–162
    examination of, 161
    reassembly of unit, **162**
    recovering, 162–164
    removal of sleeping unit, 161
Cording. *See* Welt
Corner blocks, 37
Corners
    curved, 90–91
    cutting, 90
Couches. *See* Convertible Sofa; *see also* specific chair styles, e.g., Overstuffed; Channel-back
Coupling pipe clamps, 69, **69**
Crayon, 18
Cross ties on springs, **81, 86**
Crown seat, **82**
Curved needles, 15, **15**
Cushions
    alignment of corners in, **110**
    filler boxings for, 114–115, **115**
    front boxings for, **113,** 113–114
    full T, 110, **110, 115,** 115–116
    half T, 110, **110**
    measuring, 110–111, **112,** 113
    parts of, **111**
    rough cut, 112
    square, 110, **110**
    stuffing, 116
    true cut, 112
    wedges for, **111,** 112, **113**
    zipper boxings for, 53, **53,** 113–114, **114**
Cuts, upholstery, 96–97
    45-degree, **9,** 96, **96**
    square, **9,** 96, 96–97
    V cut, 97
    wide Y cut, 96, **96**
    Y cut, **9,** 96, **96**
Cutting diagrams
    how to prepare, **5,** 5, 57
    for kitchen and dining room chairs, **121**

for overstuffed chair, **127**
for wing chair, **136**

Dacron, 32, **32**
Danish modern furniture, **73,** 73–74
Deck, **50,** 50–51
Decking fabric
    flannel duck, 50, **50**
    self-decking, 50–51
Denatured alcohol, 37
Diamond tufts, **155, 157, 158**
Dining room chairs. *See* Kitchen chairs
Disinfectants. *See* Sterilizing
Double sewing, 99, **100**
Double welt. *See* Welt
Dowels
    in frame repair, 36
    plugs, 36, **36**
Down, **32,** 32–33

Edge roll
    for hard-edge seat, 76
    for soft spring-edge seat, 76
Edge wire, **77**
Enlarged holes, repair of, 69–71, **70**
Equipment, 20–21. *See also* specific item, e.g., Sewing machine

Fabric preparation supplies. *See* specific item, e.g., Welt; Zippers
Fabric preparation tools. *See* specific item, e.g., Shears; Stapler
Fabrics
    durability of, 41
    labeling pieces, **49,** 49–50, **50**
    matching, 57, 59
    measuring, 54–56
    plaid, 42–43, 59
    plastic, vinyl, 43
    print, 42–43, 59
    striped, 42–43, 58
    velvets, **41,** 41–42
    yardage requirements for, **58**
Fabrics, sources of
    factory outlets, 40
    mail-order catalogues, 39
    shops and department stores, 40
    upholstery supply houses, 39
Feathers, **32,** 32–33
Figure-8 knot, 80, **80**
Finishing knot, 78
Flax stitching twine, 33
Foam rubber, 31
Footstools
    attached pillow, **170,** 170–172, **171, 172**
    hard-edge foam, **172,** 172–173, **173**
Fox edging, 76
Frame refinishing supplies, 34–38. *See also* specific item, e.g., Dowels; Glues; Stains

Frames
  attachment rails on, 65, **66**
  disassembly of, 67–68
  foundation, 65
  reassembly of, **68,** 68–69
  redoweling joints, 68, **68**
  repair, 69–71, **70**
  supplies, 34–38
Furniture moving, 45

Garage sales, x
Garbage days, as source of used furniture, x
Gauge, for making boxed pleats, **106**
Gimp, scroll, 22, **22,** 97
Gimp tacks, 22–23, **23**
Glues
  hide, 36
  white, 37

Hair stuffings
  curled, 30
  rubberized, 30–31
Half-diamond tufts, **155, 158**
Hammers, 12, **12**
Hand packing, 95
Hand stitching, 99
Hard-edge foam footstool, **172,** 172–173, **173**
Hard-edge seat, 102, **102**
Heavy 17-oz. burlap, 27
Helical springs, **25,** 25–26, 85, **86**
Hem stitch, 77
Highchairs, reupholstering, 124
Horses. *See* Upholstery horses

Icepick, 16, **16**
Inside fabric pieces
  arms, 52, **53**
  back, 51, **51**
  wings, 54
Inverted V skirt, 103–105, **104**

Joining welt ends, 92, 93
Joints. *See* Frames
Jute webbing, 26, **26,** 72

Kapok, 32
Kick-pleated skirt. *See* Skirts
Kitchen chairs
  boxed style, **120**
  cutting diagram for, **121**
  frame repair, 119
  measurement chart for, 120
  pattern for, 122
  plywood repair, 120, **122**
  pullover style, **120**
  recovering with vinyl plastic, 119–123
Knots
  figure-8, 80, **80**
  finishing, 78

  square, 80, **80**
  starting, 77, **77**
  three-turn slip, **77, 78**

Labeling fabric pieces, **49,** 49–50, **50**
Lacquer, 38
Lacquer thinner, 37
Lags, 70, **70**
Leather, 43
Leg repair, 69–71, **70**
Lighting a work area, 44
Linings, skirt, 103

Machine sewing, 90–94
  curved seams and corners, 90–91
  seam lines in, 90
Mallets
  rubber, **18,** 18–19
  wood, 13, **13**
Marshall springs unit, repair of, 82–83, **83**
Matching fabrics
  horizontal pieces, 60
  patterns, 60, **61**
  plaids, 60
  seams, 60–61
Measurement charts
  how to make, 5, **5**
  for kitchen or dining room chair, 120
  for overstuffed chair, 126
  for wing chair, 136
Measuring fabric, 54–56
Mechanism, recliner, **164,** 164–165
Moss, 30
Moving furniture, 45
Muslin, 28–29, **32**

Nails
  finishing, 35
  No-Sag, 25
  ornamental, 23, **23**
  rozen boxed, **35,** 35–36
Needlepoint, 43
Needles
  curved, 15, **15**
  straight, **15,** 15–16
Nomenclature of fabric pieces, 49–54
No-Sag (Zig Zag) springs
  clips, 25
  nails, 25
  repair of, **84,** 84–86, **85, 86**
Nylon fabrics, 41
Nylon thread, 33

Office chairs, reupholstering, 124
Ornamental nails, 23, **23,** 97–98
Outside fabric pieces
  arms, 53, **53**
  back, 52, **52**
  wing, 54

Overstuffed chairs
    cutting diagram for, **127**
    disassembling, 126
    examination of, 126
    measurement chart for, 126
    recovering, 130–134, **131, 132, 133**
    seat-decking assembly for, 128
    spring repair in, 129
    sterilization of, 125
    stuffing in, 128

Packing and pintacking, 95
Paint and varnish removers, 37
Partitions for down cushions, 33, **33**
Patterns, using fabric pieces as, 90
Pins, upholsterer's, 16, **16**
Pintacking, 95
Pipes. *See* Channel-back chairs
Piping. *See* Welt
Plaid fabric, 42–43
Plastic wood filler, 38
Platform rocker, repair of, 83–84, **84**
Pleats, 97, **97**
Polyfoam. *See* Polyurethane foam
Polyurethane foam, **31,** 31–32
Polyurethane wood finish, 38
Pull strips, 93–94, **94**
Pullover arm, 101
Pullover back, 119–123

Railroading fabric, 41–42, **42**
Rails, attachment, 65, **66**
Recliners
    disassembling, 164
    fabric for, 165
    mechanism assembly and repair, **164,** 164–165
    recovering, 165
Regulator, stuffing, 16, **16**
Reupholstering
    definition of, *ix*
    process, in basic steps, 4
    supplies, 22–38. *See also* specific item
Ripping tools
    claw chisel, 12, **12**
    ripping chisel, 13, **13**
Rocking chairs
    building a foundation, 169
    refinishing of, 169
    repair of, 168–169
    upholstering, 169

Sagless webbing stretcher, 14, **14**
Sandpaper, 38
Saw horses. *See* Upholstery horses
Scissors. *See* Shears
Scratch remover, 38
Screwdrivers, 19

Screws
    flathead, 35, **35**
    roundhead, 35, **35**
Seat border, 50, **50**
Seats, 49–50
    crowned hard-edge, 102, **102**
    hard edge with cushion, 102, **102**
    recovering, 8, **9**
    soft spring-edge, 102–103, **103**
Secondhand furniture stores, *x*, 40
Section-assembled chairs and couches
    assembly and disassembly of, 165–166
    recovering, 166
Sewing machines
    home, 20
    industrial, 20, **20**
Shears, upholsterer's bent, 18, **18**
Shellac, 38
Show wood
    condition of, 34–35
    refinishing procedures for, 35
Silicon spray, 123
Single sewing, 99, **100**
Sisal, 31
Skewers, upholstery, 16, **16**
Skirts, 54
    attaching to chair, 105
    box-pleated, **55,** 105–107, **106**
    closing, 106
    hemming, 106
    kick-pleat or inverted V, **55,** 103–105, **104**
    lining, 103
    marking and sewing pleats in, 103–107
Slip knots
    figure-8, 80, **80**
    three-turn, **77, 78**
Slow step-by-step method, *x*
Sofas. *See* specific chair style, e.g., Tufted; Channel-back;
    Overstuffed
Sources of supplies and services, 39–40
Spring-edge seat repair, 80–81
Springs, 23–26, 79–87
    anchorage, 80
    coil, repair of, 79–80
    double coil, 24, **24**
    helical, **25,** 25–26, 85, **86**
    No-Sag, 25, **25,** 84–86, **84, 85, 86**
    sewing to webbing or burlap, 87
    single coil, **24,** 24–25
Square cut, **9, 96,** 96–97
Square knot, 80, **80**
Squaring fabric, 58–59, **59**
Stains
    oil, penetrating, 37
    with shellac, 38
    with varnish, 37–38
    with wax, 38
Staple gun, **17,** 17–18
Stapler, paper or plier type, 18

Staples, 17, **17**
Stapling fabric, 96
Sterilizing
    sprays, 88
    tags to indicate, **63**
Stitches
    blind, 99, **99**
    hem or running, 77
    overthrow, 76–77
Straight needles, **15,** 15–16
Stretchers, webbing, **13,** 13–15, **14, 15**
Striped fabric, 57, 58–59
Stuffing regulator, 16, **16**
Stuffings, 30–33
    cotton felt, 30
    Dacron, 32, **32**
    feathers and down, **32,** 32–33
    foam rubber, 31
    hair, 30
    kapok, 32
    layers of, 88–89
    moss, 30
    polyurethane foam, **31,** 31–32
    removal of, 88
    replacement of, 89
    rubberized hair, 30–31
    tow, 30
Supplies
    basic reupholstery, 22–33. *See also* specific item, e.g.,
      Tacks; Springs; Gimp
    fabric preparation, 33–34. *See also* specific item, e.g.,
      Threads; Welt
    frame and wood refinishing, 34–38. *See also* specific item,
      e.g., Dowels; Glues; Stains
    sources of, 39–40

T cushion, 110, **110, 115,** 115–116
Tack hammer, 12, **12**
Tack lifter (puller), 12, **12**
Tacks, upholstery, **22,** 22–23
Tape, blind-tack, 28
Threads
    flax stitching, 33
    for hand sewing, 33
    for machine sewing, 33
Three-dimensional furniture forms, 29, **29, 30**
Three-turn slip knot, **77, 78**
Tools, 11–18
    basic reupholstery, 12–17. *See also* specific item, e.g.,
      Tack Lifter; Claw chisel
    fabric preparation, 18. *See also* specific item, e.g., Shears;
      Chalk
    frame repair and refinishing, 18–20. *See also* specific item,
      e.g., Mallets; Clamps
Tow, 30
Trimming knife, 16, **16**
Tufted-back chairs
    attaching buttons to, 157–158

full-diamond pattern in, **155. 157**
half-diamond pattern in, **155, 158**
pattern for, from old fabric, 155, 156–157, **157**
pleating in, 158, **158**
removing old cover, 156, **156**
Tufting, history of, 155
Tying springs
    four-way, eight knot, 80–81, **81**
    knots used for, 80
    return, 80–81, **81**
    two-way, four knot, 80–81, **81**

Upholsterer's tack hammer, 12, **12**
Upholstery cuts. *See* Cuts
Upholstery horses
    building, 44, **45**
    use of, 44–45

V clamps, for rubber webbing, 26
Varnish, 38
Varnish removers, 37
Velvet nap, 41–42
Victorian lounge chair, 166, **167**
Vinyl plastic, 43, 93, 119

Webbing
    jute, 26, **26,** 72
    rubber, 26–27, **27,** 73, **73, 74**
    steel, 27, **27,** 73–74, **74**
Webbing stretchers. *See* Stretchers
Welt
    bias-cut, 91–92
    chart, 57
    cord, 34
    cylinder, 91, 92
    double, 23, **23,** 97
    how to make, 91–92, **92**
    joining ends of, 92, **93**
    materials for, 91
    measurements for, 56–57, 91
    sewing to fabric pieces, 92
White tag, **63**
Wing chairs
    building a foundation, 138
    cutting diagram for, **136**
    examination of, 135
    frame repair, 136–138
    measurement chart for, 136
    pattern for, from old fabric pieces, **137**
    recovering, 138–139, **140,** 141–144, **142, 143, 144**
Wings
    inside, 54
    outside, 54
Wire, spring edge, **77**
Wood bleach kit, 37
Wood filler, 38
Wood forms, 29, **29**
Wood panels, reupholstering, 99, 101

Wood refinishing supplies, 34–38. *See also* specific item, e.g.,
    Stains; Dowels
Wood slats, **73**
Wooden shaped edges, 102, **102**
Workshop requirements
    height for working, 44–45
    lighting, 44

Yardage requirements, **58**
Yellow tag, *x,* **63**

Zig Zag springs. *See* No-Sag springs
Zipper boxing, 53
Zippers, upholstery, 34, **34**